THEORY AND INTERPRETATION OF NARRATIVE

James Phelan, Peter J. Rabinowitz, and Robyn Warhol, Series Editors

FOR ANITA

REAL MYSTERIES

NARRATIVE AND THE UNKNOWABLE

H. Porter Abbott

THE OHIO STATE UNIVERSITY PRESS
COLUMBUS

Library of Congress Cataloging-in-Publication Data
Abbott, H. Porter.
Real mysteries : narrative and the unknowable / H. Porter Abbott.
p. cm. – (Theory and interpretation of narrative)
Includes bibliographical references and index.
ISBN-13: 978-0-8142-1232-5 (cloth : alk. paper)
ISBN-10: 0-8142-1232-8 (cloth : alk. paper)
ISBN-13: 978-0-8142-9335-5 (cd-rom)
ISBN-10: 0-8142-9335-2 (cd-rom)
[etc.]
Fiction—History and criticism. 2. Narration (Rhetoric) 3. Knowledge, Theory of, in literature. I. Title. II. Series: Theory and interpretation of narrative series.
PN3383.N35A234 2013
808.3—dc23

2013016965

Cover design by Thao Thai
Typesetting by Juliet Williams
Type set in Adobe Minion Pro

♾ The paper used in this publication meets the minimum requirements of the American National Standard for Information Sciences—Permanence of Paper for Printed Library Materials. ANSI Z39.48–1992.

9 8 7 6 5 4 3 2 1

I wanted to write a real mystery
—Tim O'Brien

CONTENTS

ACKNOWLEDGMENTS

THE SEEDS for this book were sewn in three essays: "Unreadable Minds and the Captive Reader," *Style* (2008); "Immersions in the Cognitive Sublime," *Narrative* (2009); and "Garden Paths and Ineffable effects," in Frederick Aldama's *Toward a Cognitive Theory of Narrative Acts* (2010). For all their studied autonomy, they were at heart three different takes on the same subject, with the same over-arching set of interrelated themes. To bring this out, both their differences and their sameness, the three parts of this book rewrite, extend, adapt, expand, extensively supplement, and basically rethink these three essays. I am grateful to the publishers of *Style, Narrative,* and the University of Texas Press, respectively, for permission to use portions of these essays in this book. I am also grateful to the University of Gdansk Press for permission to reprint material from the essay "So, It's not only Unspeakable, It's Unknowable. But Is It Unnarratable? Beckett and the Apophatic Tradition," which appeared in Tomasz Wiśniewski's *Back to the Beckett Text* (2012).

Along the way, I've had opportunities to test-drive my ideas before captive audiences, notably in a conference at Purdue University in 2007 ("Theory of Mind and Literature"); a Project Narrative workshop at The Ohio State University, also in 2007; another conference in Sopot, Poland, in 2010 ("Back to the Beckett text"); and several of the annual conferences of the International Society for the Study of Narrative. They all made a difference.

In the actual writing of this book, I once again owe the most to Anita Abbott, my beloved dedicatee and first among readers, who read two drafts of this work and saved me from countless errors, obscurities, and failures of plain common sense. I was also blessed with three uncommonly dedicated and astute readers for the press—Jim Phelan, Peter Rabinowitz, and an anonymous third—each of whom in their different ways combined an exacting critical eye with a willingness to enter into the spirit of what they read. My thanks to Alan Palmer, the most congenial of sparring partners, with whom I enjoyed a two-stop road show in the fall of 2007, and to Lisa Zunshine for serial invitations to serve on cognitive panels. She, like Alan, provided a well-developed theory of fiction for my contrarian bent. Thanks, too, to Barbara Abbott, whose informed and uncompromising intelligence alerted me to dangers as I wandered into the field of linguistics. Edward Branigan, who is as positive in spirit as he is complex in mind, gave me good tips as I worked on Part Two of this book. Finally, my thanks go to Sandy Crooms and the staff of The Ohio State University Press, whose efficiency and friendly attentiveness did much to lighten the long slog of getting a book into print.

Introduction

FAIL BETTER

Sometime in the mid-1980s, a student asked me "Did Beckett really say that? 'Fail better'?" He was smiling, and I, smiling, assured him that Beckett had indeed put those two words together. They had appeared a few years before in Beckett's last long composition in prose, *Worstward Ho* (1983), and now as it seemed had already gone viral. Global culture, even without digital assistance, was doing its work, digesting Beckett, and here we were, my student and I, enjoying a moment of this rapid and complex process. I doubt Beckett ever smiled when he wrote, but there was probably something like a wry internal smile when he hit upon this combination of words, since humor was an indispensable element of his "divergent intelligence."[1] His multi-layered astringent wit was a kind of soil out of which his work grew, giving it a combination of intensity and depth and wisdom and (dare I say it?) beauty that has rarely been matched. By contrast, my student and I were enjoying a joke: the comic

1. I found this apt concept in Malcolm Gladwell's *Outliers,* where he contrasts it with the "convergent intelligence" ordinarily measured by standard IQ tests. Unlike convergent intelligence, there is no measuring divergent intelligence since there can be no right answers were one to test for it. The more powerful it is, the more surprising its results.

absurdity of two things that don't go together, framed by wonderment at the strange doings of this strange man (Did he *really* say that?).

As such, our exchange was an instance of the process of culling, recombining, and disseminating "memes," or cultural bits, that Richard Dawkins controversially proposed as analogous in their working to genes (Dawkins 1989: 192ff). In American culture, in addition to its memetic life as a lame joke, "fail better" has also been commonly appropriated as a way of saying "keep trying, never give up," with the adjunct "learn from your failures and eventually you will succeed."[2] Among literary scholars, it has at times been parsed to mean that the success of Beckett's art requires failing by the customary standards of artistic success. And, as literary history, this idea does apply to Beckett as modernist, if not to its function in *Worstward Ho.* "Failing," interpreted as a vigorous and continually evolving refusal to meet the expectations of the artistic marketplace is one of the hallmarks of modernist achievement.[3]

Much has been written about what Beckett meant when he said that "to be an artist is to fail as no other dare fail" (Beckett 1983: 145). And as failure is one of the commonest tropes in his oeuvre, much more will continue to be written on the subject. But commentary rarely probes the actual experience of something like "fail better," especially when it's put back in context. In *Worstward Ho,* written when he was seventy-seven, Beckett produced an extended valedictory fanfare in which failure is the dominating motif. It is a rich, rhythmic, complex work of art in which words are made to circle an absent center. This is my take on the work and, as such, it provides me with an opening note in this prelude to a book about the art of not knowing. Read in this spirit, the oxymoronic combination of "fail" plus "better" is felt as a momentary neural jamming in an art where words are constantly being abnormalized by their syntax. For this art to work, then, the reader must set aside, on the one hand, the self-sufficiency and distraction of the joke; and on the other, the joke's opposite, that is, the explanatory attitude. In the experience of reading the actual text, *Worstward Ho,* these normalizing frames of mind get in the way.

2. Paula M. Krebs draws explicitly on the authority of the name behind the phrase: "I had a colleague who had a poster in his dining room with Samuel Beckett's 'Ever tried. Ever failed. No matter. Try again. Fail again. Fail better.' We may tell ourselves that, but we don't tell our students. Maybe we should post it in our classrooms, not our dining rooms" (Krebs 2012). Krebs's appropriation was echoed by the actor Peter Dinklage in his 2012 commencement address at Bennington College: "Don't bother telling the world you are ready. Show It. Do it. What did Beckett say? 'Ever tried. Ever failed. No matter. Try again. Fail again. Fail better'" (Pérez-Peña 2012).

3. The multiple ways in which culture can recursively normalize intentional artistic failure has been especially problematic for Beckett, given his spectacular cultural success. After *Godot,* this meant working against cultural standards of success to which his own work had contributed.

They obscure the full force of "fail" in combination with the force of "better." This is what must be felt.

So, I go get the text and open it up:

> Worsening words whose unknown. Whence unknown. At all costs unknown. Now for to say as worst they may only they only they. Dim void shades all they. Nothing save what they say. Somehow say. Nothing save they. What they say. Whosesover whencesover say. As worst they may fail ever worse to say. (Beckett 1996: 104)

"Say what?" my student says and pretty much hits the nail on the head. He and I experience a cluster of gaps opening up where some thing or some word should be but isn't *and won't ever be.* In this textual world, it both is and is not "enough still not to know" (ibid.). The striking verbal oddity, then, of "fail better" does its work best when it is felt as an oxymoron that cannot be undone, a real mystery poised on the cusp where the inexplicable meets the need to relieve it. It is but one example of one tool among multitudes in Beckett's finely calibrated and always absorbing art of not knowing.

WHAT THIS BOOK IS ABOUT

Beckett returns in chapters 1 and 4 of this study, and in those I will give you a better understanding of two different strains of his art of not knowing, of how they work and why we should give them any of our valuable time. But what prompted this book-length study was my growing realization that other authors, who don't deploy the trope of failure and in fact compose in quite different ways, have been eliciting their own versions of this same fundamental effect. Beckett is such a repository of brightly shining limit cases that it is easy to overlook the fact that his particular innovations belong to a broader, more diversified range of strategies devised by other authors intent on arousing different versions of the same effect. You could call this effect the "palpable unknown." It is an intended effect, and the art of arousing it is what this book is about—how readers (and, by extension, viewers and auditors) of narrative can be made not only to know that they don't know, which is a matter of understanding, but also to be immersed in the condition of unknowing, which is a matter of experience.

It also asks and tries to answer the question: Why should an author want to do this? It is a question that falls within a larger question that literary scholars and critics of the *avant-garde* are constantly badgered with: Why practice an art that deliberately fails to meet readers' expectations? Narratives after all are marketed within a highly determinate process of production, selection, and consumption. As Darwin wrote of natural selection, this process works "with unerring skill" (Darwin 1952: 87). And if, like natural selection, the market for narrative commodities is a case of emergent behavior and thus in key ways irreducible, immeasurable, and unpredictable, the chemistry of mind and text that makes it work is nonetheless something producers and consumers know a lot about. This includes, among other things, the enduring appeal of the narrative triad of suspense, curiosity, and surprise (Sternberg 1978). It is this understanding of the way narrative works that allows critics to deploy the "we" construction ("at this point in the novel, we begin to sense that something has gone terribly wrong"). Readers, in other words, effortlessly learn to respond to narrative as they are expected to respond. And though the competence of readers stretches over a wide range, narrative only exists because we share an experiential understanding of how narrative achieves its effects.

So if, now to adapt Wordsworth's lines, narrative is so "exquisitely . . . fitted to the Mind" ("Prospectus," ll. 63–66), why would an artist want to mess with that fit? What is to be gained from this? Over the course of the twentieth century, these questions have become more pressing as the ascent through the rarified air of high modernism achieved lift-off into the impossible worlds of postmodernism. And it has elicited any number of explanations. These include predictable dismissive explanations like the need for ever-fresh modes of inscrutability in marketing for a cultural elite that seeks status rather than the natural pleasures of narrative.[4] On the undismissive side, however, there has been much worthwhile theoretical work on texts that resist the reader to varying degrees. This work can be loosely gathered under the concept of defamiliarization.

RESISTING THE READER

The idea that literature can be a productive way of defamiliarizing the familiar has a distinguished pedigree though it is most commonly associated with

4. See particularly Ellen Dissanayake (1992), Steven Pinker (1997, 2002), and E. O. Wilson (1998), whose critique comes out of an understanding of what comes naturally to our evolved sociality. Pinker has also suggested that willful inscrutability might confer an advantage in sexual selection (the artist as romantically inscrutable, garbed in the plumage of inscrutable art). At this level of speculation, it is not hard to put other sorts of evolutionary spin on narrative misbehavior: e.g., "Avant-gardes are always cults of difficulty—Cubism, 'The Waste Land'—by which a rising generation exploits its biological advantages, of animal health and superabundant brain cells, to confound the galling wisdom and demoralize the obnoxious sovereignty of age" (Schjeldahl 2005: 162).

the work of Viktor Shklovsky, who gave us the concept of plot (*syuzhet*) as the means by which the telling can be used to defamiliarize the story (*fabula*). In this kind of reader resistance the focus is on the conscious management of narrative as an instrument of disruption with insightful rewards for the hard-working reader. Thus, Shklovsky's coinage, "ostranyenie" (*остранение*), often translated as "making strange," is also "showing the strangeness of,"[5] and in this regard it is keyed to the larger purpose of breaking habitual templates and seeing with fresh eyes. This general idea of yielding insight by resisting the easy transport of the reader of conventional texts, slowing the reader down and increasing reflexive awareness, can be found in a broad range of diverse conceptions of reader/viewer resistance from Bertolt Brecht's *Verfremdungs-effekte* (1935) to Austin Wright's "recalcitrance" (Wright 1989) to Michael M. Boardman's "urgent innovation" (Boardman 1992) to James Phelan's "the difficult" and "the stubborn" (Phelan 1996, 2007, 2008, 2011) to David S. Miall's "dehabituation" (Miall 2006) to Vicki Mahaffey's "challenging fictions" (Mahafey 2007) and Criscillia Benford's "the inassimilable" (Benford 2010). In the same spirit, modernist texts imported into narrative the more demanding and textually self-conscious modes of poetry (Lodge 1977), even as T. S. Eliot argued that poetry itself must be difficult to be successful. More broadly, these modernists were elaborating what Coleridge contended when he wrote that "Genius produces the strongest impressions of novelty" in rescuing truths that "lie bed-ridden in the dormitory of the soul" (Coleridge 1983: 60). Or more broadly still, these resistant texts provoke what the cognitive sociologist Paul DiMaggio has called "deliberative cognition," a natural cognitive endowment that involves overriding "programmed modes of thought to think critically and reflexively." As such, these texts arouse that degree of heightened attention that is regularly called into play when "existing schemata fail to account adequately for new stimuli" (DiMaggio 1997: 271–72).[6]

5. In his translator's introduction to Shklovsky's *Theory of the Novel*, Benjamin Sher explains his use of the term "enstrangement" for *остранение* to capture the process of exposing the strangeness of "an object or image . . . by 'removing' it from the network of conventional, formulaic, stereotypical perceptions and linguistic expressions (based on such perceptions)" (xix). For an ambitious critical overview of the whole extended subject of defamiliarization, see Sternberg 2006.

6. For a penetrating analysis of how the "nonstandard" in literary discourse not only challenges thought but makes us conscious of the "standard" that informs our thought and language, see Margolin 2003. As so often in treatments of how literature can profitably resist the reader, Margolin references Beckett as a model of how far a writer can go in this direction: "the preference of much literature for nonstandard forms of cognitive functioning, be they rare and marginal, deviant, or involving a failure, breakdown, or lack of standard patterns . . . stems from a desire to explore new possibilities, and, in some cases such as that of Samuel Beckett . . . , the very limits or minimal conditions of cognitive activity as such. This procedure provides the reader with novelty and an intellectual challenge to make sense of the unfamiliar and excep-

In my mind this general view of reader-resistant texts accords with the thread of interpretive pedagogy that Schklovsky's contemporary I. A. Richards articulated when he called a literary text a "machine to think with" (Richards 1924: 52). If the mechanical metaphor has been pretty much abandoned, the spirit and the pedagogy have swelled over the years. The effort to interpret literary texts, whether read in academic seminars or non-academic reading groups, is valued for the effort involved and the accompanying expansion of thought and feeling that is catalyzed along the way. The attitude is well expressed by the novelist Toni Morrison, whose willingness to discuss her own work and the work of others is as inexhaustible as it is interesting: "I like to think of a class as ending with really interesting questions. Just as when I'm writing, I don't like my books to end, but rather leave the reader with questions that will prompt them to circle back into the text. A good book may prompt you to go out and learn more about something that hasn't interested you before" (Denard 2008: 200–201).[7] Morrison's formulation is particularly apt because it articulates the way discussing reader-resistant texts not only feeds the lives that are lived outside the fictional worlds they create but also feeds back into the experience of those fictional worlds. Done well, reading and interpretation join hands. This is a view of the teacher's craft that I fully endorse and over many years have sought to live up to in my own imperfect way.

There is also a dark version of reader-resistant narrative that, in effect, universalizes a condition of innate opacity for all texts. This is a quality that texts acquire not by any intention of the author but by their condition as texts. In this view, the yield for hard-working readers can only be perplexity as they seek the veiled meaning that Hawthorne can never let them see in his story of "The Minister's Dark Veil" (J. H. Miller 1991). The hard work of interpretation, pursued with sufficient understanding of this universal condition, leads in only one direction: to cognitive darkness. The insight acquired is a lack of sight, the revelation of an inescapable condition of unknowing that is unacknowledged or pasted over in conventional texts, as it is in our lives outside the text. This is the problem of the absent signified that, in different ways, played a central role in the theorizing of Jacques Derrida, Jacques Lacan, and

---

tional and, in addition, makes him or her aware *ex negativo* of the presumed standard case" (287).

7. Asked why she distances herself from feminism, Morrison replied: "In order to be as free as I possibly can, in my own imagination, I can't take positions that are closed. Everything I've ever done, in the writing world, has been to expand articulation, rather than to close it, to open doors, sometimes, not even closing the book—leaving the endings open to interpretation, revisitation, a little ambiguity" (Denard 2008: 140).

Paul de Man, and that leads to a process of interpretation without end. It is a resistance built into the walls of the prison-house of language in which we are all confined and that will allow no semiotic capture of "the real" (Lacan) or the "hors-texte" (Derrida). In Frank Kermode's elegant formulation, the hidden is the "secrecy" that feeds on the very effort to abolish it: "We are most unwilling to accept mystery, what cannot be reduced to other and more intelligible forms. Yet that is what we find here: something irreducible, therefore perpetually to be interpreted; not secrets to be found out one by one, but Secrecy" (Kermode 1979: 143).[8]

This sounds a lot like the subject of this book as described above, but it is not. I'll get to the difference in a moment, but first it is helpful to note that what many poststructuralists were saying about the illusion of language's transparency and our persistence in maintaining this illusion despite the news that whatever we write can be handily deconstructed connects with what some neurologists were, and are, saying about the way our minds work. On this view, we are by our nature, as Kermode writes, most unwilling to accept a mystery that cannot be resolved. In *The Mind's Past,* Michael Gazzaniga refers to an "interpreter" in the left hemisphere of the brain that works tirelessly to make sense of the world, even before we are aware of what we think. "[T]here is something very special about the left brain. It reflexively generates a notion about how things work even when there is no real event to figure out. There is no stopping it" (Gazzaniga 1998: 156). The object of this constant, largely unconscious, application of recognizable form on what is otherwise inexplicable is to maintain a familiar world within which we are secure: "The interpreter tells us the lies we need to believe in order to remain in control" (138). In religious discourse, even the term "mystery" itself can be evidence of a nameable cause, the reality of which is implicated in the mystery. To proclaim that God moves in mysterious ways is, at the least, to proclaim that there is a Mover at work, making mysterious moves. What *is,* in short, is conceived as effect, and what Gazzaniga calls "figuring out" is primarily working backward, however imperfectly, to an assessment of cause. The result is a story, simple or complex, and its mode of representation is narrative. In Antonio Damasio's words, "the mind's pervasive 'aboutness' is rooted in the brain's story-telling

8. Robyn Warhol (2005) has proposed the useful category of the "supranarratable" (230) for moments in film that are best conveyed by a strategy of concealment. An example she uses is an off-camera kiss, the intensity of which would suffer diminishment could we actually see the lovers. What I am dealing with in this essay is the narrative effort to deal with what is beyond narratable knowledge or expression. As such, its object is closer but not identical to what Allon White referred to as "the necessary not-said of the text" in Meredith's "sudden ellipses," Conrad's "metaphysical enigmas," and James's "cultivated obscurity" (A. White 1981: 28, 130).

attitude" (1999: 189).[9] Narrative, in other words, is the principal cognitive act of understanding, doing its busy work throughout the days of our waking lives, in law and gossip, in science and politics, in history and the news. Nassim Taleb calls it "the narrative fallacy" (Taleb 2007: 62–84): "an ingrained biological need to reduce dimensionality" that makes it "impossible for our brain to see anything in raw form" (64, 65). Taleb spreads his net pretty widely when he calls this operation "the narrative fallacy," but he is simply echoing what in their different ways Sartre, Barthes, Hayden White, and others have observed: that to narrativize is to apply meaning where otherwise meaning would not exist, binding events through chains of explanatory causation.[10]

But if our constitutional need to impose understanding where we do not understand is relevant to this study, the extreme constructivist view of all understanding is not. For it stands to reason that if our communications among ourselves, our readings of intention, and our descriptions of the world we live in were hopelessly sealed off from reality, we would not have survived as well as we have. Our knowledge and its means of conveyance are, in other words, good enough.[11] In fact, the extreme constructivist view that I have just taken up has lost much of its *cachet* among humanists as it has (if it ever had) among scientists of cognition. It has been broadly criticized as a reductive product of an Enlightenment bequest—the false dichotomy between objec-

9. In contrast to Gazzaniga, Damasio locates this narrative faculty at a deeper, prelinguistic level of "wordless narrative" (2010: 204). It is, he writes, a "strategic management of images" that likely evolved bottom up, early on, well before consciousness did" (174; see also Damasio 1999: 184–89). For a lucid, lively account of case histories involving neurological disorders that interfere with the capability of mentally organizing the world we live in, see Sacks 1985 (see also Young and Saver 2001; Mar 2004). In the next chapter, I'll return to the more specific role played by our narrative capability in the construction of personal identity.

10. It is not therefore surprising that causation has been a central issue in theorizing about narrative and for some (Bal, Bordwell, B. Richardson) a defining feature of narrative itself. And certainly, for fictional or nonfictional narratives of any complexity, a key part of the experience of reading (or viewing) is a constant scanning for cause and effect. If, for the most part, this operation is reflexive and unconscious, and one among many operations proceeding at once, it finds its way up into the conscious construction of what we commonly call the interpretation of narrative texts. This involves not only sorting out the chains of cause and effect within the world created by the text but also determining another kind of cause in the world outside the text—a set of intentions that brought another kind of effect—the narrative world itself—into existence.

11. As Tony Jackson puts it in reference to deconstruction's "infinitely self-disestablishing" text, "[m]y understanding of writing and representation does not have to do with this kind of theoretical absolute. Rather, I take language and narrativity as empirically established elements of *Homo sapiens* that do the work they have evolved to do, very well much of the time, but hardly in some exact or absolutely successful way" (Jackson 2009: 80). Philip Weinstein makes the same critique with a different inflection: "What happened to the space in between (the space where language's relation to the world typically operates)—representation as both determined and free, world-predicative yet open to contestation?" (Weinstein 2005: 52).

tivity and subjectivity (Lakoff and Johnson 1980; Harding and O'Barr 1987; Maturana and Varela 1998). As the psychologist Susan Oyama argues, "Our responsibility is not the responsibility of unmoved movers, absolute originators bringing order to chaos. Rather the construction is mutual; it occurs through intimate interaction." As a consequence, "[o]ur cognitive and ethical responsibilities are based on our *response-ability,* our capacity to know and to do, our active involvement in knowledge and reflection" (Oyama 2000: 149). So, to circle back, Oyama's idea of *response-ability* extends logically into the pedogogy that, as I contended above, can be made to work productively with defamiliarizing modes of reader-resistance.

But this is a book about intentionally induced states of unknowing, so I need to make sure my reader understands that I am not at all dissociating my general orientation toward the reading and interpretation of fictional texts from Oyama's more broadly applied concept of "intimate interaction"—a "constructionism" constantly inflected and corrected by the reality it works with. My focus in this book, however, is on literary texts that, in part, interrupt this process, bringing us past the limits of our understanding and at the same time inviting us to let go of the impulse to construct. They lead us not simply to acknowledge that we don't know but to feel the insistent presence of this condition. It is a humbling experience, given our bent for misestimating the extent and exactitude of our knowledge. If this bent, too, has been an evolutionary necessity, giving us the sharp sense of clarity we need in our decision making, it has also been the cause of much suffering. Fiction provides a space where we can not only reflect on this bent but, in the uncommon instances I take up in this book, know what it feels like to release ourselves altogether from its sovereignty.

THE STUBBORN

In the field of the interpretation of fictional texts, what James Phelan has called "the stubborn" is an extreme form of reader resistance that will help me clarify by contrast the even more extreme form of resistance that is my subject. Phelan first applied his useful concept to a character, Beloved, in an analysis of Toni Morrison's problematic novel of the same name, *Beloved* (Phelan 1996: 173–89). He opposed "the stubborn" to what he called "the difficult": both are forms of narrative "recalcitrance," but where the difficult finally "yields to our explanatory efforts," the stubborn does not (178).[12] Phel-

12. As Peter Rabinowitz astutely observes: "Much poststructuralist criticism . . . seems

an's treatment of the stubborn was and is part of his larger on-going effort to deal with the disparity between two kinds of engagement with fiction—the experience of the text and its interpretation—a distinction that goes way back and that is also important for this study.[13] For Phelan, as for many others, interpretation differs from the experience of reading in that it is the product of a conscious effort to develop "a single, coherent understanding" out of that experience (Phelan 2007: 212; see also Rabinowitz 1987: 1–2). This is where the stubborn does its refractory work. In his chapter on *Beloved,* Phelan dramatized the tension between the experience of reading a text and the analytical work of interpreting a text by alternating "a somewhat lyrical expression of response with abstract theorizing" (Phelan 1996: 173). The result is an "essay" in Montaigne's original sense of the term—an act of provocative incompletion.

What makes it incomplete—that is, what prevents any satisfactory transit from the experience of the text to its interpretation—is the stubborn unac-

---

quick to turn instances of the difficult into the stubborn and then to thematize them into global conclusions about the impossibility of interpretation" (Rabinowitz 2001: 207).

13. The distinction between the experience of literature and its analysis is already implicit in Aristotle's *Poetics* where he articulated two main roads that professional analysts of mimetic literature have followed ever since. The first is the approach most commonly associated with the word "interpretation." It is the one we take when we talk about the meaning of a text or of its meanings or, for that matter, of its refusals to mean. Aristotle provided a powerful way of understanding it (Aristotle 1947: 635–36, 657–58) when he compared poetry favorably, on the one hand, to philosophy (it tells a story) and, on the other, to history (it conveys ideas). That stories convey ideas is an assumption that seems almost inevitably to come with the interpreter's trade, though it can also plague the common reader who not uncommonly sees it as a distracting presumption, an intrusion on the pleasures of reading. In the century just past, some of the sharpest critics of this critical stance have been writers themselves, who in one way or another imply that the experience of the text is not only beyond paraphrase but threatened by the constraining abstraction of even the most nuanced interpretation. Asked what he thought Beckett's plays were about, the playwright Brendan Behan replied, "I don't know what his plays are about, but I know I enjoy them. I do not know what a swim in the ocean is about, but I enjoy it. I enjoy the water flowing over me" (Reid 1968: 48).

The second approach is one that gets closer to what Behan is talking about. Aristotle demonstrated it in his analysis of the well-wrought tragedy with its emphasis on the arousal and purgation of intense feeling (Aristotle 1947: 637–43). This is the experiential, processual, affective approach to interpretation with its focus on what happens to us over the course of an expressive or representational event (listening to a poem, reading a novel, watching a play). The most notable twentieth-century theorist of this approach was Kenneth Burke, though there have been some remarkable examples of theorists (Roland Barthes, Stanley Fish, Garrett Stewart) who have ramped up this focus to a microscopic, moment-by-moment tracking of the human transaction with a text. Any further intimacy with the experience of the text is the experience itself, from which any kind of commentary is a departure. And this is the problem, because the experience of the text is where the action is: the fluid, ever-evolving chemistry between the reader and the text. It is a chemistry that is ultimately beyond all analytical nets, yet without it there is no narrative to talk about.

countability of the character of Beloved herself. Reading Beloved as an individual character, a human being, is, to begin with, hard not simply because she is impenetrable ("deep down in those big black eyes there was no expression at all" [Morrison 1987a: 55]), but also because Morrison in developing this character crosses the line between realism and fantasy. Beloved was at the beginning of her very short life a living, breathing infant, though barely knowable as such. But then she returns: first as an angry, "spiteful" ghost, making life miserable at 124 Bluestone Road, and then as a "fully dressed woman," with smooth skin, a weakness for sweets, and a scar on her neck, who walks out of a stream and finds her way to 124 where she further complicates the lives of those who live there. Her multiple interactions with Sethe, Denver, Paul D, and even the community of neighbors prevent her from being pegged as the projection of the psychological state of any single character or set of characters. And finally, as a ghost in the work of an unabashedly allusive writer, Beloved seems to symbolize a congeries of different conditions, both universal and historically specific: the repressed fury of the enslaved, the evil consequences of the middle passage, the chain of guilt that binds master and slave, the power of love, its possessive insistence and capacity for madness, the dangerous simplicity of the innocent. Beloved is, in short, a problematic feast for the interpreting mind. And this is something Phelan brings out very well as he tests possible interpretations, his own and those of other scholars, against his experience of reading the text. In every case, reading trumps interpretation.

But for all the frustrating discord in this novel between the experience of reading and the attempt to create a satisfactory over-arching interpretation—indeed because of it—the stubborn, according to Phelan, does good work, contributing "significantly to the experience of the larger narrative" (179). And this is because, at bottom, it does much the same work as "the difficult," exercising and enlarging the reader's emotional, intellectual, and ethical faculties.[14] In this sense, both the difficult and the stubborn mesh with a pedagogy predicated on constructing and contesting interpretive possibilities. But the instances of narrative recalcitrance that I have brought together in this study are of a special kind and ultimately, as I shall continue to argue throughout, require the coexistence of two opposed frames of mind: the need to know and the acceptance that one will never know. This is not to say that experiencing such instances cannot be assisted by analysis and the establishment of

14. Phelan puts this similarly in a later essay, arguing that at the end of Kafka's "Das Urteil" Herr Bendemann's inexplicable judgment of his son and his son's inexplicable acceptance of it open a stubborn gap that cannot be closed but at the same time "invites us to relate the story to an ever-widening range of issues and contexts" (Phelan 2011: 17). See also Phelan's application of this concept to Frost's "Home Burial" (Phelan 2007: 211–14) and to *Lord Jim* (Phelan 2008).

an over-arching or meta-interpretive analytical frame, which is also the job of this study. But unlike the over-arching frame of Kermode, which posits unending efforts of interpretation, or that of Miller, which posits the impossibility of interpretation altogether, the frame I will be working with requires, at times, a willing immersion in modes of cognitive failure that cannot happen at the readerly distance required to explain or interpret. Like the experience of the stubborn, the experience of the palpable unknown need not forestall efforts to interpret a narrative as a whole. But if an interpretation does aspire to account for the work as a whole, it must find a place for this special experience within those efforts. To give a practical indication of the different track I am taking, let's look at the same novel Phelan used to demonstrate the stubborn but with a focus now on another aspect of our relationship to it.

THE ABSENT EPONYM

In several important ways, *Beloved* is governed by an art not of the unknowable but of the knowable, and vividly so. It is, to begin with, a book about the necessity of recovering the repressed, of "rememory," especially as this theme is played out in the lives of Sethe and Paul D. It is also an effort to do the same for its resistant audience. For this reason, Morrison actually thought *Beloved* would be her least popular novel because "it is about something the characters don't want to remember, I don't want to remember, black people don't want to remember, white people don't want to remember. I mean it's national amnesia" (Bowers 1990: 75). And, finally, *Beloved* is an act of making known not only what we don't want to remember, but also what we otherwise would not know. It does so by publishing in rich and powerfully moving detail what could not be published when it happened. As Morrison has written herself, nineteenth-century slave narratives were composed under constraints that disallowed what she could now allow herself to write.

> [P]opular taste discouraged the writers from dwelling too long or too carefully on the more sordid details of their experience. Whenever there was an unusually violent incident, or a scatological one, or something "excessive," one finds the writer taking refuge in the literary conventions of the day. . . . Over and over, the writers pull the narrative up short with a phrase such as, "But let us drop a veil over these proceedings too terrible to relate." In shaping the experience to make it palatable to those who were in a position to alleviate it, they were silent about many things, and they "forgot" many things. There was a careful selection of the instances that they would record

> and a careful rendering of those that they chose to describe. . . . My job becomes how to rip the veil drawn over "proceedings too terrible to relate." (Morrison 1987b: 109–10)

This is a job that the twentieth-century novel, with its accumulated array of narrative devices, along with its roominess and flexibility as fiction, is well-equipped to do. And by most accounts, Morrison exploits her equipment with great brilliance in the service of this job of unveiling. As Susan Bowers writes, and I think all would agree, "her novel conjures slaves back to life in many-dimensional characters with a full range of human emotions" (Bowers 1990: 62).

What I want to suggest in this brief analysis, however, is that another aspect of the deep originality of her novel is the way Morrison also works *against* the job she has set herself. To get at this paradox, I will focus on the way Morrison has created in *Beloved* a ghostly version of the eponymous novel, along with its nonfictional sub-type, the slave narrative. In this context, I am referring particularly to the eponymous (that is, protagonist-titled) coming-of-age novel that evolved out of late seventeenth-century and early eighteenth-century eponymous narratives, flourished over the next hundred years, and is often included within the genre of the *Bildungsroman,* which got its name early in the nineteenth century. It was a form that, not irrelevantly, grew in tandem with the emergent advocacy of the Rights of Man and a democracy predicated on those rights.[15] It helped shape an idea of the individual as an entity to whom by nature certain rights belonged and for whom democracies were fashioned, both to insure those rights and to provide an environment in which the individual could reach a full maturity in which to exercise them. Chief among such democracies, of course, is the one into which Beloved is born.

It was in this historical context that the slave narrative also took shape. And much has been written quite rightly about how the slave narrative served as both a resource and inspiration for *Beloved.* But the deep structure of the slave narrative also resides in the background of this work of fiction as the ghostly, skeletal framework of the eponymous coming-of-age novel. As such, this ghost of a life narrative serves a double purpose: it sets off the vitality of

15. The term *Bildungsroman* was first applied to the coming-of-age novel in 1819 by the philosopher and philologist Karl Morgenstern. The term was coined, he wrote, "first and foremost because of [the genre's] content, because it presents the hero's *Bildung* from its inception and continuation until a certain stage of completion; secondly, however, because precisely through this presentation it encourages the cultivation of the reader more fully than any other type of novel" (Morgenstern quoted in Steineke 1991: 18). Implied in this founding definition is a social context in which protagonist and reader share the opportunity of self-creation.

the way Morrison fulfills her obligation to the writers of the nonfictional slave narratives, but at the same time it sets off the way Morrison utterly undoes the African American version of the immensely popular nineteenth-century fictional genre they echoed. As Gurleen Grewal argues, where "the slave narrative privileged the individual's account of coming to selfhood—in which the single, heroic self is fixed in the 'I' of the subject and the tale ends with the victory of freedom—Morrison's narrative removes the individual from its center, giving way to a multiplicity of voices" (Grewal 1998: 103). Grewal goes on to argue that, as such, *Beloved* "invokes 'the polyphonic ideal' of Mikhail Bakhtin" (ibid.). This is true as far as it goes. *Beloved* is a very busy, musical novel with a complex multiplicity of voices and tales.

My point, however, is that Morrison complicates this shift to "the polyphonic ideal" by equally invoking expectations that belong to the eponymous coming-of-age novel. By definition and prototypically (*Jack of Newberry, Oroonoko, Pamela*), the eponymous novel features the name of the protagonist (its eponym) in its title. And this is what Morrison seems to do. For the would-be interpreter, the titular eponym signals a novel in which meaning is entangled with the growth and maturation of its central character. Morrison accentuates this traditional entanglement of character and novel by her constant repetition of the "name" of its missing protagonist. But even the name, "Beloved," is not a name but an accidental placeholder for an infant who seems never to have had a name. As such, and through its repetition, it is made to be an inescapable constancy of absence in this novel.[16]

To go back to Phelan's concept, it is not just the character Beloved that is "stubborn" but the novel itself. And Phelan would agree. This stubbornness of the book is emphasized by the medley of contradictions that concludes the novel in its last two pages, and particularly the repeated sentence, "It was not a story to pass on."[17] For the rational mind, as Phelan shows, the

16. For a twentieth-century readership, I would argue that this effect of absence is accentuated by Beloved's ghostly stand-ins. If there is a model of West African belief operating here, "that the dead live as long as they are remembered" (Grewell 1998: 107), the belief itself cannot be relied upon to persist in Morrison's audience. For all the provocative interpretive work that the two versions of her ghost generate, their very extravagance works as a sign of their constructedness—shapes imposed on what was never allowed to take memorable shape.

17. As has often been remarked, the word *pass* in this sentence can be read in different ways. Stephanie Li, for example, articulates two common alternatives: "[d]epending on how one reads the verb *pass,* this statement can be read both as an injunction to forget the past and as an injunction to preserve it" (Li 2010: 81). If the syntactical intonation of Li's second alternative requires an awkward strain that the first does not (and I think it does), the natural intonation of the first does not have to be taken as an injunction, but as a statement of fact. In other words, this was, and is, a story that cannot be passed on because what happened is irrecoverable. If this

sentence does not fully compute. Yet as an eponymous novel *Beloved* is correctly declaring that it has in fact not told a story. *Beloved* is a striking case of the absence of a story of maturation, of growing up, of *Bildung*, that provides the armature of the eponymous novel. The baby that *Beloved* should be telling the story of had neither a name nor a life to go with it and therefore could have no story to pass on. The repeated question, "already crawling?," underscores the fact that there is no record that Beloved even achieved a first movement through time and space under her own power. Lacking anything that could be construed as tellable action, that is, action performed under her own agency, Beloved was robbed of narratable being. She was erased by an act that belongs to another story with another protagonist, that of her mother. Insofar as it is an eponymous novel, then, *Beloved* can only be a project of discourse—discourse, that is, without the storytelling that gives discourse its status as narrative. There is, of course, much storytelling that goes on in *Beloved* with, as a kind of spine, the artfully delayed details leading up to Sethe's terrible act and its consequences. But the arc of a tale that binds the parts of an eponymous novel is not there because it never happened. All that we are allowed is the dead body of an infant, whose silence is doubled by Sethe when she refuses to attend the funeral service and listen to the words of the Reverend Pike. Sethe goes instead "to the gravesite, whose silence she competed with as she stood there not joining in the hymns the others sang with all their hearts" (Morrison 1987a: 171).

It is not a great leap for the interpreting mind to see in the silence of the dead infant an evocation of the silence of all the lives among the "sixty million and more" to whom Morrison dedicates her book and for whom also there can be no story. Phelan makes this interpretive move himself (189). Their lives fall into an abyss of absence that compounds that of Beloved. Morrison herself has said that "[n]othing came down orally to my generation of the experience on the slave ship" (Grewal 1998: 102). Those who died in transit—some thrown overboard in infancy as Sethe's mother did ("Without names, she threw them" [62])—plus those who survived the passage and those born thereafter who were cut down at one point or another and those who lived to complete the arc of a tellable life story – for all of these there is no record. One can, then, make the valid and important *interpretive* move of aligning Beloved with the sixty million and more, but the *experience* of *Beloved* must necessarily include the experience of this yawning absence—the absence of tellable stories and lived lives. It is plausible in this regard that all the frenetic busy-ness of

---

is not the only way Morrison intended for the sentence to be read, it should not, as I argue in what follows, be excluded.

Morrison's busy novel, in addition to the valuable interpretive work it provokes, is also intended to make this terrible silence deafening as one "listen[s] for the holes . . . the unnamed, unmentioned people left behind" (92). They are gone without a trace. For a writer who is so passionately absorbed by the vivid "fluidity" and "contradictions" of black life in America (Denard 2008: 61) and "how under the most inconceivable abuse, there is grace, there is power, and there is this tenacity" (18)—for such a writer, an absence of this magnitude must be an intolerable fact that won't go away. It adds its weight to all the known injustices. And for all the humor and grace and buoyant productivity of Morrison's prose, it adds an intimation of inextinguishable fury lying beneath her words.

Beloved's absence from her own eponymous novel, then, is an absence that both contains and is contained within an immensity of absence. It is an absence we can talk around, but even as we do, one function of this multifaceted novel is to insist on this empty silence. It is a hole that travels through the novel, lurking in its sentences and its narrative disjunctions. As Morrison's command of fiction does its valuable work, fashioning a life seeded by a few surviving contemporary words about the historical Margaret Garner's desperate act, it also sustains the feeling of not being able to know. In this sense, *Beloved* is an expression of loss without end. The word "redemption" has often been used in connection with this novel in multiple references to the death of Beloved, Sethe's act of killing her, and the deaths of sixty million and more. But none of its definitions work: "repurchasing," "reformation," "restoration," "repayment," "atonement," "releasing from bondage." As for the culmination of Sethe's story, with its achieved society of three women enclosed in the house at 124, it is in its own right powerfully evocative and says much about Sethe's complex psychology and her evolving relationship with both her daughters, the living and the dead. But, as Margaret Atwood wrote in an early review, this conclusion can only happen because "[i]n this book, the other world exists and magic works" (Atwood 1987: 47). The book's culmination and the reuniting of Sethe and Paul D that follows, include a wishful element threaded in a fictional allegory that requires what cannot be: the grown ghost of a dead child, one moreover who is in some way a real entity in a fictional world and capable of acting, as Sethe says, "under her own free will" (Morrison 1987a: 200).

From this perspective, a key function of the novel's disorienting two-page coda is to remind us that what we have read is fiction. It tells us that amid all the good work that fiction can do of making known, of building plausible characters whom we can know from the inside, of giving life to the bare facts of history; amid all this wonderful creation there is also, traveling right along with it, the absolute of what has been lost to mind. To summarize, where Phelan's concept of "the stubborn" plays a role in the energetic enterprise of interpretation, the palpable experience of what is unknown requires a space within this enterprise where the construction of knowledge stops, even as one feels the tug of the need to know. With the stubborn, the sense of both its intransigence and its textual importance, enlarged by the effort to bring interpretive order, serves a vigorous and on-going discussion of meaning. The palpable unknown, by contrast, derives from a form of recalcitrance designed to immerse the reader in a state of unknowing, robbed not only of cognitive mastery but of its resources.

THE PROBLEM OF MASTERY

Am I confident about my reading? Not entirely, at least as far as Morrison's intention is concerned. My doubts on this score relate to the broader issue of seeming to master a complex fictional text through the agency of interpretation—even as I promote the experience of not knowing as a necessary element in interpreting certain texts. But before I get into the question of what Morrison may or may not have intended, there is a little bit of housekeeping that must be done regarding the words "interpretation" and "explanation," on the one hand, and "understanding" and "comprehension," on the other—words that are often used interchangeably as ways of knowing.[18] In this book, I use the former two as subsidiary forms of the latter two, which are the overarching terms. Following Paul Ricoeur (and many others), explanation is the attribution of causal connections, and interpretation is the attribution of meaning or value (Ricoeur 1984: 118ff). As Ricoeur elaborates, these terms often overlap in the functions they refer to as, for example, when explanation affects or even determines interpretation.[19] But these two terms, in turn, refer to operations

18. In the context of this book, one thing that complicates (but does not confound) the issue is that narrative itself is a principal means of achieving what each of these overlapping terms refer to. Narrative is, as David Herman puts it, an "instrument for sense-making" (Herman 2003: 12–13). Whether or not it is at work at the most rudimentary cognitive level, giving pre-linguistic shape to our sensory input, as Damasio contends, narrative certainly does its sense-making job of work, for better or worse, many times a day in our conscious lives. History is a complex version of this way of making sense, and narrative fiction an even more complex version.

19. The *interpretation* of Mr. Garner's treatment of his slaves at Sweet Home can turn on an *explanation* in terms of his motives (compassion, good business sense, stubborn individuality, all three). Depending on the motive or motives we settle on to explain his behavior, we interpret (appraise, evaluate, attribute meaning to) Mr. Garner in one way or another. Either interpretation or explanation can be applied, as here, to a part of a work or they can be applied to the

within the larger scope of the two other terms, which are closer together in meaning and for both of which the word "grasp" is usually found in the first dictionary definition. In fact, the Latin root verb for comprehend is "prehendere"—to grasp.[20] All of these terms, then, refer to forms of grasping or mastery through the agency of one's mind. And since the illusion of such mastery is an important companion theme in this study, it is worth pursuing just a little further in relation to the issue of interpreting Morrison's novel.

Morrison has said how important it was for her as she designed the first sentence of *Beloved* to have the reader feel "snatched, yanked, thrown into an environment completely foreign, and I want it as the first stroke of the shared experience that might be possible between the reader and the novel's population. Snatched just as the slaves were from one place to another, without preparation and without defense" (Morrison 1988: 32). Slowly, with effort, the reader begins to put things together, to see the characters, to determine how they relate to each other, and to understand that there is also in this house an angry ghost who is making their lives miserable. But though the characters in this novel come vigorously alive, the cognitive dissonance incurred, not simply by the novel's willful eponymous ghost, but by the author herself, is felt by the reader right up to the end.

This dissonance, felt in the reading, should not be lost in the interpretation. To put this in other words, the dissonance should not be mastered. It should not be made to submit to what Phelan, in agreement, calls "the standard academic interpretation" with its "underlying desire for mastery" and its "determination to make texts yield up their secrets" (1996: 180). I cannot presume to say what connotations or intensities the terms "master" and "mastery" may have in the mind of a black American writer and how they may differ

work itself. But when we use the terms in the latter sense, the gap between them widens. We (academics) rarely talk of *an explanation* of a work except as a kind of stripped down biographical accounting: e.g., Morrison was inspired by the story of Margaret Garner to write *Beloved*. When we develop *an interpretation* of a work (often referred to as a "reading"), something we often do, we do so with an eye to how parts of the work relate meaningfully to each other. And, unless we are speaking of modes of interpretation that I have called elsewhere symptomatic and adaptive (H. P. Abbott 2008: 104–9), the ideal is to develop an interpretation that can provide an inclusive understanding of how all the parts work together in a meaningful way. I have also argued elsewhere that when we seek to do this, we are, implicitly or explicitly, reading intentionally—that is, according to the intentions of an author, implied or real (H. P. Abbott 2011; for two excellent, contrasting overviews of the complexity of this subject, including the various kinds of interpretation, see Hogan 1996 and Iser 2000).

20. To "comprehend" is, then, to grasp together ("com-prehendere"). As such, "comprehension" is both more and less spacious than "understanding": more spacious, in that it suggests a complete understanding of something and its common antonym, "incomprehension," suggests an equally complete blank; less spacious, in that one speaks commonly of having a number of understandings or misunderstandings of a subject.

from those in the mind of a white American reader. But there is an element of freedom from the mastery of interpretive nets, an "openness," in this novel as in all of Morrison's novels that is important to her. As she puts it, it is "a quality of mystery in the books that I recognize and underscore" (Denard 2008: 138). In this reader's mind, it is a freedom that resonates with the complex thematic braid of freedom and imprisonment that runs through her work and particularly through *Beloved.* In the novel's storyworld, physical imprisonment goes hand in hand with interpretive imprisonment, as when the sheriff, gazing on the scene of murder before leading the murderess to jail, sees in it "testimony to the results of a little so-called freedom imposed on people who needed every care and guidance in the world to keep them from the cannibal life they preferred" (Morrison 1987a: 151). It is more than a stretch to align the sheriff's interpretation of Sethe's behavior with a suppositional reader's closed interpretation of *Beloved,* except in this: that both are examples of taking cognitive possession. I believe that Morrison, in her novels, takes preemptive care to avoid being possessed in this way, though these measures will only work for a reader willing to allow such dispossession.

So far, in this section, I have shifted my focus to the interpretative challenge that Phelan has isolated—that is, the stubborn recalcitrance of the conflicting avatars that go by the name of "Beloved"—because it helps to make clear how I will be using certain key terms in this book and also because the issue of unreadable characters will return in part three. But in addition it helps bring out by contrast the different way in which the felt absence that I have isolated adds its own disturbing weight to the experience of *Beloved.* It cannot be forgotten that in an important sense *no* story has been told in this novel. This contradiction creates its own counterpoint to the fictional Beloved's stubborn provocations to both explanation and interpretation. The discourse we read stretches over a void where there is *nothing* "to pass on," including the untold tale of an eponymous heroine. Sethe's child, Mrs. Garner's child, 60 million, and more are lost in that void. The mind's need to "grasp" something to work with ("already crawling?"), something to pull out of this void in order to gain even the beginnings of cognitive possession is, in this text, repeatedly and pointedly rebuffed. It is an absence that is both enormous and an enormity, both vast and terrible, and in both senses it cannot be "comprehended."

Of course, after deconstruction, the idea of achieving cognitive mastery over any semiotic artifact is quaint. Yet the need to comprehend is, as noted above, an embedded stance, something we have by our nature, as well it should be. Narrative is rooted in conversation, where the listener's mastery is not only invited but is necessary to complete the speaker's thought. Without this sufficiency of interpretive grasp, we would not have had the communicative advantage that has served us so well in our competition with other creatures. It is a practice we grow up with. Accordingly, the assumption or at least the illusion that meaning is there to be mastered is hard for the trained interpreter to give up. It has been observed many times of the generation of critics now almost past, that when, say, J. Hillis Miller writes of Hawthorne's "Minister's Black Veil" that "The veil is the type and symbol of the fact that all signs are potentially unreadable, or that the reading of them is potentially unverifiable" (J. H. Miller 1991: 97) and that by extension "the story is an allegory of the reader's own situation in reading it" (105), he himself is reading the story with confidence. The rhetoric of authority comes with the trade even as it disavows authority. But I am not advocating any such holistic discrediting of interpretation just as I am not advocating the other extreme of seeking *the* interpretation. Quite the contrary on both counts. My aim is to invigorate interpretation of the texts I have selected with an awareness of the intentionally induced states of unknowing that are embedded within them or, more accurately, that should be a salient part of the reader's experience of them. If, finally, to describe these states as such is to explain why they are there and to interpret what they signify, so be it. If I have explained and interpreted Beloved's absence from her novel, I hope I have done so in a way that helps the reader feel the insistent absence of that story and those of millions—that is, to have the immediate feeling of wanting to know them and knowing we shall never know them. In like manner, I will be making explanatory and interpretive assertions all the way through this study, though in such a way as to preserve the immediate experience of these gaps as part of our larger understanding of the texts in which they play a significant role. Readers, of course, will judge for themselves whether or not I succeed in doing so.

As also noted above, I have found that, though the kind of intentionally induced narrative "failure" that I have isolated in this study is comparatively rare, there is variety in it and a corresponding variety of states of unknowing. Moreover, they can occur within narratives that are otherwise amenable to multiple interpretations, as is the case with *Beloved.* I shall argue in a later chapter, for example, that as a short story, "Bartleby the Scrivener" not only succeeds but can be interpreted in a number of valid ways. But as a character—that is, as a representation of a living human being—Bartleby is inexplicable. What Melville's short story has in common with all the other works in the subset I am focusing on is an element that requires a change in reader/spectator orientation from an absorption in the forward-moving dynamic of narrative to an immersion in a state of bafflement. At the same time, the readerly distance required for representation to do its work gives way to a sense of *being in* an experience of what is unreadable. This is another subsidiary theme of this book. At these moments in our reading, we are, in Gertrude Stein's words, no longer concerned with "about" but "is." This "isness," as I hope to show, must be understood as a cognitive state. The reader becomes a willing captive of an art in which the pressure of narrative expectation is felt even as the contract of its fulfillment has been abrogated.

THE UNKNOWABLE

It remains to distinguish my approach from that of Philip Weinstein in his *Unknowing: The Modernist Work of Fiction* (2005). Weinstein's wonderful series of interlocking meditations provides a historically framed account of "the modernist drama of unknowing." The heart of his study is a discussion of Kafka, Proust, and Faulkner as revisionary novelists intent on releasing narrative from the failed Western "project of knowing" (5). The story they seek to expose and undo is the realist story of growing up, that is, "the subject coming to know" (25), in which figure stands out clearly against ground, time proceeds with a dependable progressive linearity, and maturation is measured by a steadily enlarged understanding of both the self and others. Weinstein's modernists assist in a "signature event" of literary and intellectual history when the tight bond of "subject/space/time" that gives realist fiction its world and its power was broken to reveal a condition of "unknowing." Theirs was not only a project of demolition but also a "heroic," if doomed, effort to achieve in fiction the "moment-by-moment" experience of life as it is lived in a plotless, futureless world of "unconvertable alterity" (166).[21]

The first difference between my approach and Weinstein's is that for the most part I set aside Jameson's rule: "always historicize" (Jameson 1981: 9). This is not to dispute the enormous and largely unconscious shaping power of ideology, but to assume that there is also a transcultural, transhistorical human.[22] Where Weinstein's orientation is toward ideological changes over

21. For Weinstein, the deep challenge for these authors is that their target is "a narrative we cannot do without, yet one whose disturbing priorities we cannot ignore. . . . Once the Enlightenment in its thought and practice had delegitimized the authority of crown and church, it could put in its place only a story of adventuring subjects, each with an unforeclosed future. The telos of this story, for the Enlightenment, is *education:* escape from self-incurred tutelage, daring to know" (44). Yet, citing Emmanuel Levinas, "'this adventure is no adventure. It is never dangerous; it is self-possession, sovereignty.' Sovereignty, because consciousness converts—by way of knowing—the otherness of everything it encounters into aspects of its own (reconfirmed) self-sameness" (46).

22. In this, I side largely with Paul Hernadi, who stoutly debated Jameson in the pages of *New Literary History* (1981). Hernadi contended among other things that "no account of change in nature or culture can avoid postulating relatively constant factors . . . in relation to which

time, mine is for the most part toward universal human conditions and in this sense it can be called "cognitivist." My assumption in all three parts of this book is that, for key aspects of both self and other, the limits of knowledge and the difficulty of accepting those limits are a part of our nature as *Homo sapiens.* A second difference is that where Weinstein's "unknowing" requires a dismantling of realist conventions, there is no such requirement in the broader domain of my study. In fact, all the texts taken up in Part Three are by most definitions examples of realist fiction.

Finally, my focus is on an *experience* of unknowing itself—the strategies of its production and the frame of mind necessary for it to occur. In this sense, too, my study can be called "cognitivist." But "cognitivist narratology" has been, in large part, an extension of the very old field of *narrative dynamics*—that is, the study of how narrative moves us and how it draws us from one point to the next. Efforts to account for narrative dynamics go back to Aristotle and forward to the mythic structures of Northrop Frye, the psychoanalytic analysis of Peter Brooks, the reader response theories of Wolfgang Iser and Meir Sternberg, the rhetorical theories of James Phelan and Peter Rabinowitz, the cognitivist approaches of Monica Fludernik and David Herman, and the affective narratology of Patrick Colm Hogan (2003, 2011), to name just a few.[23] But the subject of my study, the palpable unknown, is where narrative halts. And by this I do not mean those points where narrative gives way for a while to other text types—description, meditation, commentary, learned exposition—all of which absorb our attention while we are at the same time aware that the narrative motor is still running (H. P. Abbott 2000). The palpable unknown, by contrast, is a place where the narrative motor stops, where there not only is no narrative but no way for narrative to get in. As I described it above, it is a hole in the narrative that travels through it and stays in the

---

change becomes noticeable." In his landmark 1938 lecture on the notion of "self" as a category that evolved by stages out of the Roman concept of the person, Marcel Mauss anticipated Hernadi's critique by taking care to dissociate his focus (and that of "the French School of Sociology") on culturally determined concepts of the self from the equally legitimate focus on the "sense of self (moi)" that is, as it were, our birthright as human beings. "[I]t is plain," he wrote, "that there has never existed a human being who has not been aware, not only of his body, but also at the same time of his individuality, both spiritual and physical" (Mauss, ed. Carrithers et al. 1985: 3).

23. The awkward coinage "cognitivist" is a short way of referring loosely to work in the study of literature, film, drama, narrative (or more broadly culture) that to a greater or lesser extent draws on research in the cognitive sciences. In the many instances in which it features the transaction between the reader/viewer and the text, this approach could also be called "cognoformalist." For of necessity it must accommodate both sides of the transaction—how the reader responds and how the elements of the text generate that response—which is what I have tried to do in this book.

mind afterward. To steal another oxymoron from Samuel Beckett, but this time to redeploy it, it is a "moving pause." How we relate to it is the key aspect of fiction's "mind work" that I want to bring into focus.[24]

But however "cognitivist" one may wish to describe this book, I hope it will be clear to my reader that it is first and foremost a study of the writing and reading of narrative. And if I succeed in my goal, then there will certainly be material here for a diversity of other approaches, including those that historicize.

THE PARTS OF THIS BOOK

What follows is divided into three parts: Unimaginable Unknowns, Inexpressible States, and Egregious Gaps. The two chapters of Part One deal with narrative inferences of two vividly contrasting types of the unimaginable unknown. I call the experience they engender the "cognitive sublime." In chapter 1, the experience of the cognitive sublime is a secular extension of mystical discourse that goes way back. I begin with Beckett's version of the discourse because it involves the most extreme type of unknowability—the inability of the inquiring intelligence to account for its particularity as an inquiring intelligence. Chapter 2 shifts the focus to the equally ancient and exotic enigma of origins—the productivity of the new under the sign of its creator (the signature).

Part Two (chapters 3 and 4) turns attention toward the mystery of affective states,[25] the nature and complexity of which can only be intimated. Here inexpressibility is an integral part of the experience of the unknowable. These two

24. "Moving pause" is lifted from Belacqua Shuah, the protagonist (*soi-disant*) of *More Pricks than Kicks,* who "had a strong weakness for oxymoron" (Beckett 1972: 38). "Mind work" is lifted from Kay Young, who used it in a fine recent volume in this series, *Imagining Minds* (Young 2010). Young uses the term in a much broader and richer sense than I do here and at the same time restricts her demonstration texts to selected nineteenth-century English novels. But her term derives from a premise we both share: that narrative fiction can *perform* where the sciences of mind and body can only theorize (Young 2010: 4). It performs, moreover, not only by representing the interaction of embodied minds but by engaging the embodied minds of its readers and viewers.

25. One could as well use the compound "affective/cognitive," since, increasingly, the two are seen as inseparable concepts. In Damasio's words, we have a "mind with feeling" (Damasio 2010: 20; see also, *inter alia,* Varela et al. 1991, Lakoff and Johnson 1999). In common parlance, we tend to associate cognition with understanding and affect with feeling, so that, for example, in the sentence "What part of 2 + 2 = 4 don't you understand?," one might say that 2 + 2 = 4 is a matter of cognition while the notes of sarcasm, exasperation, and humiliation in the sentence are matters of affect. Yet understanding the baby math of 2 + 2 plays its affective role in the rhetoric of humiliation, while conversely to understand (cognize) what's going on must include a feeling response to the sentence's affective notes (see Palmer 2004: 19–20).

chapters bring the focus down to a molecular level of narrative syntax and the syntax of narrative. At this level, we will examine deliberate failures to meet fundamental syntactical expectations in an art calculated to generate states of mind inaccessible through grammatical narrative discourse. Chapter 3, which deals with a unique form of asyntactically generated "neural sport," paves the way for chapter 4 in which I deal with several stunning examples of syntactically layered prose poetry, or better, "lyrical narrative."

Beside their intrinsic value, Parts One and Two provide a context for the concluding three chapters in that each features limitations of the knowable and the expressible that come with the mere fact of our existence as selves. They are, as it were, a birthright. In these four chapters also, perhaps unsurprisingly, the demonstration texts are each, in one way or another, a sharp departure from the realist tradition of prose fiction. By contrast, the narratives of Part Three are drawn from the realist tradition, and my focus is on enigmas, not of the self, but of the other. Accordingly, I take up a collection of narrative gaps and unreadable minds whose refusal of access plays a central role in the narratives in which we find them. Explicit in this part, but implicit in the other two, is an ethical theme that I develop more fully in the final chapter.

I like the way these three parts of my book come together and I hope the reader does, too. I hope it is also clear that, taken together, these three parts of my book are not at all meant to be a comprehensive anatomy of the subject. In my reading of *Beloved* in this chapter, for example, I have taken up another subdivision of the palpable unknown—the feeling of an absolute erasure of lives. I would not be surprised if readers were to experience similar evocations of loss, clinging with the same grievous depth of effect, in the literature of the gulag, the Holocaust, the disappeared, the killing fields, and of others who have been forcibly erased without record.

PART ONE

Unimaginable Unknowns

CHAPTER 1

Apophatic Narrative

APOPHASIS

> No form belongs to Him, not even one for the intellect. . . . What meaning can there be any longer in saying: "This and this property belong to Him?"
>
> —Plotinus

> And if He is neither goodness nor being nor truth. What is He then? He is nothing. He is neither this or that. Any thought you might still have of what He might be—He is not such at all.
>
> —Meister Eckhart

> For how can that be expressed which is neither genus, nor difference, nor species, nor individual, nor number; nay more, is neither an event, nor that to which an event happens?
>
> —Clement of Alexandria

These kinds of questions have been asked for a long time. They belong to a larger set of expressive impossibilities that is still very much alive in many different modes of discourse—Buddhist, Romantic, Holocaust, poststructuralist, quantum physical.[1] It includes an endless diversity of what is called the *ineffability topos,* which among other things is an ancient commonplace in protestations of love. You can find good examples on the lips of Goneril and Regan in Scene One of *King Lear* as they protest the unspeakability of their love for their father.[2] In the long western tradition of mystical discourse, the pursuit in words of what is beyond words is referred to as *Apophasis,* literally "speaking away" or "unsaying," and commonly understood as "self-negating discourse" or even "a total cessation of discourse" (Franke 2007: 1–2). Its development as a central philosophical idea can be traced back at least to the Neoplatonists, and its most influential deployment in the Christian tradition can be found in the apophatic, or negative, theology of the late-fifth century Syrian monk Pseudo-Dionysius the Areopagite and the thirteenth-century Dominican monk Meister Eckhart. Their work was richly redeveloped by many hands in Christian mysticism, and their influence is still very much alive in our own epoch and can be found in the work of Martin Heidegger, Jean-Luc Marion, Jacques Derrida, and Samuel Beckett.

On the face of it, the issue of the breakdown of *narrative* in the face of the inexpressible would appear to be logically subsumed within apophatic discourse, since almost invariably apophatic discourse has focused on the failure of language itself, as, for example, in reference to the entity misnamed "God," which precedes language and is therefore nameless.

> If I have spoken of it, I have not spoken of it, for it is ineffable. (Meister Eckhart, cited in Clark 1957: 87)

> God should not be said to be ineffable, for when this is said, something is said. . . . [T]hat is not ineffable which can be called ineffable. (Augustine, tr. Robertson 1958: 622–23)

Or, as Wittgenstein put it, "Whereof one cannot speak, thereof one must be silent" (2007: 27). So. No words, no narrative. Moreover, the words used most

1. "Brahman has neither name nor form, transcends merit and demerit, is beyond time, space, and the objects of the sense-experience. . . . Supreme, beyond the power of speech to express" (Shankara, cited in Alston 1956: 506). "[T]he ultimate 'objects' of nonclassical theories [of physics are] inaccessible, unknowable, unrepresentable, inconceivable, untheorizable, indefinable, and so forth by any means that are or ever will be available to us, including, ultimately, as 'objects' in any conceivable sense of the term" (Plotnitsky 2002: 3).

2. In the Renaissance, the device would be recognized as a subclass of the trope of *adynaton* (literally "without power"). Technically, this trope is not limited to the attempt through words or narrative to arrive at the unknowable (the subject of this chapter), since these two daughters profess to feel what it is they cannot express. I'll take up a different class of the inexpressible in chapters 3 and 4.

commonly to describe, not the indescribable itself, but the outward condition of the mystical experience, are words like *cessation, stillness,* and *silence.* These would seem *a fortiori* to disqualify concepts like *narrative, narration,* and *narrativity,* not to mention the entire fourth dimension of time, without which, again, there is no narrative.[3] As Clement of Alexandria writes, what is sought "is neither an event, nor that to which an event happens" (Clement of Alexandria, *Stromata,* chap. 12; cited in Hawkins and Schotter 194: 2).

Apophatic theology accords with a commonplace in the Bible, that is, that God is neither to be named nor seen. According to Gregory of Nyssa, the Lord's specific instruction to Moses in this regard was to forbid "that the Divine be likened to any of the things known by men, since every concept which comes from some comprehensible image by an approximate understanding and by guessing at the divine nature constitutes an idol of God and does not proclaim God" (Gregory of Nyssa; cited in Franke 2007: 143). At best, one must settle for the four letters of the Tetragrammaton (YHWH). Arguably, then, the extraordinary conception of Jesus as both God and man functioned to get around this prohibition. By providing an image of the unimaginable, complete with a powerful narrative, it accommodated the insistent narrative needs of human understanding—needs that would be most keenly felt when trying to understand what was more important than anything else. Certainly the stories of Mohammed, of Mary, and of all the saints serve as legitimate alternative foci of religious veneration that are both nameable and equipped with the intellectual and emotional resonances of story. But as a literal representation of God (Jesus is Lord) Christ and His story fall in a special class among the Abrahamic religions, one that by virtue of its seeming self-contradiction has unsurprisingly provoked an enduring intensity of theological controversy.

Milton boldly took this contradiction a step further in *Paradise Lost* when he portrayed not only the figurable Christ, but His unfigurable Father as well. In so doing, he made the absolutely unknowable a character in a story. God the Father appears in a pretty uninteresting segment of the larger story, as stories go, but He is still rendered in narrative form. In Book 3, we see Him, sitting "High Thron'd above all highth," with his eye bent upon "His own works and their works at once to view" (Milton III: 57–59: 196). His eye then travels from point to point, first beholding "Our two first Parents, . . . / Reaping

3. Silence of course can be time-bound and, as such, can play an important role in creating the narrative suspense of music. In this way and others, silence in music is arguably as important as sound. Similarly, silence plays a diversity of meaningful roles in the rhetoric of oral presentation and, for that matter, in the conversation of our daily lives. But dead silence, silence outside of time and without end, is a different thing altogether.

immortal fruits of joy and love" (65–67: 197); then surveying "Hell and the Gulf between, and *Satan* there / Coasting the wall of Heav'n on this side Night / In the dun Air sublime" (70–72); and finally, "to his onely Son foreseeing," he proceeds to tell the story of the Fall of Man, responding at points to His Son's queries and interjections. In the teachings of Pseudo-Dionysius, there is a role for a positive (kataphatic) as well as a negative (apophatic) theology. But Milton's "accommodation" to our cognitive limitations, goes way beyond that role. By the standards, at least, of Dionysian discourse what Milton achieved was a displacement rather than an intimation of the Divine.[4]

Of course most of the action in this scene is talk, and in this, at least, Milton follows biblical precedent. If we are not allowed to see the God of the Old Testament, we certainly hear Him. As an oral presence, particularly in His engagement with Moses, He is a forceful and exacting character, playing His role in a dramatic, narratable interaction with His chosen emissary, cautioning, ordering, making promises. And in truth, it is hard to see any alternative to such narrativization of an unknowable and unspeakable entity if, that is, you are going to have any markers of divine authenticity in the complicated business of setting up a covenant with all its attendant rules and consequences. And surely there is much antecedent tradition of invisible deities speaking, either in their own voice or the oracular voice of a human agent. Gods, of course, can do anything they want to do, including interventions in our affairs with whatever accommodation our limited minds require. It is only when the issue of divine unknownness and its discursive consequences are at a premium that such interventions amount to a problematic trade-off.

This problem, I would argue, extends also to the indirect evidence of divine power through the narrativization of its effects (thunderbolts, plagues, floods). To read such effects is to invite a triangulation of qualities that may come to dominate one's understanding and thus limit the unknowable with the contours of a divine thisness. Astronomers do the same thing when they triangulate the nature of an invisible planet through the subtle perturbations it causes in the star it circles. Reading this rhythmic dance, they infer limits of planetary thisness. When you think about it, this way of reading the divine nature through its effects can actually be applied to the full text of all

4. Dionysian standards have not, of course, always been followed. In painting, God the Father has made frequent appearances in human form, most notably on the ceiling of the Sistine Chapel. But narrativized, set in motion as it were, Milton's God was also going to fill out as a character, revealing a personality, aspects of which have rankled critics from the start. In a subtle defense, Ralph Rader argues that this defect and others, though "definite and real . . . . do not interfere with or disrupt our experience of the poem so much as they mark for us the limits of its perfection" (Rader 2011: 53).

the things in existence. You can't make a world without inviting inferences as to what kind of an entity You are. Finding a language that both acknowledges and baffles such inferences is a challenge, one that is approached in the wonderful passage in the first book of Kings when Elijah stands upon Mount Horeb:

> And, behold, the LORD passed by, and a great and strong wind rent the mountains, and brake in pieces the rocks before the LORD; but the LORD was not in the wind: and after the wind an earthquake; but the LORD was not in the earthquake:
>
> And after the earthquake a fire; but the LORD was not in the fire: and after the fire a still small voice. (I Kings 19:11–12)[5]

I want to come back to this attempt to both say and unsay in narrative form, but first I want to acknowledge one way in which narrative most commonly works in relation to the unsayable, and that is in the life-writing about, and self-writing of, mystics. Here narrativization turns away from the effort to capture, directly or indirectly, what William James described as "states of insight into depths of truth unplumbed by the discursive intellect" (W. James, ed. Marti 1983: 380).[6] Instead, it treats the process leading up to it and what happens afterward. As André Kukla observes, though Saint Theresa of Avila can write of this process "as a life-changing experience," what she "cannot do, according to her own report, is state the content of her insight" (Kukla 2005: 10). In apophatic discourse, the story of Moses is especially important in this regard. In his *Mystical Theology,* Pseudo-Dionysius uses it as a central text, a story with a black hole through which Moses plunges into "the truly mysterious darkness of unknowing" (Pseudo-Dionysius, tr. Luibheid 1987: 137). In terms of gap theory, which I will develop more fully in chapter 5, we are focusing here on permanent or unfillable gaps. But like the gap I isolated in Morrison's *Beloved* and like many of the other gaps in the following chapters, they are of a special order: they are gaps the reader must be constrained not to fill, yet to feel their quality of unfilled unfillableness.

---

5. Eyal Segal has informed me that in the original Hebrew, the sense of paradox is sustained even to "a still small voice," for which, he writes, "a more literal translation would be 'a voice of thin silence.' An even more literal translation, which doesn't take English grammar into account, would be 'voice [*kol*] silence [*demama*] thin [*daka*],' since the Hebrew has only three words (no indefinite article and no 'of,' which is only implied), and the adjective follows the noun" (email communication, 4-20-2010).

6. After more than a century, James's chapter on "Mysticism" in his *Varieties of Religious Experience* remains one of the most useful and pleasurably readable overviews of the commonalities of mystical experience and what can or cannot be inferred from them.

For Pseudo-Dionysius, Moses's ascent of Mount Sinai symbolized what Thomas Aquinas later called the *via negativa,* a negative way that culminates in seeing, not God, who is unseeable, but the clearing away of all else from Him. As such, it is a specialized form of self-consuming narrative that Pseudo-Dionysius speaks of as *aphaeresis,* "the process whereby the soul systematically negates itself along its mystical journey towards God. As an epistemology, it empties the clutter of the finite mind to clear a space for divine illumination" (Ludwin 2001: 123). In *The Divine Names,* Pseudo-Dionysius describes this space as a place that excludes the possibility of any kind of story. It is a place "not only as invisible and unencompassed, but also as at once unsearchable and untrackable; for, there is no path for those who penetrate into its infinite hiddenness" (Franke 2007: 163). The same idea guides Dante as he approaches the end of the *Paradiso.* A contemporary of Meister Eckhart, deeply influenced by the apophatic mysticism of poets like Bernard of Clairvaux and Richard of Saint Victor (Franke 2007: 313), Dante created a narrative doomed to bring an end to its narratability.

> Substance and accidents and their relations,
> Are yet fused together in such a manner
> That what I am talking of is a simple light. (Dante 33, tr. Sisson 1980: 89–91)

With no further possibility of "a flight for my wings," he writes, "At this point high imagination failed" (Dante 33: 139–42).

APOPHATIC NARRATIVE

All of which brings me back to a point I made above: that there is no opportunity for narrative in the place the mystic yearns to get to. To misuse a term from the theory of black holes, there is an *event horizon* beyond which nothing can be seen and time is abolished. The whole process resonates with Peter Brooks's analysis of the many ways in which the power of narrative derives from its condition as a journey governed by the magnetic pull of death. And yet for the mystic the termination of narrative once the event horizon of the unknowable is crossed is not a death but some kind of persistence of being out of time. It is very much like what happens in the transition from *Malone Dies* to *The Unnamable* in Samuel Beckett's *Trilogy* where being seems to persist after the cessation of narrative in a space that is, as Pseudo-Dionysius described it, "unencompassed," "unsearchable," "untrackable"—or, as a voice asks (and it is all a "question of voices now"), "Where now? Who now? When now?" (Beckett 1965: 291).

The almost perfect fit here between the fifth-century Syrian monk and the twentieth-century Irish protestant *manqué* is no accident. Beckett was strongly drawn to the work of the apophatic theologians, especially that of Meister Eckhart, whose sermons he read and reread throughout much of his adult life.[7] Apophatic theology provides a highly suggestive frame for his work before the *Trilogy*, in which he can be seen gesturing toward a narrative structure governed by versions of a "negative way." This is perhaps most notable in his first completed play, *Eleuthéria*, in which the central character, Victor Krap, could be described as a soul systematically divesting itself of everything that defines its life in this world to wind up at the end of the play curled up in bed in a state of complete, inert, inactivity, "his scrawny back turned on mankind" (Beckett, tr. Brodsky 1995: 191). The relentless and far more ambitious march of the *Trilogy* was begun immediately after the completion of *Eleuthéria* in the same year, 1947. It was broken only by the writing of *Godot* after Beckett had completed *Malone Dies*. In context, his most famous work appears to be a pause, or as he described it, a place of clarity and order where he could catch his breath before descending into *The Unnamable*.[8]

There are, however, two major differences between Beckett and his apophatic predecessors, of which the first is that he lacked the one certainty that comes with faith. Despite his enthusiasm for the sermons of Meister Eckhart, Beckett could not assume that there is *anything* lying or not lying on the other side of the knowable. What there is of any relevance lies on this side: the baffling sense of importance that attaches to being when being is self-aware—the feeling of somehow having been selected to be oneself with neither explanation nor prior consent. This is the engine that drove his periodic returns to an apophatic art. The other difference between Beckett and the theologians is that Beckett continued to draw on the resources of narrative for this endeavor. He did so despite the fact that in *The Unnamable*, as in his apophatic writing thereafter, narrative is a technical impossibility since there is neither the time nor the space to sustain a story, much less a beginning or an end.[9] What

7. For work focused directly on the resonances of apophatic mysticism in Beckett's oeuvre and its possible influence, see Buning 2000, Johansson 2000, Wolosky 1995, and Wynands 2007. See also Baldwin 1981, Barge 1988, Bryden (1998: 181–88), and van der Hoeden 1997.

8. "I turned to writing plays to relieve myself of the awful depression the prose led me into. . . . Life at that time was too demanding, too terrible, and I thought theater would be a diversion" (Bair 1978: 361); "Le travail du romancier est dur; on s'avance dans le noir. Au théâtre, on entre dans un jeu, avec ses règles, et on ne peut pas s'y soumettre" (Mignon 1964: 8).

9. Beckett's formal experiments were anticipated by the experiments of apophatic theolo-

Beckett contrived was a way of straddling the event horizon of the unimaginable unknown by driving narrative beyond its natural limits. This brings us back to Elijah and the paradox of a self-cancelling narrative that took place on Mount Horeb. In Beckett's hands, the paradox of apophatic narrative takes shape as an urgency of pursuit that resides in the language itself. This is still action, indeed frenetic action—a headlong rush of words—but it is action that draws much of its energy from the impossibility of narrative and the absolute absence of a storyworld. Narrative in this state is a long way from the narrative mode adopted by Pseudo-Dionysius when he represented the process of *aphaeresis* in Moses' ascent of Mount Sinai. It lacks the distance enjoyed by such an act of representation. It is instead experiential in the most immediate way, a bizarre apophatic quest powered by a narrative yearning that draws the acceptant reader into its struggle.

To relocate narrative excitement from a represented world to language keyed to the absence of that world, Beckett was driven constantly to remake the language of narration itself.

> A place. Where none. A time when try to see. Try say. How small. How vast. How if not boundless bounded. Whence the dim. Not now. Know better now. Unknow better now. Know only no out of. Into only. Hence another. Another place where none. Whither once whence no return. No. No place but the one. None but the one where none. Whence never once in. Somehow in. Beyondless. Thenceless there. Thitherless there. Thenceless thitherless there. (Beckett 1996: 92)

Here in *Worstward Ho,* the reader is made to float in a place that is no place, where the coordinates of time and space have given way to an urgency of directionless pursuit toward an unknowable end. What is left of story is the adventures of a voice, unfolding from one word to the next. It is a voice in the first-person present, yet without a person to go with the narration: "Say a

---

gians as they struggled to achieve in language what Kierkegaard called "[t]he supreme paradox of all thought," that is, "the attempt to discover something that thought cannot think" (Kierkegaard, tr. Swenson 1936: 29). For example, one ingenious solution hit upon by the apophatic theologians to deal with the problem of saying without saying is the device of hyperphasis or hyper-predication. One finds it in the writing of Pseudo-Dionysius and later in the "hyperphatic theology" of the ninth-century Irish mystic Johannes Scotus Eriugena. It involved appending the words "more than" ("super," "plus quam") when attributing traits to an unknowable God. God is not, for example, merciful but "more-than-merciful," not omnipotent but "more than omnipotent." In this way, one skirts the danger of limiting the divine nature by naming its traits. God is "superessentialis," more-than-being. Indeed, God is more-than-God (Franke 2007: 182). Whether Beckett had this and other necessarily odd apophatic locutions in mind when, in *The Unnamable,* he found himself hovering at the edge of the sayable, I cannot say.

body. Where none" (89). What the voice yearns for is what the reader yearns for as well, what his or her neural circuits are designed for, a world, fictive or real, in which narrative action can take place. Instead, action is narration, beginning self-reflexively in the present imperative—"On. Say on. Be said on" (89)—and ending in the past tense—"Said nohow on" (116). The initial "On" tells us that it is not a true beginning but a continuation, while the last "on" tells us it is not a conclusion but, for now at least, a loss of energy. It is the nonexistent end of what Gilles Deleuze called an art of "exhaustion."[10] The only thing that gives these words their minimal narrativity, their urgent pell-mell rush, seemingly in spurts, with no time for the little helper-words that ordinarily give sentences their clarity, is the yearning for a genuine narrativity in a genuine world. In short, there is no longer any possibility of "accommodating" the modes of human cognition, of allowing the reader to nestle into the kind of satisfying narrativity that Milton and his enthusiasts settled for. They, like the self-deceiving Devil himself, had only built themselves a Kingdom in "this hell of stories" (Beckett 1965: 380).

Deprived of certainties of any kind, such an experience of apophatic narrative is the experience of what, in this chapter and the next, I am calling the "cognitive sublime." When I first hit upon the idea of a "cognitive sublime," and used it in an essay (H. P. Abbott 2009), I was not aware of Alan Richardson's happy coinage "the neural sublime," now the title of a revisionist and provocative book on the English Romantics (2010).[11] Richardson argues for greater recognition of the influence of Burke's physiologically based concept of the sublime on Romantic poetry and thought as opposed to the influence of Kant's transcendental concept of the sublime. The neural sublime is a strictly materialist concept of the sublime as "a corporeal experience that, in the last analysis, depends on changes in the central nervous system, a stretching and subsequent relaxation of the nerves" (A. Richardson: 26). As such, the concept allows me to differentiate the concept of a "cognitive sublime," which I apply to the effects dealt with in this chapter and the next. In what I have chosen to examine in the work of Beckett and García Márquez, there is no materialist finality. If they achieve their effects by having some serious fun with our neural circuitry, it is not meant to limit wonderment in this way, since there is as yet no confirmation that matter is all there is. This, of course, also goes for the so-called spiritual, transcendental, noumenal, and like suppositions. But in Richardson's reading, the absence of the immaterial is absolute. When

10. "Il s'épuise en épuisant le possible, et inversement. Il épuise ce qui *ne se réalise pas* dans le possible" (Deleuze 1992: 57–58).

11. See also Cynthia A. Freeland's cognitivist approach to the sublime in "The Sublime in Cinema" (1999), an essay which Richardson cites.

Shelley in his essay "On Life" takes us to "that verge where words abandon us, and . . . we grow dizzy to look down the dark abyss of how little we know," Shelley, in Alan Richardson's construction, offers "no compensation aside from that awful vacancy and accompanying dizziness . . . we are left blinking in the sublime darkness of an overtaxed brain" (32–33). By contrast, if Shelley describes what I am distinguishing as the cognitive sublime, the lack of knowledge is more acute, since there is always the possibility (for good, or ill, or whatever) that there is more going on in that abyss of darkness. In short, if readers read in the mode I am promoting, they experience a textual transaction that conveys the felt quality of extratextual unknowing.

THE DEICTIC MAZE

Once in the Q & A following a keynote address by Gerald Edelman,[12] he was asked if he thought we could ever create a machine that was conscious. His answer was, Yes, in the next thousand years or so this could happen. Then someone else in the audience asked if Edelman thought we could create a machine that not only was conscious but also had that sense of its own unique particularity that we commonly refer to as the "I" or ego. After a pause, Edelman said, No, this we could not do. It was an interesting moment and resonated with the common intuition that even if we managed to find a way across the notorious "gap" between the brain and the mind, there would still be this additional gap referred to by philosophers as the problem of personal identity. It is a seemingly out-of-reach mystery with a distinction that chimes with that other august mystery: Why is there something rather than nothing? In the apophatic mystical tradition, the two questions often meld into one. In this tradition, however, there has been at least an answer to the question (God), however unspeakable that answer may be. For Beckett, as noted above, this confidence could no longer be maintained. Without it, he turned the mystery on an axis to focus on the listener, alone on an island in the great dark, hearing voices that may or may not be his own.

Consequently, when he set out in *The Unnamable* on his strange wanderings along the event horizon of the unimaginable unknown—wanderings that culminated in *Worstward Ho*[13]—the baffling condition of *being somehow*

12. At the annual conference of the Society for Literature, Science, and the Arts, Chicago, 2006.

13. There were shorter pieces by Beckett between 1983, when he published *Worstward Ho*, and his death in 1989. Notable in our context is his last work, the poem "What is the Word" (Beckett 1990: 131–34), written for his friend Joe Chaikin.

present works as a kind of black hole pulling at his sentences. As I have been arguing and will continue to argue with regard to Beckett and all the other writers featured in this book, what we feel in this kind of writing is only possible because the author took a big step, not only beyond analytical discourse (in this case, on the problem of personal identity), but also beyond the representational discourse of narrative. For readers who are willing (and "willing" is a key term here), he cut the distance between them and what is going on in the narrative to the point where they are no longer observing someone having a hard time, but having it themselves.

> The stories of Mahood are ended. He has realized they could not be about me, he has abandoned, it is I who win, who tried so hard to lose, in order to please him, and be left in peace. Having won, shall I be left in peace? It doesn't look like it, I seem to be going on talking. In any case all these suppositions are probably erroneous. I shall no doubt be launched again, girt with better arms, against the fortress of mortality. What is more important is that I should know what is going on now, in order to announce it, as my function requires. It must not be forgotten, sometimes I forget, that all is a question of voices. I say what I am told to say, in the hope that some day they will weary of talking at me. The trouble is I say it wrong, having no ear, no head, no memory. Now I seem to hear them say it is Worm's voice beginning, I pass on the news, for what it is worth. (1965: 345)

Here is a passage like many in *The Unnamable* that is impossible to read. The problems of reading begin to mount with its third word, the modest preposition "of." On the face of it, the stories *of* Mahood are the stories the narrating voice told *of* the creature he invented and named Basil and then renamed Mahood. And they are also stories *of* Mahood in the sense that they are stories told *by* Mahood. So far, the reader's problem would be no more than a problem familiar to readers of any number of autobiographical narratives in which "the teller and the told" (310) are presumed to be the same person. But with the next sentence, we are told that an ostensible subject all along has been *me:* "He has realized they could not be about me. . . . " The linguistic difference between "me" and "he" puts an impossible semantic burden on the preposition "of" with a simultaneous separation and inter-identification of *he, me, I, him,* and *Mahood,* which has in fact accompanied the reader for the preceding thirty-six pages, ever since the retroactive christening of Mahood. "It was he told me stories about me, lived in my stead, issued forth from me, came back to me, entered back into me, heaped stories on my head. I don't know how it was done" (309). Autobiographies have, it is true, been narrated in the third person (*The Education of Henry Adams,* Norman Mailer's *Armies of the Night,* Roland Barthes's *Roland Barthes,* J. M. Coetzee's *Youth*), but in such cases the narrating voice is usually stabilized as an implicit first-person entity who makes use of the third-person construction for a self now distanced by time from the one who narrates. What is unique in Beckett's narrative are the ways in which grammatical references of subject and object are at once inter-identified and set in conflict—a conflict moreover that is unsought ("he has abandoned, it is I who win, who tried so hard to lose, in order to please him") and that is fought by combatants who constantly betray their own cause by slipping into the enemy camp without even a change of pronoun ("I seem to be going on talking").

In his book *The Paradox of Self-Consciousness,* Jose Luis Bermudez contends that one strand of the paradox of self-consciousness is demonstrated in the philosophical effort to "elucidate the capacity to think first-person thoughts through linguistic mastery of the first-person pronoun." The effort, he argues, is doomed to "*explanatory circularity*" because what one is trying to explain is part of the explanation ("the explanandum is part of the explanans" [Bermudez 2000: 16]). It is precisely this circularity that Beckett embraces by continually transgressing the grammatical levels of the personal subject and the personal object. The blurring of these levels is a paradox that we live with throughout the ordinary course of our lives but keep as it were quarantined by the unconscious application of the rules of grammar. By crossing grammatical boundaries the way he does, Beckett not only exposes the paradox but immerses us in it. Moreover, as the grammatical levels of subject and object correspond to the narrative levels of first and third person narration, Beckett at the same time engages in what narratologists call *metalepsis,* the mixing together of narrative levels that are ordinarily kept separate simply in order to go about the business of telling a story (Malina 2000: 9; Risser 1997: 88). The effect of all this is a sustained sentence-by-sentence grammatical and narrational vertigo. And it gets worse.

By the end of this passage, two more personal pronouns have entered the referential mix for the same subject/object. On the one hand, *I/he* is *they/them,* for who else could be giving orders ("now I seem to hear them say")? On the other hand, *I/he/they* is also an implicit *you,* for who else could be the one addressed ("in order to announce it," "I pass on the news, for what it is worth")? In grammatical terms, this whole mess is a crisis of "person deixis," keyed to the necessary dependence of personal pronouns on context to determine their reference. Person deictics like *he, him, me, I, they, you* have no referential value in themselves but only in what can be determined from context. Perhaps Otto Jespersen's term "shifters" works better to express the fluid condition of these open lexical templates (Jespersen 1922).[14] Once they are established, we rely on them in turn to let us know who is talking and who is being talked about. But if I am right in my reading of this passage, its abundance of shifters all have the same referent. Or more accurately, they do and they do not, given our propensity to keep subject and object distinct. And to make our reading experience even more dizzying, the voice has included two proper names, Worm and Mahood, that appear to share the same referential ambiguity as the personal pronouns in that they are similarly maintained as referential templates without content except as temporarily deployed.

It may help to see what is going on here as a kind of narrational opposite to what Ann Banfield first labeled an "empty deictic center" (1987). In the case of an empty deictic center, deictics, largely of time and place, strongly suggest a narrating "subjective center" within the storyworld but do not provide sufficient contextual clues to know whose voice it is—as for example in Katharine Mansfield's "At the Bay":

> Ah-Aah! sounded the sleepy sea. And from the bush there came the sound of little streams flowing, quickly, lightly, slipping between the smooth stones, gushing into ferny basins and out again; and there was the splashing of big drops on large leaves, and something else—what was it?—a faint stirring and shaking, the snapping of a twig and then such silence that it seemed someone was listening. (Mansfield 1991: 97)[15]

The empty deictic center is a subjective center without a subject. But—and here is the point I want to emphasize—however unique, even disturbing, it may have first appeared, it is a condition most readers of modernist texts by authors like Mansfield and Woolf have learned to "naturalize"[16] and thus accept without much strain. It has, in short, become a narrative convention. In stark contrast, Beckett has crammed the subjective center of *The Unnam-*

14. The term, "shifters," was given prominence by Roman Jacobson, particularly in his 1971 essay, "Shifters, Verbal Categories, and the Russian Verb." In his lucid and impeccably organized *Lectures on Deixis,* Charles J. Fillmore distinguishes five categories of deixis: person deixis, place deixis, time deixis, discourse deixis, and social deixis.

15. For an interesting critique that identifies the missing subject with the reader, see Fludernik (1996: 192–207).

16. Here and elsewhere in this study, I use the term "naturalize" in the sense that Jonathan Culler used it when he adapted it from Barthes: that is, as an "operation" on the text performed by readers in order "to recognize the common world which serves as a point of reference" (Culler 1975: 135). Monica Fludernik's term for a somewhat broader version of the concept is "narrativize," but the effect is basically the same: "By recuperating such texts, by narrativizing them, readers enforce a minimal holistic (cognitive) story shape on what is threatening to become unreadable, unshapable textual fluidity" (Fludernik 1996: 274).

able with a superabundance of personal deictics, a conflict of grammatical schemata that cannot be naturalized and thus never loses its power to disturb the reader. It is the case of Rimbaud's oft-cited line, "Je est un autre" ("I is an other"), raised to the third or fourth power. In critical and philosophical discourse, Rimbaud's one-liner has commonly been absorbed as an ambiguity of selfhood (e.g., "The self is experienced as an other to the self"), but what has been lost in the process of explication is the feeling of vertigo induced by his "bad" grammar.[17]

Understandably, then, commentary on *The Unnamable* has likewise fallen back on interpretive formulae such as "the inadequacy of subject reference" or "the incompatibility of self and narrative." Whatever the accuracy of such analytical assessments (and they are often accurate), there is a risk in deploying them, since they can (and I think often do) serve as a refuge from the *experience* of what they purport to describe. This should be avoided because the very failures of language and narrative these formulae describe are tools that are essential for Beckett's success. They allow him to generate direct experience of news from the interior, our own interior. Put simply, Beckett gives us experiential knowledge of our ignorance about who we are. He has devised textual mechanisms through which we experience individually specific consciousness as a moving point of self-presence in a constancy of self-absence. We experience it as neither one nor the other but both at once and thus, arguably, impossible to realize without our constantly flipping deictic orientations from sentence to sentence and even from phrase to phrase. This is the "impossibility" of reading this text that I referred to above. Still, it is through this felt impossibility that Beckett gets us as close perhaps as most of us are likely to get to the condition of nonunderstanding that evolutionary necessity and its agent, grammar, for good practical reasons have kept from our daily awareness. After all, burdened as we are with consciousness as no other animal before us, it helps enormously to believe that we are unitary beings with a coherent self well within the grasp of language. It confers a competitive advantage.

THE UNNARRATABLE SELF

The self as a narrative construct is now a widely distributed assumption across numerous fields in which human beings are the subject of study: autobi-

17. For more on how this works in Beckett's *The Unnamable,* see H. P. Abbott 1984 (196–206).

ography, social psychology, narratology, therapeutics, popular texts of self-improvement, and much of the sociocultural history of the self that flowed in the wake of Marcel Mauss's 1938 lecture on "A category of the human mind: the notion of person; the notion of self." A more recent landmark in thinking of the self as necessarily a narrative construct is Oliver Sacks's (1987) moving accounts of two cases in which narrative capability has been disabled. They are instances of Korsakov's Syndrome, a cognitive deficit in which not only are all traces of one's life story erased but none is allowed to take shape. The victim is "isolated in a single moment of being, with a moat or lacuna of forgetting all round him" (29), and as a consequence can only, at best, engage in a bizarre project of constructing a new, situated, narratable self at every moment, "continually creating a world and self, to replace what was continually being forgotten and lost" (110). This necessary inclusion of narrative in the concept of selfhood was echoed by the philosopher Daniel Dennett (1991), and the psychologists Roger Schank (1990) and Jerome Bruner (1991), and provided with a neurobiological base in Young and Saver's influential essay on the severe existential consequences of four types of "dysnarrativia" (2001). Drawing on Young and Saver in *How our Lives become Stories: Making Selves,* Paul John Eakin makes the connection mandatory: "Individuals who have lost the ability to construct narratives have lost their selves."[18] It remained for Antonio Damasio to extend the inevitability of narrative back into a self that takes shape before the self becomes autobiographical. Before the autobiographical self, even before language, in Damasio's developmental paradigm, a "core self" emerges as little curlicues of voiceless narrative begin to organize sensations.[19] All there is selfwise before the core self is the "protoself," a self without

18. In a kind of summation, Bruner (2003) wrote that without narrative there is "no such thing as selfhood": "The emerging view is that dysnarrativia is deadly for selfhood. . . . The construction of selfhood it seems cannot proceed without a capacity to narrate" (86). Even Galen Strawson's widely contested repost that "[s]elf-understanding does not have to take a narrative form, even implicitly" (Strawson 2004: 448) ends with a celebration of lives that are lived episodically—that is, lives that are lived in a kind of narrative suspense within an episodic narrative structure with its own distinct narrativity: "truly happy-go-lucky, see-what-comes-along lives are among the best there are, vivid blessed, profound" (Strawson 2004: 449). By 2008, both the concept of the narrativized self and the concept of dysnarrativia had found their way into the motivational words of high-end real estate broker Al Lewis: "Among those with dysnarrativia, selfhood virtually vanishes. The lesson is obvious: the construction of selfhood cannot proceed without a capacity to narrate: to make-up and tell stories about oneself." http://thetopjobinrealestate.com/webcontent/13134/03%20The%20Making%20of%20Self%20through%20Narrative.pdf.

19. Susan Lohafer uses the term "neuroscenario" for something like this: "A hand reaches out, touches a flame, starts back in pain, and registers a meaning. Antiquity's child and tomorrow's infant are similarly equipped. Both have this built-in plot-making talent, although it takes several years before humans can recognize or tell a 'story'" (Lohafer 2003: 3).

narrative, originating "at the level of the brain stem rather than the cerebral cortex" and making itself known in the production of "primordial feelings" (2010: 21).

Damasio's still evolving (6) view of the cumulative interrelations of brain, body, and selfhood is complex. But the scheme of development that leads to the full orchestration of the adult human self is nonetheless a progression from primitive-to-fully-evolved human complexity, both phylogenetically and ontogenetically. If we were to propose this paradigm of development as a frame for the focus of this chapter, then Beckett's voices would enact a kind of progressive regression. That is, we experience in these voices a consciousness, richly endowed with resources of both language and narrative to an extent far exceeding those of most of us, yet seeking to disown both, or more accurately to abuse them (since they cannot be disowned) in such thorough and ingenious ways that the self behind the self—the self that knows itself only as an inexplicable persistence of individually distinct self-awareness—might at least be intimated.

So, ultimately, there is no place in Damasio's paradigm for these voices. The acute, vivid self-awareness they express is not the awareness of oneself as a narratable, usually agential, being, but rather as a feeling of one's distinctive one-of-a-kindness, of having been selected in the absence of any known selector or any identifiable purpose. It is a feeling of exclusive interiority, of having been gratuitously chosen to be oneself, rather than someone else, and to abide in a "hell of stories." Having woken up to this condition Beckett's protesting narrators suffer from a kind of failed Korsakov's Syndrome in which the patient endures not the loss of life narrative but its continued insistence. The voice of *The Unnamable* may seem to yearn for a valid autobiographical self when it imagines being carried "to the threshold of my story" to wait "before the door that opens on my story." But in the same breath it knows this is an impossibility since all stories of the self are merely fictions that mask the apophatic problem for which the word "self" is a hopelessly compromised place-holder. "[I]f it opens," he says, "it will be I," and then adds without a break in what has been a very long sentence, "it will be the silence, where I am, I don't know, I'll never know, in the silence you don't know" (Beckett 1965: 414).

To return to Edelman's response to the question of whether we could ever create not just consciousness but an ego to go with it, one could argue that an ego is, for all its impossibility, simply another evolutionary necessity. What evolution needs, evolution makes, regardless of our human inability to achieve the same thing. Therefore, at a certain level of consciousness the sensation of being an existential self, personal and immediate, is a logical necessity for driving the conscious organic machines of beings like ourselves. And so, one might say, "Voilà: self-consciousness explained." Yet such an explanation of self-consciousness is also a way of slipping past the conundrum of happening to be one of those conscious selves. It is another deployment of narrative to escape from feeling. It gives the ego a place in a story—the story of evolution. It is a story that introduces, at a certain point in its development, a new agential type, the ego-powered being, which in turn generates new complications in the narrative action.

And something like this move into an explanatory narrative can relieve Beckett's reader, too. In the Introduction to this study, I referred to Michael Gazzaniga's theory of an "interpreter" in the left brain that is constantly at work creating out of our sensory inputs the kind of coherences we require in order simply to get by in this life.[20] Most readings of Beckett have tended by example to bear out Gazzaniga's idea of a left-hemisphere interpreter to the extent that explication has neutralized the immediate effect of the inexplicable. This is not to argue that explication is a bad thing. But in the instances of these remarkable narrative texts, explication is often, I think, a response to an understandable, if unacknowledged, anxiety of losing interpretive control. Whatever terms are imported to explain why the mind is tempted to stand back while reading these texts, it is still the case that one cannot ignite them from the outside. What they have to offer lights up within the experience they catalyze. In this limited sense, these texts are no longer representations of life but the experience of life itself.

But, then, finally, to ask a question that has been hovering in the wings: Have I not been explicating? And the answer is, Of course I have. We can't get very far in this business without trying to explain things. But, as promised in the introduction to this study, I have sought in this chapter to operate at a level of explication that leaves intact the experience of unknowing. To get to that experience, to let it do its work, is an art of abandonment. In Beckett's terms, it is to experience "the rapture of vertigo, the letting go, the fall, the gulf, the relapse to darkness, to nothingness, to earnestness, to home" (Beckett 1965: 195). There can be deep knowledge in not knowing, but it is rarely attained. Our nature is set against it, since it means letting go even of one's least attempt to understand what's going on. As I have been arguing, the knowledge of explanation paradoxically cancels the knowledge freighted in the unexplained.

20. More recently, in *The Ethical Brain,* Gazzaniga has described how this hypothetical interpreter reflexively maintains the construction of a self in which the interpreter is presumed to reside: "[I]f the brain is modular, a part of the brain must be monitoring all the networks' behaviors and trying to interpret their individual actions in order to create a unified idea of the self. Our best candidate for this brain area is the 'left-hemisphere interpreter'" (2005: 148).

To appropriate the words of Molloy, knowledge enters in only when one is "beyond knowing anything." One can talk around such knowledge, as I have been doing in this chapter, but the knowledge itself is not analytically convertible to other discourses without serious distortion. It is, to appropriate Pound's epigram, "news that stays news" (Pound 1961: 29).

CHAPTER 2

Conjuring Stories

IN THIS CHAPTER, I will address the same phenomenon I addressed in the last, but from another direction and using the quite different work of a quite different writer. As in the last, I will continue to develop the distinction between a literature of representation and a literature of experience. The challenge will be greater in this chapter, in part because of the sheer brilliance of García Márquez's imagery and in part because the text I will be using, as all of his texts, elicits thematic, historical, allegorical, and other representational readings that have done and will continue to do good work. But for this story particularly (as for a few others by this author) the case can also be made for a shift in our relationship to the text to allow it to do the work it does best. Accordingly, the difference between the two modes—representational and experiential—structures the first two sections of this chapter. As in the last chapter also, the unknowable that is a condition for what I have been calling the cognitive sublime resides not simply in the text but also in ourselves. If the words "in" and "self" raise numerous real difficulties in philosophy and current work on cognition (Hutto, Herman 2008, Edelman and Tononi, Minsky, Penrose, Koch, Crick, Wegner, Klein and Gangi 2010), the point can be rephrased thus: though this particular experience of unknowing can be textually induced, the condition that gives rise to it is still with us when we close the book. This human condition is an exotic of the near at hand—always present but rarely attended—with which we may be reacquainted through the intentional production of non-understanding that is my subject in this book.

Toward the end of this chapter, I will extend my general argument regarding an art of unimaginable unknowns in two ways. First, I will draw again on Beckett's work to help make the case that prose—a craft strictly of words—gave both of these artists a special leverage in crafting the immediacy of reader experience that I credit them with. Then in conclusion I will suggest that for both of these authors it is the irreducible particularity of their art—the signature they leave—that serves as a marker of the two complementary enigmas they so effectively draw the reader into: that of personal being and that of origination.

REPRESENTING THE UNKNOWABLE

I shall start with J. G. Ballard's brilliant short story "The Drowned Giant" (1964), which can serve as a kind of control text before I move on to another brilliant short story by Gabriel García Márquez. In Ballard's story the unknowable—a handsome giant with "the mass and dimensions of the largest sperm whale" (Ballard 1971: 34)—is a constant reference in the text. It is "knowable" to the extent that it can be seen and touched, which happens frequently in the story, but how it came to be and where it came from are entirely inexplicable. The story begins with the discovery of the giant, washed up on the beach after a storm. Ballard's control of the tone of the narration is what gives the story its special edge:

> On the morning after the storm the body of a drowned giant was washed ashore on the beach five miles to the northwest of the city. The first news of its arrival was brought by a nearby farmer and subsequently confirmed by the local newspaper reporters and the police. Despite this the majority of people, myself among them, remained skeptical, but the return of more and more eyewitnesses attesting to the vast size of the giant was finally too much for our curiosity. (33)

The narrator is a professional in the knowledge business, a "researcher" at work with colleagues in a library. In keeping with his *métier,* his first sentence locates the event in time—"after *the* storm"—and space—"five miles northwest of the city"—and those that follow proceed in a voice of precise neutrality. Moreover, it takes more than newspaper and police reports to arouse him and his co-workers (though in this regard they are like "the majority of people" in the city). And what they are aroused to is not wonder, but "curiosity." Nonetheless, once arrived at the scene, he and his colleagues are sufficiently perceptive to be "dissatisfied with the matter-of-fact explanations of the crowd," and step down onto the beach to get a better look. This is a nice touch, since what is perhaps even more wonderful than the giant is that anyone could have a "matter-of-fact explanation" for what it is and how it got there. As for the narrator, these "explanations" are not even worth recording.

One of the signs of Ballard's mastery of his craft is the way he can thread the professional objectivity of his narrator with a voice and selective eye that provide, in counterpoint, the emergence of a sensibility that is distinguished in another way from that of the multitude:

> At first the estimates of its size seemed greatly exaggerated. It was then at low tide, and almost all the giant's body was exposed, but he appeared to be a little larger than a basking shark. He lay on his back with his arms at his sides, in an attitude of repose, as if asleep on the mirror of wet sand, the reflection of his blanched skin fading as the water receded. In the clear sunlight his body glistened like the white plumage of a sea bird. (ibid.)

On the one hand, he notes the optical illusion that would have reduced the "exaggerated" estimate of its size to "little larger than a basking shark" (that is, little larger than the second largest fish in the world, making it roughly thirty feet in length, or in other words, not so big a deal). On the other hand, he responds in his dispassionate way to the giant's humanity and his beauty—"He lay . . . in an attitude of repose, as if asleep on the mirror of wet sand. . . . In the clear sunlight his body glistened like the white plumage of a sea bird." Further on, he records how "the lips were parted slightly, the open eye cloudy and occluded, as if injected with some blue milky liquid, but," he continues, "the delicate arches of the nostrils and eyebrows invested the face with an ornate charm that belied the brutish power of the chest and shoulders" (35).

Without apparent judgment he records how the crowd, hesitant at first, was soon emboldened to begin "clambering all over the giant, whose reclining arms provided a double stairway," while children and gangs of youth have special fun sitting in his ears and bellowing in the caverns of his nostrils. At the same time, the narrator writes of how he "stopped to examine the outstretched right hand," and "tried to read the palmlines that grooved the skin, searching for some clue to the giant's character," some "trace of the giant's identity and his last tragic predicament" (ibid.). He notes how "the delicate flection of the fingers and the well-tended nails, each cut symmetrically to within six inches of the quick, argued refinement of temperament, illustrated in the Grecian features of the face, on which the townsfolk were now sitting like flies" (35–36). In time, as he continues to report, swastikas and other graffiti appear, carved into the giant's skin, and various body parts disappear and then reappear in commercial and municipal venues around the city. Huge squares of the giant's "blubber" are rendered in a vat, his bones are ground up for fertilizer, while his "immense pizzle, . . . stunning in its proportions and sometime potency," winds up in a "freak museum" where it is "wrongly identified as that of a whale" (42).

As the work of decay and plunder proceeds, interest in the giant dissipates, until eventually he is remembered, "if at all, as a large sea beast." Here's how the story ends:

> The remainder of the skeleton, stripped of all flesh, still rests on the seashore, the clutter of bleached ribs like the timbers of a derelict ship. The contractor's hut, the crane, and the scaffolding have been removed, and the sand being driven into the bay along the coast has buried the pelvis and backbone. In the winter the high curved bones are deserted, battered by the breaking waves, but in the summer they provide an excellent perch for the sea-wearying gulls. (ibid.)

In this final paragraph, the effect of complete vacancy echoes the trivializing of this wonderful being, of origin unknown, and the steady loss of interest that has been charted through the story as the people of the town return to their daily round. The irony of the last sentence, in which the reader's expectation of summer crowds, drawn by the giant's bones, is voided by gulls using them as a perch, is especially well calibrated to crystallize the story's judgment on the townsfolk's failed capacity for wonder.

For the narrator, who does have a capacity for wonder, the giant is a symbolic representation of a kind of unreachable Platonic domain. He is a sign of existence "in an absolute sense, providing a glimpse into a world of similar absolutes of which we spectators on the beach were such imperfect and puny copies. . . . The enormous breadth of the shoulders, and the huge columns of the arms and legs, still carried the figure into another dimension, and the giant seemed a more authentic image of one of the drowned Argonauts or heroes of the *Odyssey* than the conventional portrait previously in my mind" (37, 38). In this way the narrator, whose mind is more capacious than the common run, still finds its own way to domesticate what it cannot account for. Questions of where the giant came from and how it came into being in the first place give way to the role the narrator gives it in his personal metaphysics. In that system, the giant takes up residence as a symbol.

The focus in Ballard's story, in other words, is on the limitations of the townsfolk and the appropriative imagination of the narrator, both of which are understandable, rather than the giant, who is not. As such, the story lends itself easily to interpretation, while the giant operates primarily as a signifier—quite literally an embodiment of the unknown.

EXPERIENCING THE UNKNOWABLE

Ballard's story is an especially apt text for my object in this chapter because my featured text, Gabriel García Márquez's "The Handsomest Drowned Man in the World," develops out of the same material premise. Indeed, "The Drowned Giant" may well have been the spark for "The Handsomest Drowned Man," which appeared four years after Ballard's story. In the interval between the two, the Latin American Spanish translation of Ballard's story appeared in 1966, in the periodical volume, *Antilogía de la literatura fantástica,* under the title "El ahogado gigante." García Márquez, a voracious reader, may well have read it before writing "El ahogado más hermoso del mundo," which was published in 1968. If my reading of "The Handsomest Drowned Man" is persuasive, then it is arguable that this story can be seen not only as deriving from Ballard's story, but as responding to it as well.[1]

In this story, we begin again with the discovery of a handsome and larger than normal corpse that washes up on the beach. But the story pointedly opens with its emergence from the sea as a succession of possibilities in the minds of children as they watch it approach:

> The first children who saw the dark and slinky bulge approaching through the sea let themselves think it was an enemy ship. Then they saw it had no flags or masts and they thought it was a whale. But when it was washed up on the beach, they removed the clumps of seaweed, the jellyfish tentacles, and the remains of fish and flotsam, and only then did they see that it was a drowned man. (García Márquez 1999: 247)

Here, as often in García Márquez's fiction, the focus is on the need of the imagination to interpret what it sees and the pleasurable productivity of that gift. The men who lug the drowned man from the beach, feeling that he weighs "almost as much as a horse," tell each other that "maybe he'd been float-

1. It may not necessarily be a consciously intentional response, but it is worth noting that, in addition to their other similarities, the Spanish titles of both stories begin with the same noun (*El ahogado*).

ing too long and the water had got into his bones" (ibid.). When they get to the nearest house and see how "there was barely enough room for him in the house, . . . they thought that maybe the ability to keep on growing after death was part of the nature of certain drowned men" (ibid.).

In another sharp contrast to the thrust of Ballard's story, García Márquez foregrounds the joy that something so extraordinary can arouse. Cleaning him up, the women witness the same process of emergence that the children did when the drowned man first materialized out of the sea.

> They took the mud off with grass swabs, they removed the underwater stones entangled in his hair, and they scraped the crust off with tools used for scaling fish. As they were doing that they noticed that the vegetation on him came from faraway oceans and deep water and that his clothes were in tatters, as if he had sailed through labyrinths of coral. They noticed too that he bore his death with pride, for he did not have the lonely look of other drowned men who came out of the sea or that haggard, needy look of men who drowned in rivers. But only when they finished cleaning him off did they become aware of the kind of man he was and it left them breathless. Not only was he the tallest, strongest, most virile, and best built man they had ever seen, but even though they were looking at him there was no room for him in their imagination. (248)

This, I think, is the thematic heart of the tale. Where the men see only an inconvenience, "wanting to get rid of the bother of the newcomer once and for all" (251), the women see something that is wonderful precisely because it exceeds all possibility of explanation.[2] The drowned man is something that, at this moment in the tale, their minds cannot accommodate. "There was no room for him in their imagination." This is the nature of the truly wonderful, and these women have the capacity to see this and to give it the reverence it rightly deserves. In due time, being only human, they go on to name and in other ways appropriate the beautiful giant ("Praise the Lord . . . He's ours!"). With such a catch, their collective imagination goes into high gear, inventing the life and mourning the death of what must have been a spectacular husband.

So far I have, in my turn, been interpreting this story. I have been reading it as an imagined response to Ballard's story. In this reading, Ballard's vision of a community's indifference to the wonderful except as it can be used for mate-

2. Any further extended treatment of the difference between this story and Ballard's should include the fact that there is not a single woman, identified as such, in "The Drowned Giant."

rial advantage is replaced by a community of women in a state of passionate wonderment that generates a legend, a masterwork of imaginative artifice that grows ever more fabulous in time. The story, of course, like all powerful and complex stories, suggests a number of other workable interpretations. One can read it, for example, as an allegory of the origins of the sacred.[3] Or one can read it as a commentary on feminine erotic desire and the inadequacy of the masculine as it is normally found in its living, diurnal character.

What I like about my reading, however, is that it resonates with what is happening almost everywhere in our transaction with the text itself. If, within the story, the reader is kept alive to the mystery the villagers cannot accommodate—that is, the mystery of where and how the drowned man came into being—García Márquez, by the quality of his writing, keeps the reader attuned to the mystery of where the narrative itself came from. The reader, if she or he permits, is made to feel from one sentence to the next that there is some source of playful, unpredictable productivity that cannot simply be capped with the word "imagination." It is a wonderful power that can come up with such exotic gems as "that haggard, needy look of men who drowned in rivers" or "the deepest waves, where fish are blind and divers die of nostalgia" (251) or a village with "so little land that mothers always went about with the fear that the wind would carry off their children" (248) or women who could imagine a man with "so much authority that he could have drawn fish out of the sea simply by calling their names" (249) or the youngest and most stubborn among them, who might "live for a few hours with the illusion that when they put his clothes on and he lay among the flowers in patent leather shoes his name might be Lautero" (248–49).

In the business of interpretation, there are always words or phrases that serve as sufficient end-points, place-holders where the mind can rest, and certainly "wonder" is one of them: as in, What's it about? Ah, yes, "wonder," or "the capacity for wonder," or "the productivity of the imagination," or "the origins of the sacred." But what I am trying to get at here requires, to start with, an acknowledgment that we still don't know much at all about the continual productivity of this unfolding storyworld. We can only wonder. And my argument is that in this story (as in other fiction García Márquez wrote from this point on in his career, but particularly *One Hundred Years of Solitude*), this is the effect he wants to keep alive. Here, for a final example and to complete our comparison with Ballard's tale, is how the story ends.

3. As has been frequently noted, the women give the drowned man the name Esteban [Stephen] who was the first Christian Martyr.

> [T]hey were going to paint their house fronts gay colors to make Esteban's memory eternal and they were going to break their backs digging for springs among the stones and planting flowers on the cliffs so that in future years at dawn the passengers on great liners would awaken, suffocated by the smell of gardens on the high seas, and the captain would have to come down from the bridge in his dress uniform, with his astrolabe, his pole star, and his row of war medals and, pointing to the promontory of roses on the horizon, he would say in fourteen languages, look there, where the wind is so peaceful now that it's gone to sleep beneath the beds, over there, where the sun's so bright that the sunflowers don't know which way to turn, yes, over there, that's Esteban's village. (253–54)[4]

As in so much of the author's fiction, and especially in his "tales for children," of which "The Handsomest Drowned Man" is a prime example, the element of surprise is so insistent and so persistent that it keeps bringing attention back to the enigma of its origins right up to the end, resisting in the process any single act of externally imposed interpretive control.

There are, certainly, other ways to accommodate the story's multivalence without giving pride of place to a single, necessarily inadequate and constraining act of interpretive domination. One way is to see the story as an intended example of an "open form" or "open work," to use Umberto Eco's (1989) terminology, in which the reader is invited "to create for himself the meaning of the narrative elements" (Davis 1987: 167). To use John Ashberry's description of Stein's "impossible work," the text can be seen as an "all-purpose model which each reader can adapt to fit his own set of particulars" (Ashberry 1957: 251). Readers, of course, can do anything they want, but to see the text as an open form narrative is still to invite acts, however multiple, of externally imposed control, interpretive moves that run counter to García Márquez's insistent unpredictability. In my reading, by contrast, the sheer ludic quality of his final swerves in this story ("his astrolabe, his pole star, and his row of war medals and . . . he would say in fourteen languages") sustain the atmosphere of unpredictability that began with the discovery of the drowned man and that apparently has not yet ended.

---

4. "[S]e iban a romper el espinazo excavando manantiales en las piedras y sembrando flores en los acantilados, para que en los amaneceres de los años venturos los pasajeros de los grandes barcos despertaran sofocados por un olor de jardines en altamar, y el capitán tuviera que bajar de su alcázar con su uniforme de gala, con su astrolabio, su estrella polar y su ristra de medallas de guerra, y señalando el promontorio de rosas en el horizonte del Caribe dijera en catorce idiomas, miren allá, donde el viento es ahora tan manso que se queda a dormir debajo de las camas, allá, donde el sol brilla tanto que no saben hacia dónde girar los girasoles, sí, allá, es el pueblo de Esteban" (García Márquez 1978: 145).

It is also possible to read the kind of textual reflexivity I am analyzing here in terms of the now venerable idea of textual indeterminacy that has been frequently applied to modernist and postmodernist texts. By way of support, one might give special attention to the ambiguity of "so that" ["para que"] in the above passage, as it is coupled with the use of the imperfect subjunctive in the verbs that follow ["despertaran," "tuviera"]. This would appear to be an ambiguity designed to make it impossible to say whether the action now being described occurs in a hypothetical future world or in a future extension, now gone by, of the tale's actual world. Such indeterminacy, combined with the playful set of impossibilities that proliferate through the text, would add weight to the idea that García Márquez's work is governed by a nonreferential aesthetic requiring a separation of the work from the world. To borrow Marjorie Perloff's words, what representation there is seems "to exist nowhere outside the text itself" (Perloff 1981: 9). It is a hermetic game in which "the focus shifts from signification to the play of signifiers" (23).

That there is a current of excitement running through this story, and much of the other fiction by García Márquez, that is not referential in any traditional sense is a position I strongly agree with. And it is certainly possible to see his disruptions and indeterminacies as marks of a modernist or postmodernist effort to turn our attention to the words themselves and how they really work without the film of familiarity. But in my view García Márquez's continuing swerves put the deep focus on the enigma of invention. What is experienced emerges, as it were, through the text from a source beyond the extradiegetic narration: that is, from the hidden source of the author's unpredictable productivity. In this work, the cognitive sublime is felt as a moment-to-moment emergence of something as thrilling as a beautiful body arising (like Venus) out of the sea. The ambiguity of "para que," then, is a way of fusing "is" and "maybe," of the actual and the possible, in a mind where sometimes "the sun's so bright that the sunflowers don't know which way to turn."

LA REALIDAD

García Márquez has said that "there is not a single line in my novels that is not based in reality" ("No hay en mis novelas una línea que no esté basada en la realidad" [Mendoza and García Márquez 1994: 47]). But he has also repeatedly linked the productivity of the real with the productivity of the imagination and the power of invention. In his own interestingly contradictory words, "the imagination is nothing but an instrument for the production [elaboración][5] of reality. But the source of creation is always, in the end, reality" ("la imagination no es sino un instrumento de elaboración de la realidad. Pero la fuente de creación al fin y cabo es siempre la realidad" [41]; see also [78]). It is an entanglement of "insatiable creativity" with "unbridled reality" that he restated in his Nobel Prize acceptance lecture (García Márquez 1982) and that, if I read it correctly, suggests a kind of symbiosis in which the same word, "la realidad," is made to stand both for what exists before perception and for how it is produced by perception. As such, it also suggests that the real is always coming to us afresh and therefore is necessarily always magical.[6] It is an insight, in his view, that children come by naturally, but that adults lose over time. In another "tale for children," "A Very Old Man with Enormous Wings" ("Un señor muy viejo con unas alas enormes"), García Márquez portrays a whole cast of adult interpreters who seek through explication to domesticate the real. An ancient man with enormous wings, who crash-lands in the muddy courtyard of Pelayo and Elisenda, is defined variously as a castaway sailor, a Norwegian with wings, an angel "coming for their child" (García Márquez 1999: 218), and the devil masquerading as an angel. As in "The Handsomest Drowned Man," the inexhaustible need of the adult mind to explain the inexplicable, regardless of the facts (whatever these may be), is matched by the inexhaustible capacity of the story itself to surprise us. We learn of "a poor woman who since childhood had been counting her heartbeats and had run out of numbers; a Portuguese man who couldn't sleep because the noise of the stars disturbed him; a sleepwalker who got up at night to undo the things he had done while awake" (220). All of which keeps the reader from settling until, at the end, the tale's titular subject escapes from his own story, passing "over the last houses, holding himself up in some way with the risky flapping of a senile vulture" (225).

These two stories were both written just after García Márquez resumed writing his most famous work, *Cien años de soledad* (*One Hundred Years of Solitude*), in 1965. Many have noted that this novel was a kind of watershed

5. How you read the word "elaboración" in this context can make a difference. I have chosen to translate it as "production" in keeping with what I take to be the spirit of García Márquez's comments here and elsewhere, but "development" or "transformation" or even "elaboration" might work as well.

6. What keeps the widely used literary description "magical realism" from fading into a dead oxymoron is the still productive instability of its two words (Faris 2004; Bell 2010). In the continuing effort to deploy magical realism as a discrete literary mode, scholars have tended to give weight or priority to one or the other of these contesting words, "magical" or "realism." If my take on the reader's experience of García Márquez tends to emphasize the "magical," I hope it is clear that it does so by introducing an extraliterary, nonformalist element, the enigma of emergence or, if you will, the mystery of origins.

for him, and he himself has claimed that, though he began it as a young man it had remained an "inchoate nebula" ([1971] 2006: 9) until 1965 when he had "a sudden—I don't know why—illumination on how to write the book" (García Márquez 1999: 342; 2006 [1982]: 120). And though the change in his style was actually more gradual, in his own words his earlier books "constituted a kind of premeditated literature, which offered a vision of reality that was too static and exclusive. However good or bad they may appear to be, they are books that end on the last page. They are too limited [estrechos] for what I believe I can do" ("constituyen un tipo de literatura premeditada, que ofrece una vision un tanto estática y excluyante de la realidad. Por buenos o malos que parezcan, son libros que acaban en la última página. Son más estrechos de lo que yo me creo capaz de hacer" [Mendoza and García Márquez 1994: 75]). It was an interesting way to put the change in his art, but it aligns well with the case I have been making. For all the importance he placed on having a story well in hand before setting pen to paper (2006 [1988]: 157), he has also said that a story comes to him "complete in a fraction of a second": "There's nothing deliberate or predictable in all this, nor do I know when it's going to happen to me. I'm at the mercy of my imagination" (García Márquez [1971] 2006: 42–43).

By the mid-sixties, García Márquez had found a way of conveying this quality *in the writing itself*—a quality of writing without "premeditation" that, as in the case of Beckett, worked in concert with an exquisite sense of artistic form. In other words, he had found a way of sustaining this thread of inexplicable, never-ending productivity even as he granted the affective pleasures of a story with a beginning, middle, and end. What this means for the reader is to avoid those interpretive moves that would dull or dampen this magical effervescence and the mystery of origins that seems inseparable from it. As I noted at the outset of this chapter, there is no question that García Márquez has produced richly provocative "machines to think with."[7] But, however open his texts may be to thematic readings, what should dominate, if we allow it, is the feeling of a never-ending unpredictability, a productivity of "la reali-

7. Understandably, when asked if the story of Macondo is meant to be a history of Latin America or a metaphor "for all men and their ailing communities," García Márquez (like Beckett when asked similar questions) can be a little cranky: "Nothing of the sort. I merely wanted to tell a story of a family who for a hundred years did everything they could to prevent having a son with a pig's tail, and just because of their very efforts to avoid having one they ended by doing so" (2006 [1971]: 39). But he will also make thematic assessments such as "the idea that solitude is the opposite of solidarity, . . . I believe that is the essence of the book" (12) And he has even conceded that early in his career he learned interesting things from some of his critics, especially the "professional . . . well trained" readers in the US (13). But he has since given up on the critics "because they were conditioning me" (38).

dad" that surpasses any understanding of what it is and where it comes from. Because the sheer insistence of his wonderful swerves is built into the form of the narrative itself and at the expense of any naturalizing moves that would displace the immediacy of textual experience with the satisfactions of understanding, his stories keep the reader delightedly immersed in the mystery of their coming into being. What can kill this is "solemnity," the solemnity of critics who fail to "approach the book in the same way it was written" but instead dress it up "with the hat and robe of a bishop." That, he says, "is truly terrible" ([1971] 2006: 16).

READING AND THE AFFORDANCES OF AN ART OF WORDS

García Márquez has steadfastly refused permission to film *One Hundred Years of Solitude,* despite handsome offers and despite his own deep involvement in all aspects of cinema (Taylor 2010: 165). In part this refusal derives simply from the way García Márquez approaches the craft of writing, that is, as a distinctly literary *auteur* who (like Beckett) requires the greatest possible control over his medium. Working in film, he found that "the writer is merely one cog in the huge machinery" (162). But about *Cien años,* specifically, he has made the claim that it is "anti-cinematic": "In 1966 I said to myself 'Damn it! I'm going to write against cinema!' . . . I wrote a novel with entirely literary solutions, a novel which is, if you like, the antithesis of cinema: *One Hundred Years of Solitude!*" (164). Up to that point, he claimed, his works had been "hindered" by a cinematic frame of mind characterized by "an excessive eagerness to visualize characters and scenes, a very precise relationship between the time of the dialogues and action that take place, and even an obsession with signaling points of view and framing" (ibid.). As for the vaunted visual quality of his prose, he has said that this is in fact a deception that arises from "the magic of the words" (165)—a magic that, in Claire Taylor's apt phrasing, is "ironed out" when transferred to "a predominantly *visual* medium" (169; original emphasis).

This strong sense of a special advantage of prose fiction is a point where Gabriel García Márquez—a novelist who became deeply involved in cinema yet continued to write prose fiction—connects with the very different Samuel Beckett—a novelist who became deeply involved in theater yet, like García Márquez, also continued to write prose fiction.[8] Both of these artists were

8. To round out the symmetry, García Márquez has written one play (*Diatriba de amor contra un hombre sentado*) and Beckett wrote one film (*Film*).

acutely aware that what is added when a written text is scripted and then built out into the live bodies of actors and the physical properties of a set is the insertion of the intervening materiality of a staged world. Film may be more a simulacrum than theater, but it nonetheless shares with theater a visual clarity and immediacy that the art of words is not bound by. Theater, with its necessary deployment of the materiality of our "actual" world, can have what Alain Robbe-Grillet, referring specifically to the impact of Beckett's *En attendant Godot* (*Waiting for Godot,* 1953), called "presence on the stage" (Robbe-Grillet 1965). If film can only achieve a visual simulacrum of this "presence," this effect is also, as García Márquez has argued, quite different from the "deceptive" visuality of words (Taylor 2010: 165). To get at the deep alignment of these two very different artists of prose it is instructive to look at the curious evolution of Beckett's dramatic oeuvre.

Robbe-Grillet's cogent insight was given full theoretical and historical enlargement in Martin Esslin's landmark study, *The Theatre of the Absurd* (1961). Esslin wrote convincingly of the ways in which dramatists like Beckett, Genet, and Ionesco, implicitly or explicitly, had reacted to the work of Sartre, Camus, Giraudoux, Anouilh, and Salacrou, by exchanging the exhausted mode of the "theatre of ideas" for a theater of presence. Instead of staging disquisitions on the absurdity of life, they staged the absurdity itself.[9] "The theatre of the absurd has renounced arguing *about* the absurdity of the human condition; it merely *presents* it in being—that is, in terms of concrete images of the absurdity of existence" (Esslin: xx). It was a powerful argument in 1961 and it remains so fifty years later. It also seems to account for the continuing power of these experiments in stagecraft. Despite the outrage that greeted them, they connect with viewers in a deep, visceral way that the plays of Sartre, Camus, and Giraudoux do not.

But one of the many curious things about Beckett's theatrical oeuvre is the way he seems progressively to have abandoned what seemed to connect so well with the theater-going public. I'm overstating somewhat. Beckett continued to draw on the power of theatrical presence in his work for the stage, but increasingly it derived from a single figure (or a head, or a face, or in one instance, a pair of lips), isolated and severely limited in its range of action. At

9. This is exactly the burden of those oft-quoted lines Beckett wrote to hearten his baffled and stressed-out friend and director, Alan Schneider, as the latter struggled with the meanings of *Endgame:* "If people want to have headaches among the overtones, let them. And provide their own aspirin. Hamm as stated, and Clov as stated, together as stated, nec tecum nec sine te, in such a place, and in such a world, that's all I can manage, more than I could" (Beckett 1983: 109; see also H. P. Abbott 1996: 170–71). Beckett's stance in this instance chimes with García Márquez's impatient response, cited above in note 7: "I merely wanted to tell a story of a family who for a hundred years did everything they could to prevent having a son with a pig's tail. . . . "

the same time, the verbal element of these plays increased proportionately, often as a single voice, often from a source outside the visual scene. When Esslin made his famous assessment, Beckett's latest dramatic pieces were *Krapp's Last Tape,* the first *Act without Words,* and the radio play *Embers.* So, Esslin could not have anticipated the way in which diegesis—verbal narration—would invade Beckett's mimetic art to the point where, in works like *Not I, That Time,* and *A Piece of Monologue,* the visual consisted of a single body or body part while words poured out in a stream from beginning to end.[10] What, then, was gained by constricting the visual mimetic and transferring the action to the verbal diegetic? Performed well, these pieces certainly have their own strange piercing beauty. And though they don't enjoy the global *cachet* of his earlier drama, pleasing the audience was never something Beckett actively sought. Still, the question remains: Why did a writer as finely (and famously) attuned as Beckett was to the limitations and affordances of modes, media, and genres pursue this hybridization of verbal and visual modes? What was the deep appeal of prose diegesis that he would deliberately have it encroach on the theatrical effect of presence on the stage? What did it uniquely afford?

The short answer is that it afforded a *lack* of presence or, rather , it afforded a different kind of presence—presence separated from what could be seen. Call these the voices of ghosts, as many have, but my case is that for Beckett the appeal of this paradoxical effect had already gone deep, beginning with the *nouvelles* of 1946 and then deepening in what Hugh Kenner called the five-year "siege in the room" as Beckett wrote out the Trilogy (Kenner 1961). What he worked at was an art of unbodied words, and its lack of presence was a resource that never lost its grip on him, even as he turned to the contrasting clarity and order of an art form made of real people present on a stage in the real world (Mignon: 8).[11] What he did in his late plays was to bring this

10. The later plays in which the visual is limited to one figure are *Eh Joe, Not I, That Time, Footfalls, Ghost Trio, . . . but the clouds . . . , A Piece of Monologue, Rockaby,* and *Nacht und Träume.* A few have more than one figure, but again with a positioning and range of motion that is very limited (*Come and Go, Ohio Impromptu, What Where*). The only break in this pattern is the short play *Catastrophe,* with its two interacting characters (and its third stationary figure), which was contributed on request for an event honoring Vaclav Havel at the Avignon Festival in 1982.

11. I have argued (H. P. Abbott 1999) that it helps to imagine this art—that is, fiction made solely of words and as such coming out of the dark (Reid 1968: 53; Juliet 1986: 19)—under the aspect of human evolution. From this perspective, the prose diegesis of Beckett's work from 1946 on connected his reader experientially with an enigma that must have accompanied the deep cognitive and ideational shift that took place when humans began using words to tell stories. In making this argument, I drew on neuroscientist Merlin Donald's (1991) speculation that hominids acted before they talked (see also Mithin 2006; Walsh 2011). More precisely, he made the case that there was a mimetic stage of communication before the emergence of grammatical language with its reliance on an arbitrary symbology and a capability to represent

disembodied quality up on stage together with a body to which it is somehow linked yet at the same time separate. If one might infer that what we hear belongs to the body or body part we see and that its source may be somehow "inside" the body, in one's immediate experience of the play it is elsewhere. Elsewhere and nowhere, sourceless. And when, in a kind of violent reversal, Beckett coordinated words and the movement of a pair of lips in *Not I* (1972), there's nothing else: "whole body like gone" (1984: 222). And in this way *Not I* augmented the same mystery by bonding it with another, that of emergence: "suddenly . . . words were coming . . . imagine! . . . words were coming . . . " (1984: 219).

What prose fiction contributed was silence, releasing words from what one might call their aural materiality. Beckett was certainly overstating when he once said, "The best possible play is one in which there are no actors, only texts. I'm trying to find a way to write one" (Bair: 513). But it is the case that he kept writing actual texts without actors—that is, prose fiction—right up into 1989, the last year of his life. And there were many of these, including the one hundred plus pages of the "second trilogy" (*Company, Ill Seen Ill Said,* and *Worstward Ho*). My argument is that what Beckett lost in writing all this highly poetic prose was inseparable from what he gained. Without even the minimal purchase of a visible image and an audible voice, Beckett released his texts from the "presence" that Robbe-Grillet and Esslin so rightly praised. In doing so, Beckett was taking a different route to the experience of a different kind of presence, a singularity of being which, for all its material embodiment would seem to be disembodied.[12]

Without the actual presence of a teller to give it some kind of anchorage in this world, writing creates a place where, in the words of Maurice Blanchot, "here has collapsed into nowhere, but nowhere is nonetheless here":

---

things and events solely in a mental arena (see also Abbott 2000b). My highly speculative argument was keyed to the transition from the mimetic to the linguistic stage of development and the deep cognitive shift in narrative consciousness that at some level of awareness must have gone with it.

12. The literature on the far-reaching impacts of a mediating technology of linguistic visual signs starts at least as far back as the critique of writing by Socrates and his student Plato, and has continued extensively to the present day (Kenyon, Innis, Havelock, Ohmann, Ong, Goody, Chafe, Kellogg, Martin, Olson, Amodio, Jackson). If the practical advantages of this innovation are many, the disadvantages begin with the loss of sight and sound. As Socrates was the first to point out and as Walter Ong (1982, 1986) has influentially elaborated, this meant that writing as a vehicle of meaning had to cope with two key absences: for the author at the time of writing, the absence of a reader; for the reader at the time of reading, the absence of an author. For each, the other must somehow be summoned up in the imagination for the intention of meaning to be produced on the one hand and recognized on the other. If there was, and still is, good reason for Socrates to complain about the way the technology of writing separated writers from their words, what I am arguing here is that, for a certain end, this less is more.

> To write is to enter into the affirmation of solitude in which fascination threatens. It is to surrender to the risk of time's absence, where eternal starting over reigns . . . where the image, instead of alluding to some particular feature, becomes an allusion to the featureless, and instead of a form drawn upon absence, becomes the formless presence of the absence, the opaque, empty opening onto that which is when there is no more world, when there is no world yet. (Blanchot 1982: 31, 33)

Blanchot's Gallic melodrama notwithstanding, he hits the mark. In Tony Jackson's much more succinct formulation: "Writing removes speech from the body" (Jackson 2009: 110). With oral delivery, even when it is a written text being read, the reader's living presence conveys an illusion of a unitary materiality of origins that gets in the way of the special effect of the cognitive sublime that I have been focusing on in this chapter and the last.

The unity of a human being, of course, as it is displayed in its visual and aural presence, is an evolutionary necessity that we depend upon in the ethical, legal, mercantile, and other social relations of our everyday intercourse. Among other important things, it maintains our sanity. And by and large, we rely on the same illusion when we read. It's one of the reasons the "implied author" has been such an obsessive issue in the scholarly interpretation of narrative. But by the same token, writing can threaten the illusion of authorial wholeness. In the last chapter we saw what excellent use Beckett made of this and other resources of prose to evoke the real mystery of individually distinct self awareness. But at the same time, now to connect with my central point in this chapter, the silence of prose fiction can also magnify the enigma of the text's coming into existence. This is an enigma that, like the other, takes place in the dark.[13] If I am right about the (seeming) immateriality of this darkness, then it is a darkness that is harder to initiate and sustain in the physicality of theatrical and cinematic media. Together these two enigmas comprise the commonality that I have been seeking to isolate in works by both Beckett and García Márquez: the experience of a mystery compacted in the two meanings of "originality"—emergence and singularity.

If the art of these two writers is abetted by their uncommon gifts, it is an art that applies to all of us in common. This is my larger argument. If we work with this art, it can reintroduce us to ourselves, for the two meanings bonded in the word "originality" describe the universal condition of continu-

13. The Japanese novelist Haruki Murakami has claimed that his fiction comes out of a "'black box' to which he has no conscious access" (Anderson 2011: 63): "The Little People [of *1Q94*] came suddenly. I don't know who they are. I don't know what it means. I was a prisoner of the story. I had no choice. They came, and I described it" (40).

ally becoming none other than the singularity of oneself. As Heidegger put it: "I am always somehow acquainted with myself" (1993: 251). This is an enigma we can forget about, talk about, explain, reject, or take for granted—but it persists in the absence of a narratable (autobiographical) identity and even through the ravages of Alzheimers (Klein et al. 2003). What Beckett and García Márquez have done to a fine excess is to weave this thematic thread into the fabric of their art. In Beckett's case, the wonder of this human condition is spiked with moods of isolation and a burden to be borne; in García Márquez's case, it is spiked with exuberance. García Márquez is a very different author from Beckett, one disinclined to navigate the depths of personhood to anything like the same extent. But as I hope to have shown, the delightful improbabilities that pop up in his stories from one sentence to the next recreate in the willing reader the wonderment of their arrival on the page—the same wonderment that a huge and handsome drowned man and a very old man with wings ought to create as they arrive in a storyworld, as it were, out of the blue.

Finally, and as a condition of this property shared by these two authors, the multitude of their particular *differences* is critical. For if the question of origins defies the convenience of a named entity—be it Beckett, García Márquez, the daemon, the muse, or the Holy Ghost—what emerges from the silence of the text, however unexpected, bears the unmistakable imprint of its singularity. This is the signature, which in both cases is as recognizable as it is unpredictable. In scholarly discourse it has, inevitably, acquired an adjective, however cobbled and infelicitous as "Beckettian" or "Garciamarquian" ("Garciamarquiana/o"). But the signature is "what remains," to use the words of Jacques Derrida. It remains after all the critical thinking and scholarly talking inspired by the text has run its course. Derrida's words applied specifically to the Beckettian, but they could as well apply to the Garciamarquian: "The composition, the rhetoric, the construction and the rhythm of his works, . . . that's what 'remains' finally the most 'interesting,' that's the work, that's the signature, this remainder which remains when the thematics is exhausted" (Derrida 1990: 6).

PART TWO

Inexpressible States

CHAPTER 3

Sentences & Worlds

IN CHAPTERS 1 AND 2 I addressed textually induced experiences of noncomprehension that occur when the mind is directed toward an unimaginable unknown. I called these experiences the cognitive sublime and argued that they aroused a state of unknowing that is available to us not only in our experience of certain texts but also in our condition as human beings. In other words, whether they come upon us or we actively seek them out, the experience is of an unknown that abides with us in our daily lives.

In this chapter, the unknowable is entirely fabricated and as such differs from what is unknowable in the narratives examined in the other chapters of this book. It derives from a form of "neural sport"—a deliberate jamming of our mental circuitry whereby we are cut adrift from deeply embedded ways of knowing and enter states of syntactical and narrative impossibility that abide only in our transaction with the text. The result is an epistemological breakdown that is palpable. It lets us know through experience, rather than through abstract discourse or representation, one way in which our minds need "to make sense" of a represented world. "Sense" in this context is a kind of order that in turn confers a kind of comfort. Its willful violation is disturbing and, with regard to the works we'll look at in this chapter, has often been condemned out of hand. Understandably so. But reader/viewers who don't withdraw from this neural disturbance, enter into an experience of impossibility registered in the overworked synapses of their minds. They feel how deeply they depend on the syntactical and narrative leashes that tie the mind to its cognitive moorings. And for this reason alone it is a salutary experience.

But this chapter also serves two other functions. One is to introduce a useful alignment between syntactical and narrative expectations.[1] The principal template I'll use to make this alignment is the garden path of a garden-path sentence (this will come clear below). The other function is to lay the groundwork for chapter 4. The tools of analysis that I deploy in this chapter will help me in the next where I take up a more complex artistic challenge in dealing with states of inexpressible mystery. Though these latter states are unknowable in the sense of lying beyond the reach of our means of expression, they are, like the cognitive sublime and unlike the neural sport I deal with in this chapter, states that are available to us in the natural course of our lives.

To accomplish my goals in this chapter I have put together two artists, the writer Gertrude Stein and the filmmaker Michael Haneke, who would appear on the face of it to be strange bedfellows. Yet, in the two very different works I have selected, they have produced versions of the same effect, one at the molecular level of syntax and the other at the molar level of narrative. As with all the works dealt with in this study, these two works can also yield a handful of credible intentional readings (along with, as always, an infinitude of readings ranging from the somewhat credible to the absurd). And again, as was the case with my treatment of works by Beckett and García Márquez, I will be showing a way in which these authors replace, in whole (Stein) or in part (Haneke), an art of representation with an art of induced cognitive states.

1. Depending on one's definition of narrative, the sentence is where one finds either a building block of narrative or its most minute example. There are some scholars who grant narrative status to even the most minimal sentences with a subject, a transitive verb, and an object (Genette 1980; B. Smith 1981; Prince 1987; H. P. Abbott 2008. Prince was to complicate his basic definition of narrative in the second edition of his *Dictionary of Narratology* 2003). Someone said somewhere that where the verb introduces time, narrative simply extends it. But I do not intend to revive here the goal of structural narratologists like Svetan Todorov to analyze the structure of narrative as a kind of extended sentence. Of course, a sentence can present a complete narrative ("After leaving the smoking ruins of Troy, Odysseus had many adventures until at last he arrived in Ithaca, slew Penelope's suitors, and with the help of Athene enjoyed peace thereafter into his old age"). But without invoking a structuralist framework, it is still possible to see in the syntactical expectations aroused by much shorter and simpler sentences, the operation of narrative expectations at a molecular level of action.

GARDEN PATHS

To get to my subject, let's first clarify what a garden-path sentence is. Here's one:

Fat people eat accumulates.

This is a perfectly grammatical sentence. But by inviting us at the outset to apply an inapplicable syntactical template, it reads like nonsense. We are led down a garden path (hence the term) that dead-ends and it is only by a recursive effort (going back and finding the right syntactical path) that we find its meaning. On first reading, customary usage will invariably read the word "fat" as an adjective modifying "people." But doing so will then require "accumulates" to be read as a noun (what fat people eat). The only way to restore "accumulates" to its proper status as a verb is to read "fat" as a noun. Then it makes sense. Garden-path sentences usually rely on words like "fat" that can have more than one grammatical status (or meaning), but also, and often crucially, on a little bit of grammatical discourtesy as well. The writer has left out a couple of helper words that any editor would note: "*The* fat *that* people eat accumulates." Here are a few more:

The man who hunts ducks out on weekends.
While the boy scratched the big and hairy dog yawned loudly.
The daughter of the king's son admires himself.
They told the boy that the girl met the story.
All women who like a man who paints like Monet.
The old man the boat.[2]

The term "garden-path sentence" was coined by the linguist Mitchell Marcus (Marcus 1974, 1980) as central evidence for "the incremental parsing of natural language" or "discourse-as-process." The argument is that, to some extent at least, we understand a sentence incrementally, that is, word by word, rather than exclusively as a whole. This is still an area of some contention, but garden-path sentences do foreground a challenge in the field of computational linguistics and particularly in the development of computer-

2. Many of these were taken or adapted from www.site.uottawa.ca/~kbarker/garden-path.html. A quick Google search will give you other sites with fine examples. For a good general discussion of garden-path sentences and the challenge of disambiguating them, see Pinker 1994: 207–17.

ized translation programs, which generally rely on whole sentence reading. At the same time it underscores how much the disambiguation of sentences can be assisted by an understanding of context—something that it is very hard to train a computer to do. On your PC, you often see this inability to disambiguate even mild garden-path effects when Word, trying to be helpful, warns you with green underscoring that there is a problem with your grammar when in fact there isn't.

There can be a pleasure in reading garden-path sentences, and one might make the same kind of evolutionary argument for this pleasure that Lisa Zunshine makes for the way novels hone our mind-reading capability: they "test the functioning of our cognitive adaptations for mind-reading while keeping us pleasantly aware that the 'test' is proceeding quite smoothly" (Zunshine 2006: 18). With garden-path sentences, what is pleasurably sharpened is our ability to disambiguate challenging sentences. They fine-tune our language motors. This is, no doubt, why jokes often deploy the garden-path effect:

> Time flies like an arrow, fruit flies like a banana.
> Take my wife, . . . please!

It is fun to play like this with language, and I think the pleasure is sharpened by the way such a sentence tempts linguistic chaos in the split second before we parse the sentence correctly and restore linguistic order. When you get the joke, chaos is brought under control by your own acuity. It is one of the ways to achieve the excitement of living on the edge. The risk is not as great as taking a curve at high speed on a motorcycle, but losing control of one's language can be hard on the mind. How painful it is anyone knows who has struggled with a language poorly understood amid a group of native speakers.

IMPOSSIBLE SENTENCES

In one's own language, a struggle with garden-path effects is usually provoked by the incompetence of the would-be communicator or the challenge of meeting economies of space, as in news headlines ("Officer shoots man with knife").[3] But sometimes it can be inflicted intentionally by a writer of certified competence. Here's a sentence, one of many, by a canonical modernist:

---

3. Changes of usage over time can also introduce garden-path effects where contemporaries would have had no problem. Modern readers no longer familiar with the expression that begins the following sentence from *Barchester Towers* might find the sentence incomplete: "Some few years since . . . a liberal clergyman was a person not frequently to be met" (Trollope nd.: 19).

> Any little thing is a change that is if nothing is wasted in that cellar. (Stein 1998: 350)

In this instance, the garden-path effect takes hold in the phrase "that is if" at which point readers must abandon the expectation of some kind of modifier of "change" (e.g., "Any little thing is a change that is welcome"). Instead they must retroactively insert a different grammatical understanding of "that is" that leaves "change" unmodified and introduces a contingency that in the world of the sentence would abolish change altogether. The grammatical discourtesy in this case is the absence of two commas that would signal the sentence's altered course ("Any little thing is a change, that is, if nothing is wasted . . . "). What makes this sentence different from other garden-path sentences is that this substitution does not deliver the relief that ordinarily comes with "getting" the meaning. And this is because there is insufficient information through which we can establish full confidence in our reading. The nouns and the verbs are in this regard referentially impoverished.

Context gives us some help. The sentence comes from the section of Gertrude Stein's *Tender Buttons* titled "Rooms," and a cellar is a room, so in this limited sense it belongs. But the deictic modifier ("that") points to a specific cellar that we know only through this sentence. Context also helps somewhat in figuring what qualifies as "any little thing." "Any" is a repeated modifier of things in the neighboring paragraphs ("any smile," "any coat") amid an abundance of other things, though some not so little ("a can," "a cape," "a hill," "a curtain," "a package and a filter and even a funnel") and some not so concrete ("a measure," "a success," "a religion"). We also learn that "when there is a shower any little thing is water" (348). But all this does not help (me, at least) to understand what it is in the cellar that might be "wasted," nor how the presence of waste would keep things from being (making?) "a change." The lexical strangeness of this sentence is so deep that it might even elicit a third path in the mind of a reader desperate to bring some kind of closure ("Any little thing is a change that is *as if* nothing is wasted . . . "). But it doesn't help.

So, whatever pleasure we may take in the sentence's grammatical and lexical swerves and indeterminacies, it is not the same pleasure as that of a joke. The pleasure of the joke depends on the small triumph of getting it. But here there is nothing to get without serious under- or overreading. Instead, for the mind that refuses premature closure, the pleasure of the text is necessarily threaded with a feeling of anxiety or frustration in the face of the indeterminable. Stein has certainly taken her lumps for all this linguistic havoc, even from sympathetic critics. David Lodge claimed she went too far in violating "the very essence of her medium, language." It is all "exhilarating," he wrote, but "the treatment is so drastic that it kills the patient" (Lodge 1977:

154). Wendy Steiner made pretty much the same criticism when she blamed Stein's botched syntax for robbing her of even a minimal chance to make a significant modernist contribution (Steiner 1978: 156). By contrast, those who defend Stein (and their number continues to grow) stress the way she liberated language from the "real world" constraints of reference, practical usage, and the generally accepted order of time and space. In Neil Schmitz's words, "the denotated world collapses," nouns float free from any "clarifying knowledge of the nature of things, and . . . nothing can be named and then classified, given as real" (cited in Perloff 1983: 101). This comports with Stein's own view that in *Tender Buttons* she was "doing nothing but using losing refusing and pleasing and betraying and caressing nouns" (Stein 1971: 138). In rough agreement, Brian McHale described her style as "words disengaged from syntax" (McHale 2009: 153).

But I don't believe it is possible to disengage from syntax—that is, when sentence or sentence-like expectations are cued. Certainly there are moments in this text when Stein makes rhythm and sound so predominate that the reader is truly released from the prison house of syntactical constraints.

> Alas a dirty word, alas a dirty third alas a dirty third, alas a dirty bird. (1998: 341)

> A no, a no since, a no since when, a no since when since, a no since when since a no since when since, a no since, a no since when since, a no since, a no, a no since a no since, a no since, a no since. (1998: 344)

This way of writing dominates a poem like "Susie Asado." But not *Tender Buttons.* And when sentence structure begins to take shape, as it does almost always in *Tender Buttons,* the quality of Stein's lexical swerves takes on a different coloration. Commonly the syntax of her sentences can be quite clear:

> A can containing a curtain is a solid sentimental usage. (1998: 348)

Yet it is the syntax that elicits a feeling of "wrongness." Without the perception of sentence structure, Stein's semantic disorder is much more purely a lexical romp, as it is in "Susie Asado." With the perception of sentence structure, you feel a syntactical resistance as the nouns pull away from your expectations.

> Almost very likely there is no seduction, almost very likely there is no stream, certainly very likely the height is penetrated, certainly certainly the target is cleaned. (1998: 349–50)

> A change is in a current and there is no habitable exercise. (1998: 351)[4]

Stein's irresolvable garden-path sentences, then, are simply another hard, sharp turn of the screw in this gallery of disturbing affects. In these sentences, the conflict between syntax and semantics is compounded by a conflict in the syntax itself.

> Come to season that is there any extreme use in feather and cotton. (1998: 313)

> A season in yellow sold extra strings makes lying places. (1998: 322)

> That choice is there when there is a difference. (1998: 329)

> Releasing the oldest auction that is the pleasing some still renewing. (1998: 349)

There is no avoiding an intimation of chaos when cued syntactical expectations are redirected, and, even more, the discomfort when, in the end, the syntactical uncertainties fail to resolve. In short, our cognitive grooves are too deep. Stein must have been aware of this and in fact depended on it. However much her writing may resemble the chaotic speech of aphasics suffering from Jakobsen's "contiguity disorder" and "contextual deficiency" (Lodge 1977: 148), Stein herself was no aphasic. This is an important point. From her earliest years, she was, like her readers, irreversibly stamped with linguistic competence. So she must have known what she was inflicting on her readers and depended on it as an integral part of the effect she wanted. Perhaps this is what she meant by the words "losing," "refusing," and "betraying" cited above. If syntax can be considered a restraining (paternal?) hand, then that hand is felt almost everywhere in the reader's transaction with this text. It is there in the sensation of its resistance. In fact, the feelings of liberation and play are inseparable from the feeling of syntactical constraint. To put this another way, the sensation of wildness in the nouns' constant attempts at flight is a result of what constrains them—we only know their weird excess by the syntactical tether that wants to hold them back.

---

4. It is interesting to compare Stein's sentences with Chomsky's famous example of a syntactically grammatical yet semantically meaningless sentence: "Colorless green ideas sleep furiously" (Chomsky 1957: 15). My feeling about Chomsky's sentence is that it pulls at the reader less than Stein's because the referential anarchy is so extreme it prevents the syntax from gaining any semantic traction at all.

Tender Buttons is a strange text. Well beyond paraphrase, it can only be known by entering into it. And once in it, you know it, whether you want to or not. This may be what Stein meant in "Composition as Explanation," when she wrote paradoxically of "everybody in their entering the modern composition" that "they do enter it, if they do not enter it they are not so to speak in it they are out of it and so they do enter it" (Stein 1998: 521). In *Tender Buttons,* she immersed her readers in a constant warfare of nouns and syntax, of which the unparsable garden-path sentence was ground zero. By so doing she went much further down the line than Oscar Wilde ever did in fulfilling the standard that "all art is quite useless." She takes us to a kind of evolutionary dead-end, where strategic adaptation is displaced by an art that succeeds at the expense of our survival skills. In this it accords with Stein's aestheticism and the value of "the art that lasts": such an art "is an end in itself and in that respect it is opposed to the business of living which is relation and necessity." The masterpiece, she wrote, "has nothing to do with human nature or with identity, it has to do with the human mind" (Stein 1971: 358). And this is my focus: she brings us into a space in our minds that we rarely visit. We may enjoy this or we may detest it, but it lets us feel the enormous power of syntax, to know something of how deeply our minds are invested in it, and the vertigo we experience when its power is challenged.

WARS OF THE WORLDS

In an ingenious essay, "Speak Friend and Enter," Manfred Jahn has expanded the applicability of garden-pathing from sentences to narrative. His narrative examples are James Thurber's "The Secret Life of Walter Mitty" and Ursula Le Guin's "Mazes," both of which start out by leading the reader down a narrative garden path in one kind of world only to require that world's recursive reconstruction as another kind of world.[5] As with garden-path sentences, there is a range in the way the effect takes hold and is exposed: quickly in "Walter Mitty," gradually in "Mazes." In works like Agatha Christie's *The Murder of Roger Ackroyd* (1926), John Lanchester's *The Debt to Pleasure* (1996), William Golding's *Pincher Martin* (1956), Flann O'Brien's *The Third Policeman* (1967), Ian McEwan's *Atonement* (2002), and films like Alfred Hitchcock's

5. The deep cognitive commonality that is central in the alignment of sentence structure and narrative structure may be best characterized as the "predictive process." For a fascinating defense of the incremental nature of this process in the predictive mapping of linguistic "event structures" see Altmann and Mirković 2009. It is hard not to see the same process guiding readers and viewers of narrative event structures.

Vertigo (1958), Brian Singer's *The Usual Suspects* (1995), David Fincher's *Fight Club* (1999), M. Night Shyamalan's *The Sixth Sense* (1999), and David Lynch's *Mulholland Drive* (2001), exposure of the garden path comes quite late in the narrative and with little warning so that these works almost demand rereading or re-viewing in order to understand the extent to which the world the reader/viewer had accepted as the actual world of a traditional mystery or novel or film was in fact another kind of world. This need to go back and immerse oneself in the world of the narrative constitutes a significant parallel between the effect of a narrative garden path and that of a grammatical one. In *The Third Policeman* and *Atonement,* the entire narrative world is discovered to be one in which the narration itself is a sustained act of misleading—a false path that is revealed as such near the end.[6]

In Shyalaman's *The Sixth Sense,* the garden path requires an even more radical revaluation in that it requires a revised understanding of the way the world itself works. A psychiatrist, Malcolm Crowe, discovers late in the

---

6. These examples all deploy in an extreme form what Genette, dealing strictly with prose fiction, called "paralypsis," a strategy of narratorial belatedness in which information is deliberately withheld in order to release it, together with its impact, at a later point in the narrative (Genette 1980: 51–53). In these cases, the device conceals and then reveals what has been called variously a "hidden frame," a "terminal frame" (Nelles 1997), or a "missing opening frame" (Wolf 2006). Monica Fludernik uses the ending of Pynchon's *Gravity's Rainbow* as an example, though one that works as such only if we agree that the entire narrative is here revealed to be a film Slothrop has been watching (Fludernik 2009: 28–29). I am indebted to John Evans and others who contributed to an on-line discussion of hidden frames, as I am to David Richter, who used the term "revealed frame" in the same on-line discussion and produced as an example the beginning and ending lines of Milton's "Lycidas":

> Yet once more, O ye Laurels, and once more
> Ye Myrtles brown, with Ivy never-sear,
> I com to pluck your Berries harsh and crude,
> And with forc'd fingers rude,
> Shatter your leaves before the mellowing year.
> . . .
> Thus sang the uncouth Swain to th'Okes and rills,
> While the still morn went out with Sandals gray,
> He touch'd the tender stops of various Quills,
> With eager thought warbling his *Dorick* lay:
> And now the Sun had stretch'd out all the hills,
> And now was dropt into the Western bay;
> At last he rose, and twitch'd his Mantle blew:
> To morrow to fresh Woods, and Pastures new. (Milton 1957: 40, 44; ll. 1–5, 186–93)

The transition in Milton's poem is quite gentle, a shift that causes little disturbance. And though I would say it gives us a subtly altered world, it requires none of the arduous retroactive world-remaking that a film like *The Sixth Sense* does. The example indicates that the garden-path or concealed frame strategy allows for a wide and variegated range of effect.

film that he had not survived an attack that we witness at the film's outset. Ever since that early point in the film, he, along with most first viewers, had assumed he had survived the attack. But in the actual world of the film he does not survive the attack and from that point on has been a ghost, visible and audible only to the audience and a clairvoyant child, Cole, whom he has been trying to help.[7] As such, *The Sixth Sense* is an instance of what Edward Branigan has called breaking the frame of "world knowledge" by "passing through to a world that has new laws" (Branigan 2006: 288 n.64). But unlike other instances Branigan cites (*Through the Looking Glass, Dracula*), the break in *The Sixth Sense* returns us to the world we thought we knew, but now reconstructed.[8] In its world-recreating radicalism it makes vivid what is true in the other examples above: that garden-pathing in fictional narrative is a matter of "worlds" or more precisely, "storyworlds." These worlds are what correspond to the syntactical alternatives—the two different possible sentences—in a garden-path sentence. And just as in the garden-path sentence a grammatical crisis is brought on by the pressure of grammatical impossibility, in a garden-path narrative an ontological crisis is brought on by the pressure of an ontological impossibility—an impossible world—which must give way to the actual world of the story for the narrative to be coherent. For *The Sixth Sense* to maintain its narrative coherence, the world in which Dr. Crowe appears to be alive must give way to a different world in which he has died, an enlarged world governed by different rules. Much has been written in the last twenty years about the ways in which narrative is not just a matter of linear action but of worldmaking (Hernadi 2002, Ryan 1991, Doležel 1998, Gerrig 1993, Herman 2002), but few narrative moves make us so vividly aware of this than a narrative garden path with its necessary cognitive recalibration of worlds.[9]

---

7. One problem with writing about garden paths in recent narratives is that, of necessity, one "spoils" the garden-path surprise by revealing what is exposed and how it is done. I have tried in this chapter to keep such spoiling to the minimum needed.

8. For an even more complex and disorienting reading of the garden-path complexity of *The Sixth Sense* see Branigan (2002: 110–111). Though I don't (yet) go all the way down the path he suggests, I want to thank Edward Branigan here for a very helpful reading of an early draft of my chapter.

9. Current work on the worldmaking character of narrative was anticipated by Nelson Goodman's groundbreaking and still useful *Ways of Worldmaking* in 1978. Another groundbreaker is Brian McHale's 1987 book, *Postmodernist Fiction,* in which he identified the obsessive world-making (and unmaking) of postmodernist narrative as a way of bringing into the foreground the arsenal of slights of hand and unexamined assumptions that traditional realistic narrative has relied on in its world-making.

AN IMPOSSIBLE WORLD

Central to Jahn's expansion of garden-path effects is his adoption of Ray Jackendoff's (1983, 1987) concept of "preference-rules": that hierarchy of probabilities or "non-necessary conditions" packaged in frames or scripts that give them their efficiency and "cognitive power." The frame of a restaurant or the script of a waiter's behavior contains certain data that are always true ("necessary conditions") but they are also packed with assumptions of varying degrees of probability ("non-necessary conditions").[10] Michael Haneke's award-winning 2005 film, *Caché,* for example, starts with a short garden path: a street-level view of apartments that most first viewers take for a conventional establishing shot in the film's storyworld. But the credits come and go, and still the scene persists. The camera remains fixed and nothing happens except for the passing of four pedestrians and a bicyclist. After two full minutes have passed, we hear the sound of intermittent comments of indeterminate import by people who cannot be located anywhere in the scene ("Well?" / "Nothing." / "Where was it?" / "Out front in a plastic bag." / "What's wrong?"). Finally, after just under three minutes, the camera shifts to a different angle in the same locale to follow the TV culture-journalist, Georges Laurent (Daniel Auteuil), as he emerges from the apartment, crosses the street, points in the direction from which the first shot was taken and says to his wife, Anne (Juliette Binoche, now visible in the doorway), "He must have been there." He then goes back into the apartment, after which, what seems to be the cinematographer's camera reverts to the fixed scene it began with. More dialogue ensues, and, eventually, a fast forward puts it beyond doubt that we have been watching not what is happening in the present but rather what happened in the recent past, recorded on tape.

Here, what corresponds to syntactical expectations generated at the level of the sentence are world-making expectations generated at the level of narrative by the cognitive frames and scripts (including, crucially, those belonging to the special language of film) that are cued as the narrative begins. In terms of Jackendoff's preference rules, any sustained street shot includes a high probability, though not a necessity, of pedestrians and a bicyclist. Voices without perceivable speakers are lower on the list of probabilities, yet they are still possibilities. Such voices loud enough to sound as if they are quite

10. Jahn accepts the common practice of using "frames" to refer to "*states and situations* (seeing a room, making a promise)" and "scripts" to refer to "*stereotypical action sequences* (playing a football game, going to a birthday party)" (Jahn 1999: 174; see also Albelson 1980; Stockwell 2002).

near the camera are lower still, but conceivably coming from people beside or immediately behind the point of vision. The cognitive tension increases with the improbabilities: the speakers fail to appear, they continue to make mysterious references, and, perhaps most disturbing, the scene itself grows unconventionally tedious with its lack of significant action or camera movement. Perceptive film veterans may make the "naturalizing" leap before Georges appears, grasping that the scene itself is the subject of the discourse. For some the appearance of Georges going out front on the heels of Anne's answer to his question ("C'etait où?") will do it. As for the stragglers in the audience, still crushed under the weight of improbabilities, liberation comes with impossibility: the actual world cannot go on fast forward, complete with the tell-tale streaks of a VCR tape.

As Jahn writes, garden-path effects challenge our overriding preference for "maximum cognitive payoff": "What [leads] one astray is one's anticipation of good sense, and this is itself a consequence of a human understander's unwillingness to consider nonsense, of a general horror of semantic emptiness, of a craving to make satisfactory sense of a discourse, in short, of preferring what makes sense or even most sense" (Jahn 1999: 177). Correlatively, a minor pleasure of Haneke's opening strategy comes when the viewer understands how the opening belongs to a coherent filmic universe. As in the garden-path sentence, the pleasure depends on there being an initial resistance to sense.[11] Another interesting innovation in the film is the recurrence of this (increasingly vexed) pleasure in different variations, each with its small payoff of surprise and recovery. A close approximation of the first tape turns out to be actually in the filmic present. But then a sequence seemingly in the filmic present, first through the window of a moving car, then down the hallway of a seedy apartment building to a certain door, turns out to be another tape in the filmic past. Later still, the same sequence down the hallway turns out to be in the filmic present when Georges moves into the frame to knock on the same door. A scene of Georges anchoring a discussion of Rimbaud on his television book-program turns out to be a tape that Georges is editing. In other

11. The makers of *The Sixth Sense* took considerable pains to anticipate the viewer's search for inconsistencies in the revised world. At one point Cole lists the rules that govern ghostly behavior, including "They don't know they're dead" and "They see what they want to see," which explains why Malcolm, up to the last scene, fails to recognize all the clear evidence that he is a ghost. In this regard, a considerably more ragged example of garden-pathing in film is the 2003 horror mystery *Identity*, in which a collection of travelers, stranded at a motel in a rainstorm, are mysteriously murdered, one after another. Late in the film, we discover that they are each a separate personality of a convict afflicted with multiple personality disorder. In order to escape his imminent execution, he has been frantically contriving to have them kill each other off with the exception of his one decent personality (John Cusack).

instances, exactly the same fixed-camera surveillance technique for minutes at a time will turn out to be continuations of the filmic present.

In most of these little garden paths, there is the play of probability, improbability, impossibility, and resolution that delivers the small pleasure of successful parsing. Thematically the device works very well, since much of the film is about the perils of certainty. The palpable tension of the film is in large part a product of Georges's adamant refusal to acknowledge the guilt he feels for lies he told as a child. These lies had terrible consequences for Majid, the Algerian orphan his parents had loved and might have adopted. Georges's persistent denial, dissembling, and belligerence are clearly meant to parallel the way France as a nation has failed to address its own collective feelings of suppressed guilt over its treatment of Algiers and Algerians. Haneke's garden-path editing, then, recreates this theme of the perils of certainty, but now as a condition of viewer response by repeatedly reminding us how easily we can go wrong in our assessment of what it is we are seeing.

"Every path leads to nothing," Haneke has said in reference to *Caché*, "The truth is always hidden" (Haneke 2006). Well, yes and no. On the one hand, there is extraordinary truth at the level of mimesis in Auteuil's performance of a man with his kind of professional success, harried out of the blue by anonymous tapes and pictures insinuating judgment and threatening who knows what consequences. It is a highly skilled performance, and for it Auteuil was awarded Best Male Actor in the 2005 European Film Academy Awards. In fact, across the board the acting in this film is exceptionally convincing. It is what gives the film much of its power and to this degree the film is clear. On the other hand, what is not clear is the question of guilt and how to deal with it. Terrible things were done, both in French-Algerian relations (Majid's parents died in a historically documented massacre in 1961 when a rally called by the FLN was broken up by the police and two hundred French Algerians were thrown into the Seine to drown) and in Georges's relations with Majid when his lies led to Majid's expulsion from his family. But Georges was only six at the time, and by keeping us close to him as he struggles with his literal and figurative nightmares, Haneke also keeps us from any easy judgments.

Similarly, with regard to Haneke's garden-path filming, one can say that it is not entirely true that "every path leads to nothing." Repeatedly, as the examples above show, we find the right path. Film or tape, we make our mistakes and we successfully correct them. Where we do lose our way lies not (with one significant exception) in navigating the issue of film present or taped past, but in figuring out who is doing the taping and sending the pictures. The chief suspects, Majid and his son, are pretty convincing in their denial of having anything to do with it, but, much more critically, their participation would involve major contradictions. This is a drama of attribution that we share with the Laurents and that could conceivably go on forever. Compounding this mystery is the final shot in the film, which is also the major exception with regard to answering the question: Is it in the filmic present or is it another surveillance tape (perhaps even another installment in the harassment of Georges)? It serves as a bookend with the opening shot, but with this difference: where we were allowed to recognize the opening shot as a garden path, we are not allowed to determine whether this one is. It is a shot of school steps at the end of classes with young students doing all the probable things students do at such a time, milling about, chatting in groups, getting in cars. But it is also, like the opening shot, a fixed, "unprofessional" piece of camera work, stretching through the credits, and seeming to go on forever. In this it violates both what would normally be the preference rules for conventional film and also the garden-path expectations to which we have become accustomed.

Compounding this difficulty, the Laurents' son, Pierrot, and Majid's unnamed son meet in the upper left hand corner of this scene (something missed by many first-time viewers). They descend the steps in animated and seemingly amicable discussion and then finally part, Majid's son leaving to the right, Pierrot going back up the steps to join other classmates before his own exit. This is the first we learn that these two boys even know each other. How long have they known each other? Are they friends? Are they perhaps accomplices? Have they been involved together in the plot against Pierrot's father? Or is Majid's son cultivating Pierrot in order to visit upon the son further vengeance for the sins of his father? There is simply no way to answer these questions. Haneke has said of an earlier film that it "should not come to an end on the screen, but engage the spectators and find its place in their cognitive and emotive framework" (Wheatley 2006: 33), and viewers at Cannes did their best to oblige. According to Mark Lawson, "this sequence proved to be a sort of Rorschach montage in which viewers saw what they expected or wished to see. Different observers believed that they had detected evidence of a death, a divorce or a dispute over paternity. A critic who is a conspiracy theorist saw a clue to the involvement of the French secret service" (Lawson 2006).

All this frenetic activity is interpretation by supplementation (creating meaningful coherence through strategic alterations of the text as given). And though this may be a sign of intellectual vigor, I think the better part of wisdom is not to give in to it: that is, to accept our ignorance. At the level of representation, there is much powerful material in the film that we do grasp, but there is also much that we don't. We don't know what the boys are up to, we don't know whether Anne Laurent is having an affair with one of the Laurents' friends, we don't know much at all about Majid or what else may have contributed to the grotesque and ingenious vengefulness of his suicide. After all, to accept that we don't know what we can't know, that there will always be unconnected dots, does in fact harmonize with the central theme of the film: the danger of premature judgment, of assuming knowledge of what is hidden.

But there is one more twist to this film and to what constitutes a full response to it. This brings us back to the question of who is making the tapes and sending the pictures. It also brings us back to my main theme. So far, we have been dealing with questions of what is knowable in this narrative and what remains a mystery. And certainly the question of who is doing the taping would seem a preeminent mystery. Watching the first tape, Georges and Anne see Georges as he leaves for work in the morning. He walks right toward the camera, passing to its right. "How come I didn't see him?" he asks. Maybe the camera was in a car? No, it doesn't look like it was filmed through a window. "It'll remain a mystery." But actually our problem is not that we know too little about the taping, but too much. For we have here an agent who influences the course of events;[12] who is aware of intimate details from a past known only to one, possibly two, characters besides Georges; who has a capacity to tape very close up without being seen; who can catch a key event at a time impossible to predict and from a spot that is clearly visible during the scene's enactment; who can deliver a tape through a closed security gate; and who can post drawings that not only depict intimate details of what has happened in the distant past but also strongly suggest what will happen in the future (Majid's suicide). In short, we have been garden-pathed not in our serial assumptions about *who* is doing the taping but in the assumption that it is being done by someone at all, that is, by a human agent who belongs to the film's storyworld. Rather, given the set of details we have to work with, such a participant must be something else altogether. A supernatural agent capable of intervening in a storyworld sufficiently enlarged to accommodate the supernatural? An extradiegetic agent not wholly a part of the film's world but capable of making metaleptic forays into the film's storyworld? We simply will never know.[13]

This is an altogether different kind of mystery from those belonging to the storyworld in which the rest of the action takes place. In such a world, the preference rules consistent with that world would have to govern any taping by a human agent, however hidden. When Haneke violates those rules, he

12. It is worth bearing in mind that the chain of events set in motion and sustained by this hidden daemon, including the humiliation of Majid's being jailed with his son, is quite possibly the trigger that brings on Majid's suicide.

13. Catherine Wheatley settles for the director himself: "'Whose idea of a sick joke is this?' Georges asks his wife after the second tape arrives. Well, it's Haneke's. The stalker's camera is the director's camera. And the person who is really 'sending' the tapes can only be the director himself" (Wheatley 2006: 35).

creates a different kind of mystery from the one Georges had in mind when he said "It'll remain a mystery." It is an ontologically disorienting mystery, a garden-path sequence that can't be "gotten" the way the garden paths of *Roger Acroyd* or *Vertigo* can.[14] Even while the tapes and pictures and the manner of their delivery are doing their efficient and chilling work in opening up the psychological and ethical dimensions of this film, they also introduce an eerie extradimensional element that runs crosswise to the grain of this otherwise powerfully realistic film. It also gives new meaning to the title of the film, *Caché* (*Hidden*). The often ingenious hiding of other kinds of information in this film is, like the ethical issues it raises, basically an extension of the realistic tradition in film. Even when Haneke the modernist calls on his viewers to take over the job of completing the film, filling in where he has left gaps, and in the process wrestling with the ethical questions of the film, he is asking them to join with him in a basically humanistic project.[15] But with regard to the agent behind the tapes and pictures, the viewer cannot proceed in the same way without seriously underreading. To respond fully to this aspect of the film with its manifest impossibilities is to experience a jamming of cognitive schemata that leaves the viewer stranded between worlds.[16]

---

14. *Caché* falls within the large and growing number of nontraditional experiments in storytelling that Warren Buckland has classed as "puzzle films" (2009; for more limited classes of filmic manipulations of time and space, see Cameron 2008, Laass 2008, and Elsaesser 2009). But the kind of unresolved ontological puzzle that Haneke achieves through a failed garden path structure puts the film in a much smaller subcategory. Christopher Nolan's *Inception* (2010) is arguably a candidate depending on whether it is impossible to conclude that there is a level of reality within which the multiple layers of dreaming occur. Michael Caine, for one, asserted in a BBC interview that the confusing ontology of dreams within dreams does resolve into a single coherent storyworld: "[The spinning top] drops at the end, that's when I come back on. If I'm there it's real, because I'm never in the dream. I'm the guy who invented the dream." http://screenrant.com/michael-caine-inception-ending-batman-3-benm-80670/. In written narrative, a possible, if less disturbing, candidate is Doris Lessing's *The Golden Notebook* (1962) in which one cannot tell whether the novel *Free Women* contains the notebooks or the notebooks contain the novel.

15. In an interview with Richard Porton, Haneke stresses that *Caché* is a "realistic film" (Porton 2005: 50). "Hyperrealistic" might be a better term, since much of the focus of the film is on the degree to which reality has been obscured by its simulacra. Haneke said as much in another interview: "Today we are surrounded by images that we take for reality, which is dangerous because we can be manipulated. That's why we filmed *Caché* in high-def video, to create a 'video look.' What the viewer often takes for reality isn't reality, it's just another representation of it" (Ng 2005).

16. Has Haneke's device, then, marred an otherwise excellent film? On the one hand, we have a powerful narrative, delivered in a progression that artfully builds from one intense moment to the next. The alignment of guilt and denial, both personal and national, is immensely effective. On the other hand, our attention is diverted by a stubborn mystery threading its way into the narrative, deepening as the impossibilities accumulate. In the terms I've developed, a drama of representation is increasingly made to share the same filmic space with a cogni-

EVOLUTIONARY MISBEHAVIOR

Caché is an excellent demonstration text for my purposes because it includes narrative versions of both kinds of garden path: those that can be parsed and those that can't, the latter a narrative version of the jammed garden-path effect that I dealt with in the sentences of Stein. It is not hard to find much more thoroughgoing narrative versions of unparsable garden paths in postmodern literature. There are many in a novel like Alain Robbe-Grillet's *Dans le labyrinth* (1959), including the oft-cited scene in which the minute description of a nineteenth-century etching, "The Defeat of Reichenfels," almost imperceptibly transforms into a continuation of the narrative that has preceded it. Critical response to *Dans le labyrinth* has not uncommonly attributed this and other narrative impossibilities to narrator exhaustion. But in Brian McHale's words, "this is an 'expensive' reading, in the sense that it requires us to smooth over a good many difficulties and to repress the text's own resistance to being read this way" (McHale 1987: 14). In the same way, readers of J. M. Coetzee's *In the Heart of the Country* (1977) have at times sought to "naturalize" its wealth of impossibilities as instances of narrator insanity.

In the terms I have been using, exhaustion and insanity are default probabilities that allow the reader to reframe the narrative as symptom and to relocate its action from a fictional actual world of the narrative to a fictional mental world of the narrator. In other words, naturalizing formal incoherence by inferring an exhausted or insane narrator is basically a way of normalizing incoherence as a kind of coherence, sufficiently recognizable to be labeled a product of exhaustion or insanity. And though, as McHale says, both interpretive moves require strategic reductions of the texts involved, it is certainly understandable why readers should want to make them. Narratives, like sentences, can be intolerable when they can't be parsed. Our biological and cultural evolution did not give us the cognitive engineering to accommodate them with ease. But if you are going to do justice to a novel like *In the Heart of*

---

tive drama between the viewer and the film. And, it would seem from the accounts of its first showing that it was the second drama that had everybody buzzing afterward. Nonetheless, I think the really interesting issue is one of logistics: Could Haneke have achieved the success he did in any other way? That is: Would it be possible to resolve the mystery of the agent and maintain the tension that its hiddenness contributes to the moral drama at the center of the film? The answer would seem to be No. Revealing the agent behind the camera and the premonitory drawings would both reduce the nightmarish quality of an all-knowing, irresistible, accusatory consciousness and introduce plot and character complications that would diffuse the focus on Georges's crisis of conscience. From this perspective, what I have been calling the film's ontological conflict, could be seen as an unintended collateral price Haneke was willing to pay in exchange for what he gained.

the Country, you cannot opt, as Coetzee himself put it, "for psychological realism": that is, "a depiction of one person's inner consciousness." In his words, he's playing "a different kind of game, an anti-realistic kind of game" (cited in B. Richardson 2006: 138).[17]

My argument throughout this chapter has been that such a game, whether in sentences or narratives, involves a more radical relocation of the action from the fictional actual world of the text to the mind of its beholder. It becomes a drama of cognition and at the same time a much more intimate transaction between creator and audience. Of course, it is not news that much of twentieth-century experimental literature and film has not only abandoned traditional conventions of representation but representation altogether. The idea has been around so long that Brian Richardson in his *Unnatural Voices* has called for an "anti-mimetic" supplement to narrative theorizing so that we may catch up with this common insight. And certainly the development of a cognitive dimension of such a revised and enlarged theory would help us deal with texts that, in part or in whole, have relocated the intention of the art to what it does to the mind of the reader or viewer: from what art is *about* to what it cognitively *is.* But any such supplemental adjunct to theories of the anti-mimetic or the unnatural, must be grounded in our understanding of what comes naturally to us. In short, experiments like those of Stein and Haneke are so disturbing because . . . we are what we are. Our exquisitely evolved hearts and minds are what have given us our craving for narrative and by extension the market that serves it.

There has been no dearth of plausible theories regarding the utility of this craving. But where strictly evolutionary theorizing runs into difficulties is when literature fails to perform what it is supposed to be good for, that is, notably, literature that falls in the alien terrain of these texts and other modernist and postmodernist fiction and film. When scientists like Dissanayake, E. O. Wilson, and Pinker write off these texts as various forms of perverse indulgence, they are accusing their authors of evolutionary misbehavior. In this they echo the outraged arbiters of taste whose disapproving response to works of the *avant garde* has often been a key part of an intended effect.[18]

---

17. Julian Barnes's *The Sense of an Ending* (2011) may be an example of a novel that winds up on the edge between, on the one hand, intended permanent bafflement of the reader and, on the other, closure through the retrospective application of a mental disorder to the first-person narrator. The argument for the latter reading is that there is sufficient evidence to see the narrator-protagonist as a case of impaired memory so severe that he can, without knowing it, mentally erase and replace the central event of his life's story.

18. One could make the case that the production of, and market for, such texts is a case of privileging one survival trait—the "novelty drive" (J. D. Miller 1999)—at the expense of others: e.g., cultural solidarity, the preservation and transmission of knowledge, "a mental catalogue of

There is an underlying assumption in such rebukes that what we are evolved to do is what we *should* do. But in an age in which we are learning so much about how the mind works, it is valuable to know what it feels like when you are pushed up against the limits of that mind. I think this is one object, perhaps *the* object, of the kind of neural sport we have focused on in this chapter. These instances of the unresolved garden path may be a narrow kind of art, but it is nonetheless an art that serves a salutary purpose. It is good to take a look over the edge and, in the process, to feel in the protest of our evolved wiring an intimation of how much there may be that we are not, by our nature, equipped to know. In this limited evolutionary sense, all the principal authors I focus on in this book are guilty of misbehavior.

---

the fatal conundrums we might face someday and the outcomes of strategies we could deploy in them" (Pinker 2002: 543). That such perverse texts appeal to our penchant for novelty is indisputable. But this does not necessarily mean that they can be written off as novelty for novelty's sake, nor the elitist racket Pinker has suggested (Pinker 1997: 522; 2002: 407).

CHAPTER 4

Syntactical Poetics

IN THIS CHAPTER, I return to an art that actively seeks to express inexpressible mysteries that we live with outside our textual transactions. They don't abide with us as a birthright in the manner of the unknowable I dealt with in the first part of this book. They are paradoxical states of feeling that come upon us during the course of our lives, but they are at the same time beyond our grasp. The art that seeks to approach them and that we will be focusing on is an art, as in *Tender Buttons,* that is practiced at the level of the sentence—in the present instance by two masters of slow-moving minimalist narrative. A central difference, however, between the garden-path structure featured in this chapter and the unresolved version of it that I featured in the last is that, where in the last chapter neither path worked, in this chapter both (and sometimes more) paths work. So the device we'll be looking at in this chapter is really what you might call the apparent garden-path sentence, or more accurately the multi-path sentence, since, whatever path is taken, the path arrives at its goal. I'll clarify how this works in the first section of this chapter, but in what follows thereafter I'll show how such sentences can be used in an art of syntactical layering. With the assistance of this device, the two authors in this chapter, Beckett for most of it and Janet Winterson toward the end, seek to capture complexities of feeling and thought that lie beyond the expressive power of language. They are the dominants of lyrical poetry, intensities of love and loss, which most of us come to experience at some time in our lives. As such, these authors deal with the knowable in the sense that they deal with inescapable conditions of our conscious life. But, as I hope to show, it is the very precision of their art that allows these authors to show us that we don't fully know what words like "loss" and "love" stand in for—that they signify what lies not only beyond expression but beyond understanding as well.

This is also the point in my study where we come closest to an examination of specifically lyrical effects. The exemplary passages I use are drawn from texts of indeterminate genre, for which "prose poem" may work as a category of last resort. Not only do they feature the expression of feeling but they also have the poetic concentration and atemporal character that are commonly ascribed aspects of the lyrical, as opposed to the narrative, mode.[1] That said, there are both compacted narratives here and micro-narratives in which there is an intimation of action. More important, the same process of incremental parsing necessary for the garden-path effect is also necessary for the multi-path effect. And with it comes the corresponding cognitive drama that unfolds in the reader's mind. Finally, and significantly in regard to the perennial subject of the limits of narrative, the multi-path effect seems unobtainable in longer narratives. If I am right about this, then, though there are fully fledged narrative versions of the garden-path sentence that Jahn demonstrated and comparable narrative versions of the irresolvable garden-path sentence that I have just demonstrated, there is no comparable narrative version of the multi-path sentence. The reason for this is interesting and worth pursuing. It will be my final subject in this chapter.

MULTI-PATH SENTENCES

Like the garden-path sentence the multi-path sentence can also be found in jokes:

> She was only a whiskey maker, but he loved her still.

1. This distinction between lyric and narrative is implicit in Wordsworth's "Preface to Lyrical Ballads" (1800/02) and Shelley's "Defence of Poetry" (1821; published 1840), as well as Poe's over-the-top 1846 essay on "The Philosophy of Composition." More recently the case for the atemporal and temporal distinction between the two "modes," lyric and narrative, has been given explicit development by theorists like Culler 1981: 148–54, Brooks 1984: 20–21, and a number of others. For a helpful overview see Morgan 2009: 8–11.

Here we have a sentence that on the one hand tells us of a woman whom a man loves despite her societally marginal, *déclassé* profession and on the other tells us of a socially marginal, *déclassé* woman whom a man tolerates for the whiskey she makes. Both readings work and, in this case, neither strains credibility in the sense that neither reading requires us to entertain the possibility of a world unlike our own. There are other multi-path sentences in which both readings work syntactically, but one of them requires a world with different conditions from the one we live in. These are often classified as garden-path sentences for this very reason, even though technically the sentence can be completed following either path, since both are grammatical. In the classic garden-path headline, "Red tape holds up new bridge," for example, both paths are grammatical, but one works for the world we recognize as our own while the other requires a world in which either the law of gravity works quite differently from the way it works in our world or there is a kind of tape we haven't invented yet. In a similar way, alternate worlds that lie dormant in the commonest sentences can be awoken by supplementary context: "Mary had a little lamb. The doctor fainted."

Multi-path sentences in which the alternative readings are each in themselves compatible with the way things are in our own world are actually quite common in everyday discourse:

> Someone ate every Twinkie.

In this sentence, the double meaning of "someone" is the pivot that turns the reader in one direction or the other. Depending on how this word is read, the sentence could mean that one particular person ate up all the Twinkies, or it could mean that for every Twinkie there was someone who ate it. The only way to disambiguate such a sentence is through context. If, for example, the suspects are gathered in a room and the sentence is uttered by Hercule Poirot, who has been called in to solve the mystery, then it is likely that the correct meaning of the sentence is the first. But if the Twinkies had been piled on a plate for a group of hungry children, then it is likely that the correct meaning of the sentence is the second. In short, though multi-path sentences are constantly popping up—

> He's going to sleep.
> I know the people Hortense knows.
> They are hunting dogs.

—there is usually a context that makes them clear.

In conversation, problems of contextual meaning can be quickly resolved through on-the-spot clarifications. Where serious problems arise is in written discourse. As we have already discussed, written discourse is hobbled by the way it separates senders from receivers. This can be especially problematic in questions of law:

> A well regulated militia, being necessary to the security of a free State, the right of the people to keep and bear arms, shall not be infringed.

But what is problematic in law can be an advantage in art. This is what I will focus on in what follows.

A POETICS OF SYNTACTICAL PARSIMONY

I'll start with a set of what are, technically, garden-path sentences, though ones in which the garden path is more than a false lead.

> Here without having to close the eye sees her afar. Motionless in the snow under the snow. The buttonhook trembles from its nail as if a night like any other. (Beckett 1996: 68)

Each of these three consecutive sentences from Samuel Beckett's haunting late work *Ill Seen Ill Said* sets the reader on a garden path. In the first, the garden path terminates in the phrase "to close the eye sees," in which the noun "eye" must be converted from an object to a subject in order for the sentence to make grammatical sense. The garden path in the second terminates with the word "under" since it is not the snow that she is standing in that is under the snow, but rather she herself. She is both standing *in* the snow and *under* the snow that falls on her. In both of these sentences, the "discourtesy" that enables the garden-path effect is a missing comma. The moment of hesitation in the third sentence comes in the phrase "as if a night," which threatens to run astray for want of a verb: "as if [it were] a night like any other." Technically, the verb (like the commas missing in the other sentences) has been there all the time since, once we get the sentence right, we feel its presence even without seeing it in print. But less is more. Beckett's syntactical parsimony guarantees that we also cannot *not* be aware of the verb's absence and feel the mute impedance that comes with its visual suppression.

Once you "get" these sentences (and, unlike Stein's, they can be gotten), they come together with an austere and eerily precise beauty. Eerie, because the hesitations of a first reading remain a part of the whole effect, however adept readers may get at hearing and grasping the "proper" syntax of these sentences. Precise, because in this way more is said than grammatical correctness will allow. As the title of the work implies, *Ill Seen Ill Said* is not only an intensely self-reflexive piece, but one in which the difficulties of seeing and saying are identified as a single condition: perception as expression and expression as perception. Infected throughout its system, each of the work's sentences is an instance in miniature of this "illness." In each to some degree the reader feels the struggle of seeing as saying and saying as seeing. This is no mere case of what Ivor Winters called "imitative form," in which the form of the work imitates what the work is about. "Here form *is* content, content *is* form," as the young Beckett wrote of *Finnegans Wake.* "His writing is not *about* something; *it is that something itself*" (Beckett 1929: 14). The difficulty of this text, then, is no mere signifier of difficulty but, like the difficulty of Stein, inseparable from its condition as art. And, as in Stein, the syntax of this art is critical to its success. The difference lies in our awareness that there *is* something very important lying just out of the reach of seeing and saying. This is my first point. Beckett is not playing with his reader but keeping his reader from premature closure, from settling on meaning when meaning can only be approached, not arrived at.

THE SENTENCE MAN

Beckett is a "sentence man," as Hugh Kenner originally observed, and as such the work of his maturity stands in marked contrast to the lush verbal art of Joyce the "word man." From this perspective, the verbal pyrotechnics of Beckett's apprenticeship in the 1930s was a legacy of the master, which, through constant formal exploration and exile in a foreign language, was refined to an art of syntax, "the local order of language" (Kenner 1990: 293),[2] which only grew more austere and subtle as he aged. In a powerful extension of Kenner's insight, titled "Beckett's Tattered Syntax," Ann Banfield has analyzed how Beckett increasingly relied on words whose meaning is almost entirely a register of their syntactical function. Unlike Joyce, who gathered together and even cross-germinated nouns, verbs, adjectives, and adverbs in a superabundance of semantic content, Beckett depended more and more on the "non-

2. "I could show you a Beckett sentence," Kenner wrote, "as elegant in its implications as the binomial theorem, and another as economically sphinx-like as the square root of minus one, and another, on trees in the night, for which half of Wordsworth would seem a fair exchange" (Kenner 1977).

productive" words, the pronouns and determiners that "lack highly specified semantic content, having only cognitive syntactic features" (Banfield 2004: 16). Joseph Emonds (2000) called these, collectively, "the syntacticon," and in Beckett's late work they predominate along with semantically "'light' nouns, verbs, adjectives, and prepositions," words like "be" (is, are), "one," "self," "thing," "have," "go," "let," "say," "other," "same," "mere," "such" (Banfield 2004: 16–17). Citing Emonds, Banfield notes that "the philosophical vocabulary is drawn from the syntacticon," which in Beckett's hands is the instrument of a negative quest for the beyond of language, a goal he first wrote of in his essay on Proust and, Banfield argues, never gave up. The words he drew on, especially in his late style, were "not mined in the riches of the dictionary, with its adjectives of infinite shades and qualities and nouns filled to the brim with meaning, but out of the poverties of the syntacticon" (20). The paradox of Banfield's take on the evolution of Beckett's style is that his lifetime pursuit of an art in which "the object is perceived as particular and unique and not merely the member of a family" (Beckett 1931: 11) required letting go of much of language's semantic specificity. Thus, in *Ill Seen Ill Said*, "'this old so dying woman' is never named (apart from this single definite noun phrase) but only 'pronamed' by a function word . . . with no meaning but the syntactic features of feminine gender, third person, and singular number" (Banfield 2004: 19).

I think Banfield is right. However, the paradox she discloses is compounded by another: that it is not only the semantic lightness of his language that works for Beckett but also the contortions of his syntax. This is my focus. Beckett's precision requires the serial impedances of his syntactic parsimony. And this again brings us into literary terrain that is neither representation of the world nor postmodern world-building. If I am right, Beckett's project is to return us to a feature of the world we are always in, one that is neither fiction nor fact, neither "figment" nor its "counterpoison," an object of neither the "vile jelly" of "the eye of flesh" nor that "other eye" in "the madhouse of the skull and nowhere else" (Beckett 1996: 58), and (fleshly or other) neither clearly the reader's eye, the author's, or the subject's. It is a deep "confusion" of "[t]hings and imaginings. As of always" (ibid.).

> Weeping over as weeping will see now the buttonhook larger than life (57)

Though there was enough of Joyce the punster left in Beckett to enjoy the impoverishment of "weeping willow" in "weeping will," the energy in this sentence is syntactical. It lies in the opposing tugs of "will see" and "see," plus the ambiguity of the latter. "Will see," if it could work syntactically, would become an implicit "she will see," and the sentence would resolve into a brief narrative in the third person (i.e., no longer weeping, she will now see the buttonhook). But this would make the tautological "weeping over as weeping" the subject modifier. Disambiguated, the sentence requires the verb "see" to take the imperative mode with "weeping over as weeping will" as the modifier (i.e., weeping at an end, as weeping always does come to an end, see now the buttonhook). But then who is addressed? Who is being asked to see? There are three possibilities—the reader, the narrator, the woman—each of whom is curiously encumbered. If it is the reader, then it is the reader who has been in tears and thus unable to see the buttonhook until finished weeping. Likewise for the narrator, who is also by this construction addressing himself. If the woman, then the narrator is no longer describing her and her actions but giving her directions as well.

In my view, all of these options are meant to apply. By abusing our hard-earned capabilities in this way, forestalling any imposed clarity, Beckett makes us feel what happens when the borders separating the imagined, the real, the seen, the said, and the seer are not just erased but erased *and* maintained. On the one hand, the distinctions of the true and the false, the self and the other, are constructions embedded in language. On the other hand, they seem, for all their "constructed" nature, to correspond to distinctions that have an actual nonlinguistic existence. So Beckett seeks not to abolish them, but at one and the same time to abolish and promote them. Again, the exquisite lessness of Beckett's syntax is a moreness of sensation as he pursues his project of driving language ever "worstward," seeking at every turn to "fail better."

BEYOND REPRESENTATION

It brought him (and brings us again) to *Worstward Ho,* the final text of the "second trilogy," in which the quality of music, always present in Beckett's verbal art, is accentuated almost to the point of displacing the dramas of syntactical meaning.

> Stooped as loving memory some old gravestones stoop. (Beckett 1996: 115)

An old woman in a graveyard is seen "stooped as [in] loving memory some old gravestones stoop." Or is it "stooped as, loving memory, some old gravestones stoop"? Or is it "stooped as loving memory [is stooped], some old gravestones stoop"? I would argue for all three—the memory of one loved, loving memory, and the burden of loving memory—three states of mind that are at once different and yet susceptible to melding. But at the same time, in the same sentence, Beckett has created a perfectly symmetrical cataleptic alexandrine, bookended with the strong chiasmatic chiming of "stooped" and "stoop." The sentence moves toward a pure evocation of rhythmical sound, a music that threatens (as it does at times in *Tender Buttons*) to assert its own priority, absorbing all of the interest. Yet it doesn't, and that's the important point. This is the case even when the effects are so compacted as to approach a kind of nonsensical hilarity:

> Not that as it is it is not bad. (99)
> Whenever said said said missaid. (109)
> So far far far from wrong. (110)

It has often been observed that if you repeat a word often enough it loses its meaning and becomes a moment of pure sound. Beckett loves to test the limits of this effect, but, uniquely, he does so without relieving readers of their syntactical obligations. In each of these brisk passages, modest words drawn from the syntacticon are rung like bells but only by observing the rules of the syntactical game (whenever said [is] said, said [is] missaid). And even when you do, uncertainties can remain (is it "said" that is "missaid" or is "said" meant to be read as "missaid"?) In short, the struggle for meaning and the release from it are experienced simultaneously, but you can only know this by going into it.[3]

Reuven Tsur proposed in his essay "Two Critical Attitudes: Quest for Certitude and Negative Capability" that readers and critics can be ranged on a scale between those determined to find interpretive certitude at all cost and those who adopt what Keats called "negative capability" or a capacity "of being in uncertainties, Mysteries, doubts, without any irritable reaching after fact and reason" (Keats cited in Tsur 1975: 776). The latter attitude, he argued, depends on a willingness to shift "mental sets" without settling on any one as final and requires a high degree of tolerance for "uncertainty and ignorance" (787). Tsur's distinction between these two critical attitudes complements a similar distinction between works themselves—those that invite certitude

3. In chapter 2, I argued that Beckett and García Márquez achieved effects in a medium without sight or sound that were unobtainable in media where the visual and auditory are experienced in their material form. As García Márquez insisted, the effect of his imagery in prose was unfit for a visual medium like film. I think the same is true for sound. There is no questioning the importance of rhythm and sound in the prose of these artists. But we hear, as we see, in silence. The effect may not be exactly what Keats meant when he wrote that "Heard melodies are sweet, but those unheard / Are sweeter," but writing does disembody language, and this makes a big difference of effect.

and those that require openness to a plurality of meaning. The latter certainly applies to much of the work of Beckett, and indeed Tsur's prime example of a work demanding negative capability is Beckett's *Waiting for Godot.*

But what I have been focusing on in Beckett requires, I believe, an attitude that goes one step beyond the far end of Tsur's scale—it does, that is, if I am right in thinking that the critical attitudes Tsur describes are attitudes toward representations. As such, negative capability is an openness to the meaning of what is represented, but it does not deny that representation is going on. The reading of Beckett (by Günther Anders) that Tsur features to demonstrate this attitude can therefore assert that part of the meaning of Estragon's game of "shoe off, shoe on" is that we, the audience, in our everyday lives, are doing "nothing but a playing of games, clownlike without real consequences" (Anders cited in Tsur 1975: 786). But a function of the impedances that I have been examining in both Stein's and Beckett's works is to foreclose such interpretive moves, taking their creations outside the realm of representation altogether.

Critical attitudes of whatever degree of subtlety, including Tsur's version of negative capability, tend to draw even the most bizarre artistic departures back into the realm of *aboutness.* But in Stein's definition of "Master-Pieces," she distinguished between a "thing to see," which belongs to the representable world of identity and human nature, and a "thing to be" which is the rare work of great art (Stein 1998b: 363). This was a leading principle of Stein's aestheticism much as it was a leading principle in the young Beckett's description of Joyce's *Work in Progress* that I noted above ("His writing is not *about* something; *it is that something itself*"). Such an authorial intention may have been (and may still be) more widespread than has been credited. It may account in part for why a significant number of modernist and postmodernist authors tend to avoid interpretive commentary on their own work. Indeed it often seems that there is a kind of battle going on in which the increasingly radical modernist and postmodernist departures from narrative norms can be seen as a form of evasive activity. Yet as fast as writers generate an art of *isness* through modes of unfamiliarity, the academy reconstructs an art of *aboutness* through modes of familiarity.

What I have sought to do here, as elsewhere in this study, is to limit my focus on such aboutness in order to triangulate as best I can the immediate cognitive/affective states in readers that, if their reading is done right, complete that "something in itself" that is served by the text. As elsewhere in this study, I am arguing that we have in such prose fiction an art that achieves its effects through a deliberate and constant abuse of the fine communicative instruments that most distinguish us as we do the work of species survival.

But at the same time, I have sought to show how, in these sentences by Beckett, there is a payoff that differs from what Stein achieves in *Tender Buttons*. If Beckett strains the syntactical coherence of his sentences, he at the same time preserves their semantic plenitude. As multi-path sentences, they are not to be disambiguated. What slows the reader down is the way Beckett's syntactical parsimony allows different sentences to occupy the same words in the same space. At one and the same time, then, the reader experiences both an enlargement of meaning and its inadequacy.

PROSE POETRY

It has often been said that as time went by Beckett's prose evolved into a kind of poetry. This idea can be taken in several different ways: as an increase in "density," or in "resonance," or in rhythmical patterning, or in the primacy of what is happening in the language as opposed to what will happen in the story. All apply in varying degrees to Beckett's prose as it progressed from *The Unnamable* through much of the prose thereafter. What I have been opening out in this chapter is a kind of layering of meaning for which the terms "density" and "resonance" are both certainly apt. But they are apt in a different way from the layering of meaning ordinarily attributed to poetry. To take a representative example of the way resonances in poetry are usually teased out, Yeats's "rough beast" of "The Second Coming" is at once Christ and Anti-Christ, Sphinx and *Spiritus Mundi*, human and animal, nightmare and real, horrifying and necessary, and probably a lot more. Beckett's prose can be resonant in this way, too, but his is basically the art of the "sentence man," an art in which syntax plays the vital role in stacking layers of meaning. The result is a different kind of resonance, one that derives from the cohabitation of whole sentences. If both writers achieve a richness of meaning, Beckett's sentences are harder to process than the symbolic freight riding on Yeats's "rough beast." Both kinds of complexity are irreducible, but Beckett's complexity of effect can only succeed in the cognitive strain of its irreducibility. Its complexity thrives on this aspect of its effect in a way that Yeats's complexity does not.

Yeats's "Second Coming" helps in another way to isolate the kind of strain on the thinkable that I am dealing with in this chapter. It brings us back to the common modal opposition of narrative and lyric, the one defined by the representation of events or actions unfolding in time, the other defined as a "static" mode devoted to the expression of a single emotion. The distinction is at best porous.[4] If "The Second Coming" is devoted to the expression of emo-

4. See especially Phelan's discussion of the way character and judgment emerge through

tion, it is, like many lyrical poems, more accurately described as an unfolding of emotion-in-action, the power of the poem residing in the transition from the distress of "mere anarchy" in the first stanza to the horror of the approaching beast in the second. Moreover, the temporal condition of the beast itself is made vivid in the acute narrative suspense that dominates the poem's second stanza. Five years later, Yeats would actually try to tell the whole story behind "The Second Coming" in *A Vision* (1925). His aim, in part, was to make his poetry more accessible, to show among other things how the layered complexity riding on symbols like the "rough beast" could actually be laid out in a time-chart.[5] But in works like Beckett's *Ill Seen Ill Said* time slows to a crawl. To draw on the double meaning in the title of one of Beckett's last texts, composed the year before he died, this kind of "prose poetry" is a matter of *Stirrings Still* (Beckett 1990: 111–28). In these works, suspense shrinks from what will happen in the story to what is happening now in the sentences as they unfold. If it can be called poetry, or even lyrical poetry, it is a kind of lyrical poetry that depends for its effects on our narrative awareness.[6]

WHAT LOVE IS

The same kind of hybridizing of lyric and narrative can be found in Jeanette Winterson's intense prose poem "The White Room." In a seeming definition of the kind of thing she aims for, she writes, "Love is the story."[7] It is an answer, one answer, to the question: "How to make love in time?" But it is an answer that puts a strange pressure on our understanding of story as a sequence of events since love, when it happens, unfolds in "the place where time stops." It is a room with a door. Yet even outside this room, as desire begins to take hold, time becomes compacted. Fraught with desire, she is at one and the same time "aim, arrow, and target." It is only when "the stirrings of desire" are "sacrificed . . . to time" that life is gone and clock-time rules, carrying noth-

---

the interplay of lyric and narrative in Woolf's *The Waves* (Phelan 1996: 27–42) and also Heather Dubrow's broadly conceived demonstration of the overlooked ways in which narrative and lyric work together in the same text (Dubrow 2006).

5. Technically, a three-dimensional bi-directional infundibuliform time-chart.

6. What we never seem to remember is that most of the world's verbal narrative has been conveyed in poetic form, not prose. This may account for why interesting questions like what distinguishes narrative in poetry from narrative in other modes are rarely addressed (cf. McHale 2009).

7. "The White Room" appeared originally in *The Guardian* (July 17, 2004). My citations are taken from the extensively revised 2008 version of "The White Room" that can be found on the Jeanette Winterson site (www.jeanettewinterson.com).

ing "in its hands but itself." Roused from the dead, her life "is simultaneous—whatever the artificiality of time."

If Winterson's prose poetry is at times more discursive than Beckett's, as it is in the passages I have just quoted, its discursivity works as such to frame the moments it brings us to, sentences in which her writing is no longer about something but is that something itself. These are the passages in which events go on and don't go on at the same time. Syntax bifurcates, and her strange story is told in co-habiting sentences.

> I walked into you.

In these four words, "into you" works, on the one hand, because at one and the same time what is entered, is a room, is love (figured throughout as a room), and is her lover ("you"). "[W]hen time opens like a door," she enters both her lover and this room, which "like all sacred spaces . . . does and does not exist." Despite the complexity of this expressive work, it is served by syntax that functions quite correctly. Yet with the same words in the same order the syntax creates another quite different but also quite correct sentence: "I walked into you," in the sense of "I walked right into you" or "I bumped into you." And this is to say that "you" is necessarily other, she who arouses "desire" across "the props of ordinary life," physically separate, at once watchable and touchable, but as such un-enterable. What Winterson is trying to capture in words requires this impossibility. Writing two conflicting sentences with the same words in the same order is a way of bringing her reader into an experience of its inexpressibility. Together, we approach without answering the questions: "How can we enter what cannot be entered? How can we understand what cannot be understood?"

As noted above, Winterson's prose in "The White Room" is more discursively expansive than Beckett's, but in syntactically parsimonious sentences like this she relies on the same kind of sabotage to bring the reader as close as she can to what cannot be said.

> The white room is where we made love.

In this sentence, the worn cliché "made love" conveys the desire-driven physical action of love, "skin close enough for grafting." At the same time, the cliché can be given new life by slightly increasing the accent on "made." Now the sentence says something else, which the context also supports: that in the act of love they created love, invented it, as a space in time that is both familiar yet new. Like "the circles of enchantment" in another context, it is both "magic and cliché." The two sentences are distinct, as sentences must be to be understood, yet bonded, co-existent. They also make a strange kind of micro-narrative that seems to undo its narrative status. Hinged on a transitive verb, the sentence doubles back on its customary, event-defined, physical, time-contingent construction (making lóve) to indicate a space out of time where something "goes on" without going on (máking love).

In the last chapter, I made the following distinction: that where the garden-path effect at the level of syntax is a matter of warring sentences, the garden-path effect at the level of narrative is a matter of warring worlds. In the multi-path sentences of Beckett and Winterson, however, this distinction itself is hard to maintain. Their cohabiting sentences come equipped with worlds, worlds which are themselves compacted into one world. And that world is our world. But to begin to feel the nature of this baffling world that is our world requires the continual cognitive challenge of laying down opposing threads of discourse in the same series of words, each thread with its own way of being and its own values.

> I know I loved and lost. Then I made the mistake of not loving enough, and won.

In an eerie echo of Beckett's "it is I who win, who tried so hard to lose" (1965: 345), Winterson rewrites without unwriting. As so often in the prose of both authors, it is a cliché that allows her to tell a little story and then, recursively, to tell it again.[8] In this case, Winterson rewrites the cliché ("I loved and lost") by fusing the words "won" and "lost" in such a way that they each acquire antithetical meanings within antithetical worlds of discourse and value—but without the one giving way to the other.

Let's look at how this works. Here's the cliché, a story told in a four-word sentence:

> I loved and lost.

A little more fully narrativized, it can run like this, "I fell in love and then I lost the one I loved." It leaves open possibilities like "the one I loved died" or "the one I loved left me for someone else," but it doesn't, in common usage, imply that the verbs in their negative form work in the same way:

8. The work on cliché as an asset in the creation of literary effects is extensive. See especially Lerner 1956, Zijderveld 1979, Redfern 1989, Amossy and Rosen 1982, and the collection of essays in Mathis 1998. For an excellent overview of the subject, as well as a rich investigation of Beckett's use of cliché, see Barry 2006.

I didn't love and won.

Even though this is a literal reverse translation of the story in a five-word sentence, it's a statement we wouldn't expect to hear. It's something a computer might come up with. But when Winterson intentionally puts this odd microstory together with the first microstory it gains a wry wit while bringing the cliché back to life. Together, the second inflects the first, so that "lost" becomes an outcome in the game of life where the losers must endure the heartbreak that can come with falling in love (losing one's heart) and then losing one's lover, while the winners are rewarded by avoiding the heartbreak of losing one's heart and then losing one's lover. Winning and losing are put together as a kind of contest.

But the second sentence that Winterson actually wrote was

Then I made the mistake of not loving enough, and won.

The added words unbalance the quality of strict semantic reversal, replacing one symmetry with another more complex symmetry in which "win" and "lose" undergo an ironic exchange of meaning and the cliché acquires the quality of judgment. Now loving enough to lose is to win, while to win by not loving enough is a mistake or, in other words, to lose.

Yet by rewriting, Winterson does not unwrite. Instead she creates two cohabiting worlds. The cognitive problem with these worlds is that neither is a "possible world," as the concept has been applied to narrative literature by Umberto Eco (1979), Thomas Pavel (1986), Marie-Laure Ryan (1991), Lubomír Doležel (1998), and others.[9] Possible worlds, in narratives of any complexity, are worlds that pop up in the might-have-beens, could-have-beens, and should-have-beens that sprout in the words and minds of characters as they talk and think. They pop up, too, in readers' minds as they read and as suspense builds. The key point is that these possible worlds are eliminated as a story's single possible world, its "actual world," unfolds.[10]

9. In the precise words of linguist Barbara Abbott, "[t[he universe and everything in it is a certain way, and that is one possible world—the actual world. However, one can easily imagine things that could have been different. Genghis Khan might have been thrown from his horse as a child and spent the rest of his life as a woodcutter, the US Supreme Court might have called for a recount of Florida ballots in the 2000 presidential election, the Milky Way might not have existed, one of the banana slices on my cereal this morning might have been a millimeter thicker. For each difference in the way things might have been (and all that that difference entails) we have a difference in possible worlds" (B. Abbott 2010: 52).

10. Technically, I suppose, since the possible worlds generated by the thinking and discourse of characters occur in an artifact (novel, short story, film) that has a continuing existence

They are eliminated just as a possible world is eventually eliminated from a garden-path narrative, and a possible meaning is eventually eliminated from a garden-path sentence. What I am claiming for the multi-path sentence as it is deployed here by Winterson and also in the prose poetry of Beckett is that the opposition of its meanings, and the "possible worlds" to which they each belong, does not result in the elimination of one world or the other. If one can still speak of an "actual" world in these works of art, and I believe one can and should, then it is a world that accommodates contradictory worlds of meaning and value—a world in which "won" and "lost" can at once retain and exchange meaning. And it is only by short-circuiting the need to maintain for our own world the purity of what Rudolf Carnap called a "state description"—that is, a world in which there is a "maximal consistent set of sentences" (B. Abbott 2010: 52)—that we can feel, in a kind of pleasurable discomfort, what we all somehow already intimate from our experience of the world we actually live in.

WARS OF THE WORLDS, II

I want to end this chapter by addressing the question raised at the beginning: Can we extend the concept of the multi-path sentence to larger narrative structures in the same way Jahn extended the concept of the garden-path sentence to extended garden-path narratives? After all, I have already suggested that a multi-path sentence can be seen as a multi-path micronarrative with its multiple paths all cohabiting in the same world. Why couldn't an author do the same thing on a larger scale? It's a good question. To begin, it's worth recalling that the garden-path narratives I referenced in the last chapter—"The Secret Life of Walter Mitty," "Mazes," *The Murder of Roger Ackroyd, Atonement, Pincher Martin, The Third Policeman, Vertigo, Mulholland Drive, Identity, The Sixth Sense*—all shed one of their presumptive worlds, that is, the garden-path world, by the time you've reached the end. A different kind of discrimination of worlds is found in "forking path narratives" (Bordwell 2002, Branigan 2002), narratives like the films *Groundhog Day, Run Lola Run,* and *Sliding Doors* in which the same narrative is run and rerun with different outcomes. In these films, one version of the narrative doesn't displace the others, as in a garden-path narrative, even when in the final version (*Groundhog Day, Run Lola Run*) the protagonist "gets it right." Nor do they reside together

in all its parts, these worlds undergo a continuing rebirth in the fictional actual world created by that artifact. In this sense, one could argue that they are not eliminated. But their insufficiency to constitute an actual storyworld of their own is nonetheless as evanescent in that storyworld as their counterparts in the lives we lead in our own nonfictional, actual world.

in the same actual world—not, at least, in the cognitively challenging way of the multi-path sentences that I have been describing. They invoke a commonplace of science fiction (and, increasingly, the science of cosmology): parallel universes. As for the irresolvable garden-path narrative (*Caché*), we are indeed left at the end with two narrative worlds still standing in the space of a single storyworld. But they are worlds at war. They don't go together ontologically. My conclusion in the last chapter was that in this regard Haneke was deliberately inflicting on his viewers a version of the neural jamming Stein inflicted on her readers in the syntax of her irresolvable garden-path sentences.

But so far in this chapter I have been making the case that there are artists who for certain lyrical ends can sustain multiple ways of reading a sentence or micro-narrative, ways that ordinarily would not belong together but that in these instances work together. One of the working titles of Beckett's *The Unnamable* was "Beyond Words" (Admussen 1979: 86–87), and this is where both authors are pointing. What their brief flights seek is an expressive goal that is beyond the grasp of ordinary discourse. Can we, then, find the same correspondence between sentences and worlds that we developed in the last chapter? Are there instances in which multiple worlds cohabit ontologically in the same way as different sentences can be made to cohabit in a multi-path sentence? What this would mean is that, just as individual words (nouns, verbs, pronouns, etc.) can have different meanings in the different sentences layered in a multi-path sentence, so events and characters can be read differently depending on their function in the different coherent storyworlds layered in a multi-path narrative. What we need to find, then, is a multi-path narrative that can be shown to work on the reader in the same way as Beckett's and Winterson's multi-path sentences do—that is, not only a narrative in which the same narrative details sustain two conflicting stories together with their conflicting storyworlds, but also one in which the different stories (and their storyworlds) can be held in the mind at the same time. Perhaps intuitively my reader may already be thinking that this is a tall order. But I believe it is instructive to test it out anyway.

My candidate is Henry James's *The Turn of the Screw,* since over the course of the still lengthening controversy that has trailed Edmund Wilson's reading of the novella in 1934 ("The Ambiguity of Henry James"; E. Wilson 1948), two different stories seem to recur most frequently. These are: 1) the tale of an heroic governess, alone and unaided, who discovers that the boy and girl in her charge are under the spell of two former employees of the house that are actually evil spirits, and who then sets out at the risk of her life to rescue the souls of her charges and finally succeeds in foiling the spirits, but only at the unavoidable price of the boy's life as he dies in her arms; 2) the tale of a narcissistic, sexually starved governess, possibly in love with the absent master of the house, who hallucinates the two evil spirits and their evil project, places herself in the role of heroic protector, and succeeds only in committing involuntary homicide by scaring (or possibly squeezing) the boy to death. This simplifies, of course, and omits the many twists and turns of this long debate, but over time, critics have most commonly settled on versions of one or the other of these stories.[11]

Now suppose one wants to argue that this is a multi-path narrative in which neither story is meant to be eliminated and that, to achieve a full and adequate reading of the novella, both should be experienced at the same time. That is, the story of an heroic governess in a world that includes evil spirits bent on the damnation of innocent children is somehow fused with the story of a pathologically self-absorbed governess in a world in which the evil spirits are solely the products of her imagination. There are, in my view, two basic problems with this reading of the novella. The first is that it does not overcome the duck-rabbit effect. I'll include the well-known image of the duck-rabbit so that you can feel the effect I am trying to describe.[12] The point is that, just as one cannot hold both the image of the duck and the image of the rabbit in the mind at the same time, in the same way one cannot hold the two versions of *The Turn of the Screw* in the mind at the same time. One might at best experience an oscillation between the two different stories in the same way one can between the duck and the rabbit. But they can never coincide. This is the problem of the "Gestalt shift" that Wittgenstein wrestled with in Part Two of his *Philosophical Investigations* (Wittgenstein 1997: 193–208). To use his term, we see one "aspect" or the other, and in doing so we are necessarily prevented from seeing the alternative aspect since it is blocked through the intervention of a temporary, but necessary, "aspect blindness" (213–14).

But then why does the duck-rabbit oscillation happen at this level but not at the level of the multi-path sentence? Well, the first answer to this question is that it usually does.

They are hunting dogs.

11. Full disclosure: my own experience of this tale favors the heroic governess version since in my opinion the other version requires too many unnarrativized insertions to make the story work (e.g., to account for how, never having seen or even known of Peter Quint, the governess could nonetheless hallucinate his image in exact detail).

12. From the October 23, 1892, issue of *Fliegende Blätter*. This is the first known appearance of this familiar image and was, I believe, the image the American psychologist Joseph Jastrow used, when at roughly the same period of time, he developed the concept of competing Gestalts. I think this version of the image is better than those that are more commonly circulated.

Welche Thiere gleichen einander am meisten?

Kaninchen und Ente.

This sentence can say, with reference to the dogs, that "they" belong to the type of dogs that we call "hunting dogs." Or this sentence can say, with reference to two or more people, that they are out looking for some dogs. But only through the operation of aspect blindness can we make sense of the sentence. We are forced to hold in our minds one meaning of the sentence or the other. They can't be made to coincide, however precariously. At least in my mind. There is no invitation to read them otherwise. In Winterson's "I walked into you," by contrast, there is. As in Beckett's sentences, there is an implicit invitation to shift from the literal to the figural. As metaphors the two meanings of "I walked into you" can be felt as two opposing aspects of the same condition. But they reside in the same set of words as an *unstable* co-existence of meanings. In other words, the felt hesitation between meanings is the locus of cognitive action.

This brings me to a deep difference between on the one hand Winterson's and Beckett's multi-path sentences and on the other a multi-path narrative like *The Turn of the Screw*. For, if I am right, the conflict of meaning that takes place in the examples from Beckett and Winterson can be felt because something like it is already a part of the reader's experience. It is a lived set of contradictions that they draw on, an enigma that one "knows" experientially in the same way that one "knows" the enigma of individually specific self-awareness. But this isn't the case in *The Turn of the Screw.* The conflicting readings of character and world the novella seems to invite do not draw on conflicting elements that are deeply bonded in certain emotions like those of love and loss. In skillful hands, the complexity of the latter can be elicited in short lyrical flights. By contrast, as the narrative details of James's novella pile up, they build two increasingly independent worlds, increasingly at war. As in *Caché,* we have an ontological duck and an ontological rabbit, created in the same space with the same words, but refusing to meld into one animal.

I have no evidence from the cognitive sciences to support this particular contention. And readers may find convincing examples of multi-path fusions on a full-fledged narrative scale. But at this writing, my hunch is that the experience of cohabiting paths that I sought to demonstrate earlier in this chapter—an experience that replicates our best understanding of inexpressible states we experience in the actual world of our lives—becomes exponentially harder to achieve as a narrative gets longer and more detailed. The worlds remain separate in the same way that the meanings of most multi-path sentences stay separate. And for this—the cognitive operation that keeps worlds and meanings apart—there is much support. We are wired in a way that both enables and strongly inclines us to sort out possible worlds from actual ones and possible meanings from those that are intended. This is a cognitive bent that our lives as fully functioning human beings quite literally depend upon. And like everything else having to do with the relationship between the way we think and how we get by as human beings, the proclivity to sort out possible from actual meanings and possible from actual worlds does not need to be exact to be an asset in the game of survival. In the terms of schema theory, what we seek is the feeling of "goodness of fit."[13] At the level of the sentence, there have been landmark studies (Swinney 1979; Seidenberg et al. 1982) on the manner and the sheer speed with which the mind eliminates discordant meanings that do not "fit." And though, to my knowledge, there has been no comparable study in the cognitive sciences of the same process of elimination at the level of narrative discourse, there has been extensive critical and narratological commentary on the ways we "naturalize" discordant elements—ways that involve strategic under- and overreading, and that allow for the same goodness of fit that we regularly achieve as we proceed from one sentence to

13. "Incoming information may be distorted or partially deleted, in order to achieve this fit, thus explaining some of the *errors* or *gaps* in remembered accounts. Schemas enable rapid perception, as information is assimilated to the existing composite, but they also lead to patterned and recurrent distortions" (Nuckolls 1999: 143). Indeed, the evidence (e.g., in the history of religion), would indicate that we also have a proclivity to settle for an impossible world when necessity dictates.

the next (Kermode 1979; Culler 1975; Fludernik 1996; H. P. Abbott 2008). Conversely, the way Haneke handles the device of the hidden camera in *Caché* makes "goodness of fit" impossible to achieve. But, to repeat, the game Haneke is intentionally playing (and that James for all we know might also have been playing) creates a contradiction of worlds that belongs strictly to the narrative that creates those worlds. Unlike the multi-path art of Winterson and Beckett, this game does not recreate for viewers a contradiction like those embedded in the feelings of love and loss that befall them in their extratextual lives. Of course there is an abundance of schemata available to us that are designed to override these felt complications of feeling as well. They can be found on Hallmark cards and gravestones, in popular songs and comforting sermons.

IN THE NEXT two chapters, I shall be taking up another class of naturalizing schemata. These are schemata that readers are often prone to import from their lives as social beings into their experience as readers of narrative fiction. To resist this natural tendency, there is a signal device that authors have drawn on. As elsewhere in this study, the device can be handled in such a way as to immerse the willing reader in a condition of not knowing. It is in turn a condition that we could, and at times should, allow ourselves to experience in the social and cultural world in which we live our lives. Quite simply, this device is a gap. But it is a special kind of gap, and its deployment is my principal focus in Part Three.

PART THREE

Egregious Gaps

CHAPTER 5

Untold Events

> I wanted to write a real mystery, as opposed to a mystery that's solved, and then it's not a mystery anymore
>
> —Tim O'Brien

THEORY OF GAPS

A gap in narrative, like the much more salient gaps in poetry, is any kind of opening in the text that is either permanent or requires some degree of filling in order for the text to do its work. Defined as such, gaps are endemic in narrative and have been since people started telling stories, though it was not until the late 1960s and early 1970s, with the work of Menakhem Perry and Meir Sternberg ([1968] 1986), Gérard Genette ([1972] 1980), Wolfgang Iser ([1972] 1974, 1978), Jonathan Culler (1975), Mary Louise Pratt (1977), and Sternberg (1978) that both the inevitability of gaps and the complexity of their effects began to achieve serious attention in narrative theory. Since then, the work on gaps has gained in richness and sophistication (Eco 1979, Fish, Ryan, Spolsky, Doležel, Rabinowitz 2001, Herman 2002), but as the general thrust of this work stands in contrast to the argument I stake out in this chapter and the next, a brief survey at the outset will help frame my own contribution.

In his influential book, *The Implied Reader* ([1972] 1974), Iser put the principle of the gap at the center of his narrative theorizing.[1] For Iser, gaps

1. Iser saw his work as both a development and a correction of Ingarden's theory of inde-

not only occur in all narratives, but it is *only* through them that "scenes and characters [come] to life" (39). Gaps, for Iser, are moments of indeterminacy caused by a "break" in the narrative. They are "points at which the reader can enter into the text, forming his own connections and conceptions and so creating the configurative meaning of what he is reading" (40). Whatever dynamism a story has, then, depends on the reader's creative engagement with the text, which in turn is enabled by moments of indeterminacy that allow the reader the space to do this work. "[W]henever the flow is interrupted and we are led off in unexpected directions," Iser argued, "the opportunity is given to us to bring into play our own faculty for establishing connections—for filling in the gaps left by the text itself" (280). The result is a movement beyond representation to "an experience of reality" that "only the reader" can bring about (227).

One serious problem with this view of narrative gaps, a problem that was quickly noted,[2] is that Iser limited his focus to the role of key "points" where gaps let readers in to do their work. In so doing, Iser neglected the way gaps actually riddle narrative at *all* points and the way readers begin filling them from the first words.

> When he saw us come in the door the bartender looked up and then reached over and put the glass covers on the two free-lunch bowls. (Hemingway 1966: 384)

Just to get past this first sentence of Hemingway's "The Light of the World," we have a bar to create, a bartender, the narrator and his friend (or friends, we won't know for a few lines), and an action to interpret (the bartender covering the bowls). Characteristically, Hemingway makes us work harder than most writers as we imagine what is intimated in his taut sentences. We have to infer the bartender's concern when he covers the bowls, which requires in turn inferring the appearance of the narrator and his friend. But, as in our encounters with any other storyworld, the work we perform expands and deepens from sentence to sentence. We are always imagining far more than comes from the page. Simply to understand these opening lines of "The Light of the World," we draw on what we know about bars, bartenders, drifters, tough towns in hard times, Hemingway's style, and much else. We build characters and the world they inhabit, as we fill in scenes, imagine action, and inferen-

---

terminacy and the role of textual lacunae (1931). For Iser's critique of Ingarden, see Iser 1978: 169–81.

2. By Sternberg 1978, Umberto Eco 1979, and Stanley Fish 1980, who in their different ways called for a more finely grained approach to the reader's relationship to the text.

tially construct significance and meaning. Narrative in this regard is like the universe, comprised largely of "dark" matter and energy. Just as the universe does not consist solely of the visible stars, a written narrative is not solely the marks on the page or even their explicit semantic content. We see points of light and then fill in the rest by exercising our powers of triangulation.

My analogy almost immediately breaks down, but it is instructive in this regard as well. After all, it takes no filling in to appreciate the stars. Unlike a human communicative artifact, they are not meant to be read and can be enjoyed as a visual pattern that brightens the sky. Moreover, the process of responding to the gaps of a text is a guided process in which we are not only cued to fill gaps in a certain way but also cued to leave other gaps unfilled. As I shall be focusing in this chapter and the next on a special kind of unfilled gap, it is important to make clear that permanently unfilled gaps—"ellipses," to use Genette's term in its broadest sense[3]—far outnumber the fillable kind. Moreover, their emptiness plays its own critical part in narrative success. This necessity becomes very clear when you read a novel like Nicholson Baker's *The Mezzanine,* in which the entire action consists of a one-story ride up an escalator, with the narrator straining in an insouciant if doomed attempt to account for every particle of the action, mental and physical, during the course of this ride. Baker's novel is an amusing exception that proves the rule that narrative is generally a blessed liberation from every little thing. We can be taken quickly to the important moments because we follow what Marie-Laure Ryan calls the "principle of minimal departure" (1991: 48–60), that is, unless informed otherwise, we assume the storyworld replicates the real world.

These unfilled gaps come in many different degrees of gappiness and in many different sizes. There are the gaps of space, which include all those unvisited parts of an implicated world, a world like ours that keeps pace with the action. In that space lie the children of Lady Macbeth (or their nonexistence) and the unmentionable product that made Chad Newsome's fortune in *The Ambassadors.* And there are the gaps of time, what Genette termed ellipses of duration. Some of these are gaps of discretion: Tolstoy drawing a veil when Vronsky and Anna first make love or Hardy spending a page not giving us any details of the rape of Tess. Other gaps are huge, covering years. In his *Confessions,* St. Augustine marveled at the way in which memory chooses among millions of events those moments that are essential to the story of one's life. There is always much history that a story does not need. We jump years in the

3. Genette's discussion of the way ellipses can be managed (1980: 106–9ff.) has its own richness of distinctions. For my purposes, the definition of an ellipsis is a representation of "a practically nonexistent portion of text" (109).

lives of characters like Abel Magwitch, Michael Henchard, and Dick Diver, seeing them again, changed by the cumulative effect of untold events.

But the demands of gaps that can and must be filled, like those in the sentence above from Hemingway's short story, are what give narrative its power to move us and to deepen our understanding. They are the main component of Hemingway's "principle of the iceberg," according to which the art of fiction is an art of leaving things out in such a way that they are still present, as it were underwater, contributing to the effect of the whole.[4] The implication is that those with the requisite depth of experience supply what is missing from their own understanding and in that way are allowed to see and feel anew what they already know. Hemingway's theoretical language was modernist and it echoed what Pound and Eliot were saying about poetry: that the reading of art is itself an art. The more informed the reader, the more fully and precisely are the gaps of art filled.

However elitist Hemingway's High Modernist preachments may be, it is nonetheless true that the precision with which writer and reader collaborate in the dance of meaning is what releases the power of art. It is in this regard that Sternberg's (1978) account of narrative as "a dynamic *system* of gaps" (50; emphasis added) is more in line with modernist aesthetic practice than Iser's arguably more postmodern dynamics. Iser grants the reader what appears to be complete freedom to "read something into" the breaks in a text, capitalizing on "perplexity . . . as a stimulus and provocation" (Iser 1980: 210). Gaps, in his theorizing, are synonymous with "elements of indeterminacy," without which "we should not be able to use our imagination" (283). In contrast, Sternberg (1978 and elsewhere) argues that narrative is a complex yet determinate system of "temporal ordering" reflecting at every point strategic authorial decisions to withhold or release information that in turn must be experienced by the reader in an equally complex internal process of questions, hypotheses, and answers.

Sternberg in effect is describing a contract between the reader and the writer. Each knows the rules of narrative and depends on the other to know them. Only in this way does the reader experience the plenitude of thought and feeling that is released by the arrangement of verbal signifiers over the course of any fictional narrative. This contract is similar to the "cooperative principle" that Paul Grice ([1975] 1989) contended was essential to conver-

---

4. "If a writer of prose knows enough about what he is writing about he may omit things that he knows and the reader, if the writer is writing truly enough, will have a feeling of those things as strongly as though the writer had stated them. The dignity of movement of an iceberg is due to only one-eighth of it being above water. A writer who omits things because he does not know them only makes hollow places in his writing" (Hemingway 1996: 192; see also Plimpton 1995: 235–36).

sation. We acquire the "maxims" of this principle as unconsciously as we acquire grammatical language.[5] They in turn allow us to grasp the "implicatures" that abound in ordinary verbal intercourse. The applicability of Grice's theory of conversational pragmatics to literary discourse was almost immediately developed by Mary Louise Pratt (1977) and has been extended, qualified, and elaborated by others, including Ryan (1991), Doležel (1998), and particularly Herman (2002: 173–80). Though Grice was writing specifically of conversation, to extend his theory to the experience of fiction is not much of a stretch. Fiction characteristically combines, on the one hand, multiple inset conversations with, on the other, a narrative voice that, in effect, speaks the story.[6] But however fully or successfully one can adapt Grice's theory of conversational implicature to a theory of narrative implicature, it is certainly true that by the time we get to Hemingway's famous concluding lines of *The Sun Also Rises,* what allows us to feel the weight of complex emotion riding underneath the words is the reading that got us to them:

> "Oh, Jake," Brett said, "we could have had such a damned good time together."
>
> Ahead was a mounted policeman in khaki directing traffic. He raised his baton. The car slowed suddenly pressing Brett against me.
>
> "Yes." I said. "Isn't it pretty to think so." (Hemingway 1926: 247)

That we relate to narrative gaps by filling them is supported by work on perception in cognitive science, social and developmental psychology, discursive psychology, and the psychology of perception (Goffman, Mandler, Rumelhart, Schank, Schank and Abelson, Thorndike, Baron-Cohen). In a continuing elaboration of Kant's original insight regarding our necessary involvement in what we perceive, such research has sought to describe the extent, and in some cases to infer the mechanisms, by which we internally elaborate the limited sensory input we obtain from the external world. We are designed to see, in other words, what we have a hand in shaping, drawing on an immense and highly flexible repertoire of generic structures or *schemata* that we carry within us. In Roger Shepard's calculated overstatement, perception is an "externally guided hallucination" (Shepard 1984: 436).[7]

---

5. Grice distinguishes four "maxims": of quantity, quality, relation, and manner.

6. As a refinement of the conversational model, Richard Gerrig has advanced the idea that we relate to narrative as "side participants" in a conversation (Gerrig 1993: 103–56). That is, we are neither active participants nor formally addressed, but nonetheless meant to grasp the narrator's intended meanings.

7. More fully: "I like to caricature perception as *externally guided hallucination,* and dreaming and hallucination as *internally simulated perception*" (Shepard: 436; original em-

This is what writers of fiction depend upon as they construct, from sentence to sentence and even from word to word, the blueprint for a storyworld. But, and here I come to the main job of work in this chapter, they not only depend on the fact that we do this, but they also depend on the fact that we *need* to do it. Filling in is, in effect, a kind of cognitive lust and as such it can be manipulated to create the thread of curiosity and suspense that keeps readers reading. We seem unable to tolerate not knowing what is going on. The urgency of this need to fill in brings us back again to Gazzaniga's notion of the "left-hemisphere interpreter" and the way it is always on the alert to make some kind of sense of what perplexes understanding—even at the expense of the facts.[8] So, setting aside all the permanent narrative gaps or ellipses that are necessary to exclude the irrelevant, the question remains: what happens when we come across a narrative gap, the filling of which is vital to the narrative but which cannot be filled without "amending" the text by selective underreading or supplemental overreading? This is the gap that not only keeps the narrative from closure but at the same time aggravates the need for closure. Is it possible, then, *not* to fill such a narrative gap? Can you cognize its emptiness? Should you? And what would it feel like, if you could?

THE EGREGIOUS GAP

These questions bring me to the concept of the egregious gap.[9] These are the gaps that we cannot fill but that, at the same time, require filling in order to complete the narrative. In other words, they cry out for authorial assistance in filling them. In Robbe-Grillet's *La Jalousie,* is "A . . . " murdered? In Christopher Nolan's film *Memento,* what is the full story of the protagonist's wife? Is she dead? If so, at whose hands? If not, why doesn't she intervene to aid her husband? What happens between the two acts of *Waiting for Godot?* In *Vanity Fair,* does Becky Sharp kill Jos Sedley? Thackeray famously told inquirers

---

phasis). That we are not the hopeless prisoners of our "hallucinated" constructions of reality is strongly indicated by our capacity to change our thinking despite the seduction of cultural frames and schemata. In the introduction, I referred to Paul DiMaggio's concept of "deliberative cognition," which deals with "schema failure" by overriding the routine and uncritical application of schemata that he calls "automatic cognition" (DiMaggio: 268–72). The point remains, however, that in both modes of cognition we fill in. The very effort involved in deliberative cognition shows how important this object is.

8. Researchers at Duke University have found evidence in the prefrontal cortex for what may be the location of our automatic impulse to find patterns – even in chaotic behavior (Huettel et al. 2001).

9. The term is my own (H. P. Abbott 2004). This chapter is a rethinking of the concept.

that he himself didn't know the answer. In *Wuthering Heights*, does Heathcliff kill Hindley Earnshaw? Hindley was alive when Heathcliff sent Joseph for the doctor, yet he was "both dead, and cold and stark" (Brontë 1995: 185) when Joseph and the doctor got back. For good reason, the space in which Hindley dies has become a crux in the criticism of *Wuthering Heights*, and interpreters have filled it with several possibilities of which the main contenders are: murder, involuntary homicide, and death without further assistance.

Egregious gaps have been handled in many different ways to serve different functions. Yet they share the capacity to call up immense inferential energy. This in turn would appear to confirm the rule that we are so constructed that simply to know of a gap is to try to fill it. Even an exacting theorist like Sternberg will not deny us the exercise of this all-too-human imperative—indeed, he will expect us eventually to come up with something:

> What are Iago's motives, or Raskolnikov's? Is Becky Sharp "guilty" or "innocent" in her relations with Lord Steyne? Are the ghosts purely hallucinations of the governess's disordered mind? What really happened in the Marabar Caves? All these questions point to permanent gaps in the respective works. No reader can afford to disregard them, but he will look in vain for pat explicit answers. Only through a close analysis of the text can he evolve an hypothesis or set of hypotheses by which these gaps can be filled with some degree of probability. (1978: 51)

The implication of the last sentence is that we not only have a need but an obligation to find something "with some degree of probability" to put in the unfillable gap. Peter J. Rabinowitz, an equally exacting instructor on the "rules" of reading, acknowledges a "license to fill" what is left blank. With but one exception his examples enjoy sufficient context to allow filling with more than a degree of probability. The exception is "avant-garde novelists" like Robbe-Grillet who nonetheless operate with the same expectation that readers will try to fill the gaps they have left. Indeed, they "demand that their readers fill in the blanks" (Rabinowitz 1987: 150). The operative word here is "demand," and my questions are Do they? and Should we?[10]

There is much to be said for exercising what you might call the "narrative imperative" at these moments. The finely calibrated exercise of this natural human propensity is, arguably, the best kind of training that scholars in the

10. For a provocative addendum to Rabinowitz's treatment of gaps, see his argument for the strategic use of gaps to achieve a "rhetorical realism." Rabinowitz draws on the cluster of confusing informational gaps that greet the reader at the opening of Dostoevsky's *The Gambler* (Rabinowitz 2001).

fields of textual analysis can demand of their students. An egregious gap in a complex work of fiction is an opportunity for the most intense cognitive workout, because how it is filled can have consequences for one's reading of the entire text. If one settles for the idea that Heathcliff's unbridled ruthlessness drove him to kill Hindley, this contributes to the sense of a preternatural Heathcliff, almost entirely possessed by volcanic passions of hate and love. If one opts for a Heathcliff who, seeing how far he has gone in his rage, attempts, if grudgingly, to revive Hindley, this contributes to a different Heathcliff, one less preternaturally inhuman in whom there is an element of common humanity (and thereby qualifying Catherine's cautionary words to Isabella). But if one imagines Heathcliff just sitting there, watching Hindley die, one is constructing a much colder Heathcliff—in our own epoch, a psychopath; in Brontë's, what her sister called him, a devil.

It can be a salutary exercise to see how each of these different Heathcliffs differently inflect our reading not only of Heathcliff but also of Catherine and even of Brontë's larger vision of life on earth. Is Catherine drawn by the erotic appeal of Heathcliff's sheer ferocity? Or does she know, from childhood, a Heathcliff more leavened by humanity? Or is she, like Heathcliff, possessed by a cold, dark supernatural force that would make her indifferent to the suffering of others? These are actually only three of many more Heathcliffs and Catherines that have, over the years, been generated in the critical literature. But out of that little hole in the text, were readers to claim a license to do so, there can be drawn not only support for a certain Heathcliff and a complementary Catherine but with them support for complementary versions of what it can mean to be human (at least in this storyworld), of its nature and range, of its limits or limitlessness, of how it is or is not threaded with a supernatural element, and, if so, to what degree for good, or ill, or both. Such an exercise shows how closely bonded are the concepts of narration and interpretation. To supply one micronarrative in this gap is to interpret the novel in one way, to supply a different micronarrative is to interpret the novel in a different way.

But what I am suggesting is that we leave this gap empty. When the distraught Isabella asks Nelly "to explain, if you can, what I have married" (Brontë 1995: 134), she is asking a question that Nelly cannot answer. Correction: Nelly can provide any number of answers, just as the reader can. But in the reading I am proposing, such answers risk closing down a novel that was not meant to be fully closed. And by this I do not mean that the novel is "open" in the sense that it is open to a rich multiplicity of readings, which of course it is. What I am saying is that the most accurate readings of the novel will leave this gap as empty as its author most definitely left it. This is hard. The interpreting mind, like nature, abhors a vacuum. But if you stifle the interpretive imperative (which in instances of egregious gaps means stifling the narrative imperative), that act comes with its own reading of Brontë's overarching vision: that is, that there is wisdom in accepting with a full cognitive embrace the fact that there are things we simply do not and cannot know.

If a main theme of the mixed reception of *Wuthering Heights* was the "inexpressibly painful" (*Athenaeum*) and "wild, confused; disjointed and improbable" (*Examiner*) nature of its contents,[11] what made it "a strange sort of book—baffling all regular criticism" (*Douglas Jerold's Weekly*) was the author's refusal to fill the gaps where interpretation demanded fulfillment. Brontë, to our knowledge, left no words indicating how we were to fill the egregious gaps in her novel. In a preface to the second edition of *Wuthering Heights,* Emily's sister Charlotte, more conscious of what the market would tolerate, dealt with this problem by constructing two competing versions of her sister. On the one hand, "Ellis Bell" was the untutored servant of inspiration, working "passively under dictates [she] neither delivered nor could question" (Brontë: xxxvii). Thus "[h]aving formed these beings, she did not know what she had done" (xxxv). On the other hand, Ellis Bell for all her rude imaginings was indeed a devout believer in "the Great Being who made both man and woman" and that, in His universe, Heathcliff, at least, "stands unredeemed; never once swerving in his arrow-straight course to perdition" (xxxv–xxxvi).

The latter assertion was a key move. By closing the book on Heathcliff, Charlotte sought to reassure the mid-nineteenth-century English reader regarding her sister's position on the broader metaphysical problem of the existence of evil. For a public that largely assumes the universe to be the intended product of a creator who is at once merciful, just, and omnipotent, the existence of evil as an active unpunished and seemingly unpunishable presence at large in the universe creates a metaphysical gap. It afflicts a sense of justice that may well be innate.[12] Accordingly, as Milton did for the Bible, Charlotte Brontë did for her sister's text—both in their different ways providing the source text with an in-filling interpretive supplement to show how, in the end, justice does prevail.

---

11. "Excerpts from Contemporary Reviews of *Wuthering Heights*" http://academic.brooklyn.cuny.edu/english/melani/novel_19c/wuthering/contemp_rev.html

12. Research continues to grow in support of the case for an "embodied" morality in which an innate sense of justice plays a key role See Verplaetse et al. 2009; Gazzaniga 2005; Hauser 2008.

WRITING A REAL MYSTERY

But Charlotte's sister may actually have known what she was doing when she left this egregious gap and others unfilled in her novel. Doing so, she anticipated Conrad's refusal to provide us with sufficient narrative in-filling to understand the psychology of evil as it operated in the figure of Kurtz. In the words of the novelist Tim O'Brien:

> [Kurtz] has witnessed profound savagery, has immersed himself in it, and as he lies dying, we hear him whisper, "The horror, the horror." There is no solution here. Rather, the reverse. The heart *is* dark. We gape into the tangle of this man's soul, which has the quality of a huge black hole, ever widening, ever mysterious, its gravity sucking us back into the book itself. What intrigues us, ultimately, is not what we know but what we do not know and yearn to discover. (O'Brien 1991: 180)

The formal differences between Brontë's and Conrad's texts are, of course, huge. The metaphysical gap that the creation of Heathcliff leaves open is the product of too much narrative—that is, more than can be accommodated in a single character. Kurtz, by contrast, is a case of too little narrative. Responding to this criticism, Conrad himself admitted "the fault of having made Kurtz too symbolic or rather symbolic at all" (Conrad 1999: 161).[13]

I've quoted above Tim O'Brien's take on Kurtz because of the way it chimes with O'Brien's own version of Conrad's novel, *In the Lake of the Woods* (O'Brien 1994a). In this novel, the experience of giving way in the jungle to pure anarchic cruelty is the slaughter at My Lai, an actual documented event in US history. Where we are only permitted glimpses in Conrad's novella of leaping figures, heads on stakes, a single document with four words scrawled at the end ("Exterminate all the brutes!" [117]), O'Brien draws on the actual testimony in the court-martial of William Calley.[14] As if making up for Conrad's

13. In the next chapter, I will argue that this "fault" of making a character too symbolic corresponds to a default mode of reading that construes as symbolic a character who would otherwise prove unreadable.

14. "Q: How much of the My Lai testimony is real? [A:] All of it. Richardson is made up, the rest of the testimony is real. He was the only one that mentioned Sorcerer [John Wade]. He's also made up, of course" (Edelman 1994). In the 1996 film version of *In the Lake of the Woods,* an adaptation that sticks pretty close to the novel, My Lai is changed to Son My. Historically, this is still accurate, My Lai being one of five hamlets within the village of Son My, but to most Americans it might sound made up, since My Lai was the name almost always given to the massacre. Moreover, the only testimony from the massacre introduced into the film version is that of the fictional soldier Richardson. The contrast between this adaptation and

lack of specifics, O'Brien not only recurs to this testimony throughout the novel, but extensively reimagines what went on.

> [H]e found burning hootches and brightly mobile figures engaged in murder. Simpson was killing children. PFC Weatherby was killing whatever he could kill. A row of corpses lay in the pink-to-purple sunshine along the trail—teenagers and old women and two babies and a young boy. Most were dead, some were almost dead. The dead lay very still. The almost-dead did twitching things until PFC Weatherby had occasion to reload and make them fully dead. The noise was fierce. No one was dying quietly. There were squeakings and chickenhouse sounds. (O'Brien 1994a: 107)

> The killing went on for hours. It was thorough and systematic. In the morning sunlight, which shifted from pink to purple, people were shot dead and carved up with knives and raped and sodomized and bayoneted and blown into scraps. The bodies lay in piles. (1994a: 200)

For the reader, then, as well as the novel's disturbed and disturbing protagonist, John Wade, the horror is inescapable.

Wade was a fictional soldier, of course, but O'Brien inserted him into the actual Charlie Company, where he could serve under the actual Lieutenant Calley and be present at My Lai. Haunted by the experience, plagued by guilt,[15] Wade finds a way to literally erase this part of his personal history when he is assigned to the battalion adjutant's office in the last two months of his tour. Secretly, he "reassigns" himself from Charlie Company to Alpha Company (which happened to be the actual Tim O'Brien's company) by removing all references to himself in the former, adding his name to all relevant documents in the latter, and "tidying up the numbers."

> The illusion, he realized, would not be perfect. None ever was. But still it seemed a nifty piece of work. Logical and smooth. Among the men in Charlie Company he was known only as Sorcerer. Very few had ever heard his real name; fewer still would recall it. And over time, he trusted, memory itself would be erased. (1994a: 269)

---

the original text indicates how important it was for O'Brien to include in his novel evidence of horror from a documented episode in American history.

15. The extent of Wade's active engagement in the slaughter at My Lai beyond the shooting of an old farmer and, on impulse, PVC Weatherby is hard to determine. He is pictured wandering through the havoc uttering "meaningless sounds" (1994a: 107) and occasionally the words "No," "Please," and "Go away."

For everyone else, the erasure works for seventeen years, until it explodes in the midst of Wade's campaign for senator in Minnesota. Up to that point, six weeks before the primary, the upward trajectory of Wade's political career and his carefully constructed and widely admired political persona had made victory a certainty. The revelation that he had participated in My Lai changes all this, and after a disastrous primary, he and his wife, Kathy, escape to a secluded cabin on the shore of Lake of the Woods, where they hope to repair the damage, personal and marital. It is here that the novel picks up their story.

Through multiple strategically inserted analepses, O'Brien does a masterful job opening out the complex ways in which the trauma of My Lai and Wade's fall from political grace combine with an already fragile personal chemistry, marked by obsessive secrecy and a volatile insecurity in matters of love. It is a novel of well-earned psychological complexity. But my focus here as elsewhere in this study is on how the author, like Brontë and Conrad before him, refuses to supply certain vital segments of narrative action. What most distinguishes this novel from recognizable generic types, and what has frustrated so many of its readers, is its narrative incompletion. Sometime early in the morning of their eighth day in the cabin Kathy disappears, and we never learn how or why. To reveal this to those of my readers who have not yet read *In the Lake of the Woods* is not much of a spoiler.[16] In a footnote early in the novel, our narrator, an obsessed inquirer into the truth about the Wades, lets us know that we won't know what we most want to know: "Biographer, historian, medium—call me what you want—but even after four years of hard labor I'm left with little more than supposition and possibility" (30).

Unlike Emily Brontë, but like her sister, O'Brien was highly attuned to the market and, therefore, to the risk he was taking in leaving such an egregious gap. He knew he wanted to maintain right up to the end the mystery that has been pulling the reader through the novel, but he also knew what the market for mysteries demanded—that is, that they be solved and thus, in his own words, "no longer mysteries" (Edelman 1994). As he said in an interview shortly after the book's publication, this gamble held him back from submitting it to his publisher:

> I started it in '85, wrote for two years until the end of '87, maybe into '88. Then I put it aside for a while and wrote *The Things They Carried.* It was mostly this business about the ending. I knew some reviewers wouldn't like the idea of having a mystery at the end, of leaving it unsolved, so I put

16. Indeed, this is one novel that improves on subsequent readings, guided by a fuller awareness of how it is incomplete.

> the book aside and figured I'll try to change it around sometime later. But I realized that this is just what had to be. I figured what's the point of making hypotheses and talk about mystery just to solve it in the end? What's the point of it? So I gathered my courage for two years to write a book that wasn't solved in the end. I knew I would get nailed in some places. (Edelman 1994)

And he was. As one reviewer wrote, the novel is a "beautifully written, often haunting, but ultimately disappointing book. . . . [H]as Wade always lived a lie? Did he kill Kathy and put her body in the lake? Did they escape their problems altogether? O'Brien openly asks the reader such questions, in a series of rhetorical footnotes that amount to an uncomfortable authorial intrusion."[17]

Actually, the entire novel, including the narrator's footnotes (there are no "authorial intrusions" as such), is framed as a hypothetical representation of what might possibly have happened, interspersed with evidence in the form of documented facts, witnessed events, the words of friends, relatives, law enforcement, and the testimony given at the court-martial of Lieutenant Calley. Sometimes this material is collected in chapters titled "Evidence." Other chapters are given titles like "Where they Looked" and "What was Found." And some of them are titled, simply, "Hypothesis." The latter is especially the case when it comes to developing certain alternative hypotheses regarding Kathy's possible agency in determining her fate. Their possibility has already been seeded by a number of references to her trait of disappearing without warning. In a postcard to Wade in Vietnam, she warns him: "Careful with the tricks. One of these days you'll make *me* disappear altogether" (1994a: 38). So maybe she got fed up, or sufficiently scared, and arranged for someone to pick her up early that morning and drive her out of this life. Or maybe, on a whim, she took off in the boat (which we learn is missing, along with the outboard, two oars, and a life vest). Maybe she and the boat in one way or another sank. Or maybe she's still out there somewhere on that enormous lake.

---

17. This review is attributed to Samuel Goichman and appeared in the October 1994 issue of *Publishers Weekly.* Though it has been posted on publishers' sites on-line, I have not been able to find the source text. But it is useful as a compact statement of a common response to *In the Lake of the Woods.* It did not help that the book was "tagged" in *Vanity Fair* and *Harper's* as a "thriller," a genre that, like the mystery, includes the expectation that suspense will be resolved. In his interview with Edelman, O'Brien comments on how this "necessity" of tagging a book of fiction compounded the marketing challenge he had anticipated: "People say that it's a literary thriller," but if that was all it was, "you'd have to dispense with three-quarters of the book" (Edelman 1994).

But the riveting hypothesis that builds suspense in this novel is that, in the early hours of the eighth day at the cabin, Wade finally cracks and in a fit of madness kills his wife and disposes of her body, packing it into the boat, which he sinks out in the lake. In a number of ways, O'Brien encourages his reader to feed on this hypothesis by incrementally fleshing it out in bits and pieces so that gradually we see a single story line, culminating in the last of the chapters titled "Hypothesis." This story, in the narrator's imagining, has a terrible climax in which Wade, repeating "Kill Jesus" like a mantra, pours boiling water on each of the potted plants in the cabin. He then refills the kettle with boiling water and pours it on the head of his sleeping wife. Through O'Brien's carefully staged hints, the gathering horror of this hypothetical story—"the fascination of the abomination," to use Marlow's formulation (Conrad 1999: 65)—is made to exceed even the imagined horrors of My Lai.

In his way, then, O'Brien's narrator confers the power of narrativity on the axioms that Marlow can largely only talk about: that horror breeds horror, and that the "immense darkness" (Conrad 1999: 148) a white European man can encounter in the jungle is a darkness that already lies in his heart. Like Marlow, O'Brien's narrator wants at one and the same time to approach and to keep his distance from this "truth" about us. You can see this in the Marlovian language that inflects his footnotes:

> It was the sunlight. It was the wickedness that soaks into your blood and slowly heats up and begins to boil. Frustration, partly. Rage, partly. The enemy was invisible. They were ghosts. . . . The smell of the incense, maybe. The unknown, the unknowable. The blank faces. The overwhelming otherness. (1994a: 199, fn 88)

> Nothing is fixed, nothing is solved. The facts, such as they are, finally spin off into the void of things missing, the inconclusiveness of conclusion. Mystery finally claims us. Who are we? Where do we go? (1994a: 301, fn 133)

Again, and as in Conrad, this is the narrator speaking, not the author. He is a man exhausted by an inconclusive four-year quest and the effort to put what he has found into words. As with Marlow, the pressure of a story that is both terrible and untellable brings on clouds of melodrama that puff up between us and the narrative. O'Brien's narrator even, if subtly, echoes Marlow's own "retraction" at the end of *Heart of Darkness*. In a different voice, he disowns his worst-case scenario with the claim that, finally, "it's a matter of taste, or aesthetics, and the boil is one possibility that I must reject as both graceless and disgusting" (1994a: 300, fn 131).

"Too horrible," is a better description and a better reason to want to reject "the boil" in a narrative that is supposed to be governed by standards of plausibility, not aesthetics. But if this particular hypothesis, as he continues, is not only "tasteless" but also belied by "the weight of evidence" (ibid.), then where does it come from? He goes on to add, as if to provide confirmation, that after all Wade "was crazy about her" (ibid.). But the idea of being "crazy" in love can be read in more than one way, given "the weight of evidence," and it can support almost any act of madness. So, to return to my question, why this hypothesis, and why are we forced to see and feel so terribly what only can be imagined?

> Bits of fat bubbled at her cheeks. He would remember thinking how impossible it was. He would remember the heat, the voltage in his arms and wrists. Why? He thought, but he didn't know. All he knew was fury. The blankets were wet. Her teeth were clicking. She twisted away, pushing with her elbows, sliding off toward the foot of the bed. A purply stain spilled out across her neck and shoulders. Her face seemed to fold up. Why? (273)

There is more, but even to quote this much feels like an imposition on my reader. The thing about fiction is that it "makes real." Done well, it is hard to dispose of as "fiction," even when it is a fiction of a fiction—that is, even when it is a fiction imagined by a fictional narrator. And when it is this terrible, the question that the hypothetical Wade keeps asking, "Why?," is also the reader's question. And if the reader is angry at being put through this experience, both the anger and the question are focused on the author.

So, the answer to the question I asked at the beginning of the last paragraph—"where does this come from?"—is the author. Where else could it come from? "The object of storytelling," O'Brien wrote in his essay "The Magic Show," is to "reach into one's own heart, down into that place where the stories are, bringing up the mystery of oneself" (O'Brien 1991: 183). By making us complicit in his imagining, O'Brien may, quite understandably, arouse considerable anger directed at himself, but he also does what Conrad failed to do by drawing us at least part of the way into "a huge black hole" (1991: 182) that we enter through our own willingness, however conflicted, to reimagine what he imagines. Much has been written lately about "affect" and "embodiment" in the processing of narrative: here both terms would seem to apply with narrow force. I do not think a reader can fully read this scene without inhabiting it, entering emotionally and viscerally into the minds and bodies of both the killer and his victim.

But, to repeat, it is an imagined scene and *framed* as such, which brings me to my final point and returns me to my central theme in this chapter: we do not *know* what has happened. This is not to say that, as readers, we will have our preferences in what we believe has happened. O'Brien has acknowledged as much: "Everyone can have a different interpretation. My sister went for the killing, my brother thinks they got lost. My dad says they ran off together. That's my whole family right there" (Edelman 1994). But he is also saying, by his own narrative refusal, that it is a good thing to realize that this is what we are doing: believing where we do not and cannot know. Revisiting the book is a way of reminding ourselves that we will never really know what might be pasted over when we say, "He was crazy about her."

IN THIS CHAPTER I have put the focus on the egregious narrative gap as a gap of action and on our need to know how the story, conceived as a chronological sequence of events, turns out. We require those "kernels" of action (Chatman 1978: 53–59), those key events, without which the story is incomplete. But it is hardly a new insight to assert that understanding the action is inseparable from understanding the characters involved in that action. As Henry James put it in his oft-cited words: "What is character but the determination of incident? What is incident but the illustration of character?" (H. James 1956: 15–16).[18] And this inseparability, of course, is exactly the direction in which my reading of *In the Lake of the Woods* has been trending. Without the action, we don't know the character. Still, there can be an interpretive advantage in keeping character and action separate as analytical concepts, as I have been doing in this chapter and as I will be doing in the next.

18. In "The magic Show," O'Brien includes his own iteration of this insight in a way that chimes with other comments on his craft that I have included in this chapter: "[P]lot relies for its power on the essential cloudiness of things to come. We don't know. We want to know. . . . As with plot, I believe that successful characterization requires an enhancement of mystery: not shrinkage, but expansion. To beguile, to bewitch, to cause lasting wonder—these are the aims of characterization" (O'Brien 1991: 180, 182).

CHAPTER 6

Unreadable Minds

> I know nothing, nothing! Except from the outside. I have to guess at everything!
>
> —Joseph Conrad

READABLE MINDS

Alan Palmer (2004, 2010), Lisa Zunshine (2006, 2009, 2011, 2012), and others have been building the case for reframing the action of narrative fiction as busily "intermental"—a collective reading and misreading of minds. Their work at once draws on and supports the idea that we have an evolved craving, along with a sufficient ability, to read the minds of others (loosely termed Theory of Mind). By extension, we have a corollary craving for the kind of narrative action that catalyzes this reading of minds.[1] This is where I left off at the end of the last chapter. The universal cognitive urge to find out what happened in a story—to fill a narrative gap—is more often than not an urge to understand the character it happened to or who made it happen. In this chapter, I will supplement the work by Palmer and the others with a focus on fictional minds that *cannot* be read. These are minds that vex not only charac-

1. This work extends an insight notably associated with Käte Hamburger (1973) and enlarged by Dorrit Cohn (1978) that prose fiction enjoys the distinction of a "penetrative optics" (Cohn) giving access to otherwise inaccessible thoughts and feelings. In addition to Palmer and Zunshine, others who have focused specifically on how Theory of Mind works either within representations or in readers' transactions with them are Bruner (1986), Mar (2004, 2011), Turner (1991), Butte (2004), Keen (2007), Mar and Oatley (2008), and Oatley (2011). See also Leverage et al., eds., *Theory of Mind and Literature* (2011).

ters in the storyworld but also readers in the actual world. That such fictional minds exist at all is a conundrum—if, that is, these scholars are right about the important role of reading minds in arousing narrative desire, and I think they are.[2] Readers tend to supply motivation where none seems to work, creating according to one type or another just as they tend to "naturalize" what is strange in literature, mentally domesticating it either by drawing on preexisting literary forms (Culler 1975: 134–60) or by drawing on the larger range of "real-world experience" (Fludernik 1996: 31–35 et passim). I'll discuss in this chapter ways in which unreadable minds are commonly made readable or elided, but my position with regard to the examples I introduce is that they work best when we allow ourselves to rest in that peculiar combination of anxiety and wonder that is aroused when an unreadable mind is accepted as unreadable. In this regard, my stance is at odds with efforts to make sense of the unreadable, as, for example, Jan Alber's development of "sense-making strategies" for the "impossible storyworlds" of postmodern fiction—in effect, to make the unreadable "readable" (Alber 2009: 80).

I should note at the outset that the inability to read minds can enter realistic fiction as a pathology. In *Why We Read Fiction,* Zunshine refers to fictional representations of autism or "mindblindness" (Baron-Cohen 1995). Citing the autistic narrator of Mark Haddon's *The Curious Incident of the Dog in the Night-Time* (2004), Zunshine notes that the narration "is mostly lacking in attribution of thoughts, feelings, and attitudes," though "we, the readers, supply those missing mental states, thus making sense of the story" (Zunshine 2006: 12).[3] Sociopaths belong to another type that suffers (perhaps the wrong word) an emotional deficit, which not only robs them of a full emotional life, but also robs them of the capacity to understand the emotion-filled life as it is lived by others. To do so requires an effort of triangulation that operates the way Dr. Van Helsing describes the mindblindness of Dracula, whose powerful "great brain" is yet a "child-brain . . . that do only work selfish and therefore small" (Stoker 1992: 363). In his novel *Talk Talk* (2006), T. C. Boyle brilliantly renders a sociopath who is similarly hobbled and

---

2. My qualifying word "important" is important, since reading human minds is not the only craving that draws us to fiction. Jesse Bering uses the term "purpose-based thinking," which includes the reading of minds but also extends to reading messages in inanimate objects and natural events (Bering 2011). Brian Boyd's expansive wording locates the principal appeal of fiction in the general human "fascination with agents and actions," including "hidden causes," "probable scenarios and consequences," and "other spaces of the possible we can explore" (Boyd: 198–99).

3. In the light of an emerging re-evaluation of autism and particularly the work of Ralph James Savarese (2007), Zunshine has recently retracted her view of autism as a disability distinguished by mindblindness. See especially Savarese and Zunshine 2014.

consequently incapable of understanding the tenacity of the pair of lovers who pursue him.[4] In *The Essential Difference* (2003), Simon Baron-Cohen controversially extended his early work on autism to include a calibrated range of mindblindness down into the "normal" masculine demographic. If he is right about this, both Othello and Lear would qualify for a diagnosis of mindblindness. And certainly much comedy has turned on the blindness of men to *What Every Woman Knows* (to cite the 1934 film starring Helen Hayes), that is, not only the minds of others but their own minds as well.

My subject, however, is the fictional rendering of minds that defy our best efforts to read them. The usual default reading of such a mind is as one or another generic type or stereotype, as, for example, that the character is crazy. It is important to acknowledge here that authors may, and often do, create characters according to stereotypes that are meant to be fully readable as such.[5] Authors also, though less commonly, create characters who appear to be unreadable and in consequence are stereotyped by others, yet who acquire readability over the course of the narrative. Colonel Kurtz in *Apocalypse Now* (1979) has "very obviously . . . gone insane," according to the film's unnamed general. In context, "insane" is a place-holder for the inexplicable, though here, as often, it works as a performative, that is, as an act of naming with a practical purpose.[6] Putting Kurtz into the category of the insane confers permission to "terminate" him. Captain Willard, recognizing the game in play,

4. A key 1991 study by Williamson et al. found that diagnosed sociopaths, unlike normal people, reveal no heightened affective response to emotion-laden words. "Love" and "happy" produce the same neutral response as "chair" and "fifteen." In an important follow-up, Intrator et al., using single-photon emission-computed tomography, discovered heightened blood flow in the temporal lobes of sociopathic subjects when asked to solve problems involving emotion-laden words. In other words, they had to work harder than others, given the difficulty they had understanding the emotional element.

5. Perhaps the most common of such reductive designators is the ethnic stereotype, of which the number is legion. In fiction, these more often than not are unfortunately the product of intentional characterization. But, like the designation "crazy," an ethnic stereotype can also release the needful reader from the burden of trying to read an intentionally unreadable character. This is dramatized when, in *Wuthering Heights,* Heathcliff arrives in the Earnshaw household, bringing human unreadability with him. He is a "dirty, ragged, black-haired child" who "repeated over and over again some gibberish that nobody could understand" (Brontë 1995: 36–37). He immediately elicits from Mrs. Earnshaw an available default reading of sufficient generality to handle his repellent strangeness. He is "that gypsy brat" (37). Nelly, telling this story, momentarily inhabits the self she was then by referring to the child as "it"—a default pronoun that goes further in accomplishing the same end by declassifying Heathcliff as human. In this she anticipates Emily Brontë's sister Charlotte, who writes in her preface to the second edition of *Wuthering Heights* that Heathcliff "was child neither of Lascar nor Gypsy, but a man's shape animated by demon life—a Ghool—an Afreet" (Brontë 1995: xxxvi).

6. Such a performative move is often a way of rejecting any effort of interpretation, as in the familiar student's reading: "He's like so totally weird!"

replies "Yes, sir. Very much so, sir. Obviously insane" (Milius and Coppola 2000: 13). But from there on, using Willard as its principal focalizer, the film revaluates the term "insane," transferring it to the war effort that the general represents while at the same time conferring on Kurtz a degree of complex readability. A similar revaluation can be seen in Pat Barker's superb novel of World War I, *Regeneration* (1992), in which the generic stereotype for unreadable behavior is "shell shock." A central drama of the novel is the gradual decoding of shell shock by a historically real figure, Dr. William Rivers. Rivers learns to read shell shock as a language of protest that, given the political climate and a soldier's need to "be a man," cannot be given voice. It is a protest, moreover, rooted in a sane assessment of the madness of war.[7]

In what follows, I shall be dealing with characters that by intention disallow the fall-back reading of generic stereotypes. These are characters for whom there is an insufficiency of material—be it description, dialogue, "thought report," or narrative action—to release them from their unreadability. I shall also be describing a second and a third fall-back response to unreadable minds in fiction that also have the potential to displace the immediate experience of unreadability.

READING THE UNREADABLE MIND

My first example is Herman Melville's classic tale "Bartleby the Scrivener" (1853), a story whose title character stands out against the rich social tapestry of canonical nineteenth-century fiction with its hubbub of interacting minds that Palmer has described so well. It is hard to think of another like it in Victorian fiction, and indeed all the other characters in "Bartleby" are as readable as those of Melville's contemporary Charles Dickens. Our decent, kindly narrator is a comfortable sort, "one of those unambitious lawyers who never addresses a jury, or in any way draws down public applause" (Melville, ed. Chase 1957: 92–93). His veteran scriveners, Turkey and Nippers, and the

7. One important caution is that an accurate reading of a character is by no means a complete understanding. It is an understanding that honors the information we are given. The issue of what lies in the gaps of narrative is a vexed one. As I noted in chapter 5, Ryan's "principle of minimal departure" assumes that the world of any fictional narrative matches our "own experiential reality" unless there is information included in the narrative itself that tells us otherwise (Ryan 1991: 48–60). This means, among other things, that characters in realistic fiction can generally be assumed, without specifying details, to have depths we cannot see. But see also Lubomír Doležel's chapter on "Saturation" in which he argues among other things that, unlike the gaps in historical narrative, gaps in fiction contain *only* what is in some way cued (Doležel 1998: 169–84).

office boy, Ginger Nut, are as vividly Dickensian in their look and manner as their names suggest. Together they make the story buzz with the thick "intermental" life of accessible minds that is so common in the Dickens world. At the same time, they effectively frame the mystery of Bartleby, a silent, pale, diligent copyist who could as easily play the role of a readable character except that, when requested to do any other task than copying, he politely replies, "I would prefer not to." As such, the tale unfolds like a kind of experiment in which an inaccessible mind is dropped into a conventional nineteenth-century storyworld.

Predictably, the common default reading of the unreadable mind that I mentioned above is ready to hand in this story. As Ginger Nut puts it: "I think, sir, he's a little *luny*"(103). The narrator himself is driven to think that "the scrivener was the victim of innate and incurable disorder" (111–12). But, strangely, this explanation doesn't work for him, and he must repeatedly return to the stubborn fact that "Bartleby was one of those beings of whom nothing is ascertainable." This was, he writes, "an irreparable loss to literature" (92)—a comment that is as understandable, given our evolved narrative expectations, as it is ironic, given the tale's achieved canonicity. The anxiety that Bartleby brings on in the heart and mind of his employer is caused by the way the scrivener obstructs what Ernst Mayr has called the human tendency to engage in "typological" thinking—our assumption of an inner classifiable essence that generates what we see on the outside (Mayr 2001: 165–66): to wit, the thinking of the jail's grub-man who assumes Bartleby was "a gentleman-forger" because "they are always pale and genteel-like, them forgers" (130).[8] It is a tendency that Dickens relied on extensively and provides much of the great pleasure of his work. And perhaps Melville was provocatively mimicking Dickens in this regard when he gave his character the leitmotif "I prefer not to." In so doing he throws into sharp relief the Dickensian essentializing device of the repeatable character tag. In *David Copperfield,* for example, "Barkis is Willin'" expresses a character's predictability of behavior and at the same time his *essential* depth of motivation—in this case the devotion to Clara Peggotty that rules Barkis's heart. Bartleby's tag also conveys predictable behavior but without any depth at all, either of feeling or motive. All we can imagine is that "some paramount consideration prevailed with him to reply as he did" (103).

---

8. Scott Atran (1990), Susan A. Gelman (2004), and others have developed the case that thinking in such essentialist terms is a transcultural feature of the human response to humans. In *Strange Concepts and the Stories They Make Possible,* Lisa Zunshine extends this work into the sphere of fictional representations.

Identifying the type, as Mayr argues, is a powerful cognitive imperative, and accordingly Bartleby's employer begins to infer essence from the evidence of Bartleby's isolation and poverty: "what miserable friendlessness and loneliness are here revealed! His poverty is great; but his solitude, how horrible!" (109). Seeking a prototype, he pronounces him "a sort of innocent and transformed Marius brooding among the ruins of Carthage." Likening Bartleby to the plebeian-born populist, Marius Caius, sworn foe of Roman aristocracy and unjust privilege, the narrator seeks to achieve species kinship, establishing "the bond of a common humanity. . . . For both I and Bartleby were sons of Adam" (110). Actually, for a prototype, he might have chosen the "incurably forlorn" scrivener, Nemo, of Dickens's *Bleak House* (1852), which had appeared the year before "Bartleby." A pale copyist, Nemo is so devoid of the signs of life that when he is found dead he is, like Bartleby, first thought to be alive. Our narrator, however, is too honest a man to succeed in identifying Bartleby even as this least of types. He remains a captive would-be reader, bonded to his scrivener by a need to read him, which in itself seems as enigmatic as Bartleby's unreadability. He marvels at that "wondrous ascendancy which the inscrutable scrivener had over me, and from which ascendancy, for all my chafing, I could not completely escape" (118). So powerful is it that when he thinks he is leaving Bartleby for good, "strange to say—I tore myself from him whom I had so longed to be rid of" (124).

Andrew Delbanco reads this as Melville's bearing witness "to a good man trying to become a better man in the face of another's suffering" (Delbanco 2005: 221). Delbanco's interpretive move, and there have been many like it, is an example of a second fall-back response to the unreadable mind: that is, to see its function as a way of eliciting traits of another character. In this regard, the unreadable character is read primarily as a catalyst in a drama of nonreading, with the focus on the captive reader as she/he copes with the unreadable. In this instance, Bartleby's employer is the captive reader, and the unreadable Bartleby is the catalyst who brings out the lawyer's character. All of which is quite just. And we can choose to leave it at that. But should we not give up on him as a character, that is, as a realistic representation of a human being, Bartleby's unreadability remains a problem for us, the captive readers of the text. Without narratable cause, "I would prefer not to" is a motif of such transcendent *bizzarerie* that it seems to come from outer space. Its combination of quaint diction, subjunctive formality, affectless politeness, together with the granitic resolve of its speaker's behavior, takes Bartleby one step too far from any kind of plausible integration of character—an implausibility that only grows with its insistent repetition. To adapt Andy Clark's coinage, the phenomenon of Bartleby is "representation-hungry"[9] in the sense that there remains an inexplicable distance between Bartleby's behavior and the presumption from all appearances that Bartleby is human.

Yet, as the story is fiction and not nonfiction, there remains a third common fall-back response. This requires shifting the mode of reading from determining who Bartleby *is*, or how he *functions* in the characterization of someone else, to determining what he *stands for*. The unreadable character is read neither as a character nor a function, but as an idea. It is a shift that allows meaning to rush in, which is what has happened almost invariably in the critical response to Bartleby. The narrator himself cues this symbolic mode of reading at the beginning of the narrative when he says that "[w]hat my own astonished eyes saw of Bartleby, *that* is all I know of him, except, indeed, one vague report, which will appear in the sequel" (92). The "sequel" is a paragraph devoted to a mere "rumor," that "Bartleby had been a subordinate clerk in the Dead Letter Office at Washington." "Dead letters!" our narrator exclaims, prompting, "does it not sound like dead men?" And after a brief excursus on the metaphorical potential of Bartleby's rumored employment, he concludes: "On errands of life, these letters speed to death. Ah, Bartleby! Ah, humanity!" (131). The hint is more than enough to initiate a shift to the symbolic mode. In 1949, Richard Chase developed what has become a popular reading of Bartleby as the uncompromising writer at a time when Melville, now struggling to write novels of greater weight after a brief period of popular success, was beginning to go into eclipse. Bartleby thus chooses death rather than compromise with the agents of a society that has degraded his profession. Others have hung their readings on Bartleby's plebeian status. For Laurie Robertson Lorant, "Bartleby is the ghost of social conscience haunting the precincts of the ruling class" (Lorant 1996: 333). For a third, Bartleby can be read as a protest against the absurdity of life itself—that, finally, we are all writers of dead letters. An existential Christ, his death is a final act of refusal, a protest against the whole metaphysical set-up of life on earth. "Ah, Bartleby! Ah humanity!"

These are all readings with rich potential. I have introduced them, however, to help make my point: that in this tale, a shift into the symbolic mode of reading is a necessity if its eponymous central figure is to be *read* at all. Taken as a human being, however, and not as a symbol, Bartleby remains unreadable. Moreover, it is this stubborn unreadability that gives the story its

9. The term was originally developed by Andy Clark and Josefa Toribio to refer to the problem of representation in "(1) cases that involve reasoning about absent, nonexistent, or counterfactual states of affairs and/or (2) cases that involve selective sensitivity to states of affairs whose physical manifestations are complex and unruly" (Clark 1997: 167).

narrative tension. It is as an unreadable being and not as an ultimately decodable symbol that Bartleby challenges the narrator, right up to his death. This is the drama that holds us captive and that Melville does not relieve with the enlightenment of closure. He would prefer not to, and it is this preference that makes the story work as well as it does. If in retrospect the narrator grasps at a rumor that might restore readability to the unreadable Bartleby, the very act of grasping at meaning cancels that reading with another: that the unreadable is, by and large, unendurable, and that, one way or another, readers will generally find some strategy to make it go away.

Briefly summarizing the theoretical yield so far, I've proposed three fall-back responses to unreadable minds: the generic stereotype, the catalyst, and the symbol. They are all modes of reading, but only the first purports to be a reading of the unreadable character *as the representation of a human being.*[10] And these modes can work together: a generic type can certainly *catalyze* telling responses from other characters and *symbolize* ideas. Moreover, they have yielded, working separately or together, a range of tenable readings of the text itself. The one risk they take, however, and a big one in my view, is that they so absorb attention that they displace the cognitive dilemma of Bartleby's unreadability that is vital to the narrative experience of this story.

READING THE CAPTIVE READER

In my second text, the central focus is a would-be reader held captive by an unreadable mind, but, again, for the text to work it is vital that the reader of the story share the perplexity of this would-be reader. The unreadable mind in Kathryn Harrison's *The Seal Wife* (2002) is that of an unnamed Aleut woman, who never speaks, and about whom little is known except that she is uncommonly attractive, smokes a pipe, skins small animals, sews with skill, and tolerates only the missionary position in intercourse. We observe her

10. The set of distinctions I make—between reading a character 1) as the representation of a human being, 2) as an element functioning to elicit a response from (facilitate the characterization of) another character, and 3) as an idea or symbol—very roughly corresponds in a-numerical order to Phelan's tripartite theory of the "components" of character as 1) mimetic, 3) synthetic, and 2) thematic (Phelan 1989; 1996, 29–30). Phelan argues that these three components are present in variable ratios in the make-up of characters, according to narrative (rhetorical) need. Phelan's helpful theory is clearly more comprehensive in its scope than mine, which seeks to describe reader response to a particular situation: the presence of unreadable characters in fiction that are cued as mimetic representations of real people in the actual world of the story. In the actual storyworld of "Bartleby the Scrivener," the narrator is struggling to understand a real person in his world, a struggle that is echoed in the reader as she or he struggles to understand the representation of that person in that world.

unreadability through the eyes of the novel's protagonist, Bigelow, a gifted engineer and meteorologist who has been sent to Anchorage at the turn of the last century. His job is sending daily observations by teletype to the Weather Bureau, and in his spare time he builds giant kites to test his theories about the upper atmosphere. But at the center of the novel is his obsession with this unreadable woman.

> She looks at him, neither through nor away but directly at his face in the way that she has: not surprised, not inquisitive. Not excited, not agitated. Not apprehensive. Not interested, and not uninterested, either. Not angry, not curious. Not judging. Not dismayed. Not resigned. Not amused. Not delighted, or even slightly pleased. Not displeased.
>
> There are a hundred, no, a thousand ways that other people have looked at Bigelow over the years, and none of them describe the woman's gaze. He knows all the things that it is not. What it is, is harder to say. She has this trick of just looking. (Harrison: 204–5)

As in the case of Bartleby (and Conrad's Kurtz and O'Brien's Kathy Wade) the Aleut woman is a case of unreadability by narrative impoverishment. She is a hole in the narrative, a placeholder for a nonexistent story. At one point, Bigelow goes to her house and finds it empty. "He tries to imagine what might have summoned her from her home. Illness? A death in her family, or a birth?" (82). Later in the novel, with the same lack of warning, she is back in her house. "All these heavy things, stove and bed and table and chairs—how has she done it? Who has helped her to transport them?" (181). He never learns. We never learn. It is of course possible for a reader to "read her off" as a generic racial type (as in: "She's an Eskimo, what more can you say?"). But it is specifically as an unreadable mind that she works as a catalyst in a drama of nonreading.

> He doesn't want for her to have escaped behind the lids of her eyes—it seems as if he can see her there, in the dark, folded in a place too small to admit another occupant. He's getting what he hoped, he tells himself, but it isn't at all what he expected, and a desolation seizes him. He's not joined to her, he can't reach her. (28–29)

The novel contains a narrative inset that works as a kind of experimental "control," setting off the unique appeal of the Aleut woman's unreadability. It involves Bigelow's emerging fascination for another beautiful mute, Miriam, during the interval when the Aleut woman is gone. But Miriam turns out to be a sham mystery, part of a racket, seducing men who are caught by her father *in flagrante* and then subject to extortion. Applied to them, the stereotypes seem to fit—"criminal, scoundrel, extorter" (196)—and they are duly run out of town, and out of the novel. For Bigelow, there can be no readable substitutes. It is precisely by *not* giving him the assurance that his "mind-reading muscles" are working, that the Aleut woman maintains her grip on Bigelow. As in "Bartleby," the catalytic role played by the unreadable mind casts a shadow of unreadability over the catalyzed would-be reader. If the allure of the mysterious beauty is a familiar literary topos, even a cliché (which it is), in this narrative rendering Harrison has found a vehicle for restoring the mystery's original power. As long as the Aleut woman's unreadability remains intact, the ancillary mystery of desire persists as well. And though it is Eros that brings Bigelow to her, and though "he tells himself" that "he's getting what he hoped, . . . it isn't at all what he expected" (29). It's reading her that he wants, and it is not being able to read her that keeps him wanting.

In the case of Melville's captive reader, I suggested that shifting to a symbolic reading—what I've been calling the third fall-back response to an unreadable mind—could be seen as an effort to seek relief from the unreadable, one that the lawyer-narrator would share with a long line of interpreters. This is something Bigelow does not allow himself, though for us there are several hints for a reading of Bigelow and the Aleut woman as figures in an allegory of desire. The novel's title probably comes from a North American aboriginal myth in which a seal captures a man to live with her under the sea. When he escapes and tries to return to his village, he finds that he has been so transformed by his captivity that he chooses to return to the sea for good (E. White 2002). Bigelow would seem to fall pretty neatly into the masculine role in this allegory, seeking to achieve lift-off but pulled back down by the magnetic, earthly power of the feminine. At his station high above the town, fashioning bigger and better kites, Bigelow sends them thousands of feet up into the heavens to read the secrets of the weather. Yet in his dreams "he's falling through a woman's vastness: storms and oceans, a desert, a mountain, a field in bloom, the wind moving in loops and arcs and great gusting sighs, . . . a beauty that cares nothing for the attentions of men, who crawl like ants on her face, at her feet" (90).[11]

In my reading, however, if this allegory is to work comfortably in concert

11. It is also possible to read the Aleut woman as the expression of the actual author's needs or desires. In this reading, for example, the Aleut woman conveys Harrison's experience of her own unattainable mother (detailed in *The Kiss* and *The Mother Knot*). Such a biographical interpretive move is like the symbolic in that it applies meaning from the outside, in this case drawing on an extradiegetic life story to decode an unreadable character.

with the novel's action, it must not displace the mystery at the novel's core. It provides, in other words, a soft frame for Harrison's constant focus on the absolute unreadability of the Aleut woman as a character and its role in bringing out the mystery of her captive's need to read her.

> In the dream, he dismembers her. It's easy enough; he's learned from watching her skin and cut up game. And there is no blood. Instead, a stream of writing spills from her veins, letters and runes and symbols he doesn't understand. They pour out in order, like a Weather Bureau teletype, a cipher he is to translate into meaning.
>
> Except he can't fathom the writing inside the woman. He's killed her for nothing. (70)

This unreadability is what must be felt, along with its power to captivate. This complex experience is the target of Harrison's considerable creative energy. To allow too great an encroachment of the symbolic mode of response, then, is to risk disengaging from what the novel does so well.

There are, however, tales in which the symbolic mode works, not as a way of decoding the tale, but rather as a key element in a drama of reading that goes on within the tale. This is what I will turn to next. It is a transaction between the reader of the tale and the reader in the tale that is a little more complex than what I have tried to show so far, but it should become clear in what follows.

THE UNREADABLE IMAGE AND THE ART OF THE SHORT STORY

One of Alice Munro's signature gifts as a writer of short stories is the efficiency with which she builds to a moment of insight that allows us at one and the same time to see a character anew and to see that there is more we can't see. One of her more stunning achievements in this regard is "Fits" (1986), a story in which unreadability and its power to captivate are thematized throughout. In it, an entire community is held captive by the unreadable minds of the Weebles, a retired couple, recently arrived, who are found one morning dead of a murder-suicide. Their corpses mark the end of some terrible story, forever untold. By extension, their house itself becomes a magnet drawing the townsfolk, their "cars nosing along the street, turning at the end, nosing their way back again . . . , making some new kind of monster that came poking around in a brutally curious way" (Munro 1996: 449). Inevitably, formulaic stories start packing the void left by their deaths.

> They had owed money on their income taxes. Being an accountant, he thought he knew how to fix things, but he had been found out. He would be exposed, perhaps charged, shamed publically, left poor. Even if it was only cheating the government, it would still be a disgrace when that kind of thing came out. . . .
>
> It was not money at all. They were ill. One of them or both of them. Cancer. Crippling arthritis. Alzheimer's disease. Recurrent mental problems. It was health, not money. It was suffering and helplessness they feared, not poverty. (442)

The Weebles' next-door neighbor, Robert Kuiper, trying to explain to his stepsons what happened, falls back on a version of the insanity default: "it's like an earthquake or a volcano. It's that kind of happening. It's a kind of fit. People can take a fit like the earth takes a fit. But it only happens once in a long while. It's a freak occurrence" (448). But Robert still yearns for some way of narrativizing the Weebles that works better than this or any of the other stories his neighbors have been fashioning. "If he could have believed one of them, hung on to it, it would have been as if something had taken its claws out of his chest and permitted him to breathe" (442). Robert is a special instance in this storyworld because he is held captive not only by the unreadability of the Weebles, but also by that of his wife, Peg, who first discovered the Weebles. The problem with Peg is that she fails to register an appropriate response to the dead couple. She does not scream, she does not run to tell others, she does not phone her husband. She simply goes to the sheriff and reports what she found. Then she goes to work without bothering to let her co-workers in on this hot item. The unreadability of Peg doubles that of the Weebles, and its captivating power generates a trajectory of its own. With characteristic economy, Munro weaves both of these threads together in a remarkable counterpoint on the obscure origins of human violence and the unpredictability of its eruption.

Normally "reserved," or "self-contained" (in Robert's words), Peg has stepped over a line. For her friends and workmates, not telling what she found is a betrayal of trust. Worse, it's abnormal. "What was it they were really looking for?" the narrator asks. "Perhaps they wanted from Peg just some kind of acknowledgment, some word or look that would send them away, saying, 'Peg Kuiper is absolutely shattered.' 'I saw Peg Kuiper. She didn't say much but you could tell she was absolutely shattered'" (443). What they are looking for is a "natural" narrative with its appropriate sequence of cause and effect:

Discovering bodies → Absolutely shattered

Karen Adams, Peg's co-worker, inserts herself in just such a normalizing narrative when she recounts finally getting Peg to say what happened: "I started to shake. I shook all over and I couldn't stop myself" (439).

But Robert is married to Peg so the whole problem of her nonresponse is, quite literally, closer to home. The Weebles, too, were married—married long enough to retire together. The one evening they had dropped over for a drink, they seemed normal enough. Peg and Robert have themselves been married for five years, and it has been pretty smooth sailing. So for Robert, the unreadability of the Weebles and the unreadability of Peg are bound together, since to read her is to read her reading the Weebles. This is what makes it hard for him to breathe. He senses there's something under her smooth surface, something caged that might or might not spring; he just doesn't know what it is.

> Robert was watching her, from time to time. He would have said he was watching to see if she was in any kind of trouble, if she seemed numb, or strange, or showed a quiver, if she dropped things or made the pots clatter. But in fact he was watching her just because there was no sign of such difficulty and because he knew there wouldn't be. (446)

What sends her and the whole story into a much graver key is a "discrepancy" in her narrative when she finally tells Robert how she discovered the Weebles. She says what she saw first was Mr. Weeble's leg "stretched out into the hall" from the bedroom door (447). But that isn't what she saw, and Robert knows it. He has already heard the constable's account of the scene, and it has given new meaning to the "long crusty smear" of dried blood on the coat Peg wore that morning. For her readers, Munro saves the constable's account until the end of her story, where its detonation can have the greatest recursive effect.

> At noon, when the constable in the diner was giving his account, he had described how the force of the shot threw Walter Weeble backward. "It blasted him partways out of the room. His head was laying out in the hall. What was left of it was laying out in the hall."
>
> Not a leg. Not the indicative leg, whole and decent in its trousers, the shod foot. That was not what anybody turning at the top of the stairs would see and would have to step over, step through, in order to go into the bedroom and look at the rest of what was there. (453)

Short story theorists have argued that one consequence of the shortness of short stories is that we expect "a degree of mystery, elision, uncertainty

[that] we would not in the novel" (Hanson 1989: 25). In a recent essay, Renate Brosch, with the cognitivist work of Zunshine and Palmer in her sights, has argued that because of the "reduction of textuality" in the short story, "the psychological make-up of characters becomes a mystery, and reading minds becomes a guessing game for which we collect clues scattered through the text." As such, "the reading experience" of the short story "highlights the deep desire for, and the failed attempt at, achieving intersubjectivity" (Brosch: 200). Brosch couples this contention with another: Wolfgang Iser's view that the centrality of the "image-building process" to narrative experience is accentuated in the experience of the short story. Where the novel, with its greater length, sequentiality, and detail, can build up an autonomous world in which the reader feels at home, the short story has a "poetic" density, so that a single image can dominate our understanding, tying together themes and incidents.

The interrelation of the ways short stories resist the mind-reading skills of the reader and expand the role of the image bears directly on the third fall-back response to the unreadable mind, the move into a symbolic reading. As I have been arguing, this can be a way of neutralizing the disturbing effect of what cannot be dealt with at the level of character. To be "mindblind" can be terrifying (Baron-Cohen 1995: 5), and though we are not exactly terrified when we encounter a fictional character that we don't understand, there is some comfort in being able to deal with this condition in the abstract. The temptation to move into a symbolic meaning in "Fits" is certainly strong, ending as it does with the ominous, fearful, deeply disturbing scene that comes into focus: Peg, stepping through the remains of Mr. Weeble's destroyed and bloody head into a room that possibly holds even greater horror. But Munro does two things to complicate the way in which we absorb this image. She maintains our intimate connection with Robert, focalizing through his eyes, thinking and feeling with him. But she also chooses to release this image to us only after recounting Robert's encounter with another image, also focalized through his eyes and mind. The sequence provides an implicit commentary on a man desperate to move into the symbolic mode, to read something in the landscape that can provide the solace of understanding. But strategically ordered as it is, the progression also serves to deepen the pain of mindblindness that comes with the story's final image—ours, of course, only a shadow of his.

Going out at the end of this disorienting day for a walk on the hard crust of a snow-covered field and enjoying its glittering surface and smooth contours, Robert begins to make out "a new kind of glitter under the trees. A congestion of shapes, with black holes in them, and unattached arms or petals reaching up." As he closes in, they continue to resist his understanding:

"They did not look like anything, except perhaps a bit like armed giants half collapsed, frozen in combat, or like the jumbled towers of a crazy small-scale city." It is only when he gets very close that he sees that they are "just old cars. Old cars and trucks and even a school-bus that had been pushed in under the trees," some "tipped over one another at odd angles" (452–53). The symbolic stature of this experience in Robert's mind follows directly from what we've been reading about the cold, serene, surface of his unreadable wife and the possibility that what lies underneath it is a frightening chaos of emotion and potential violence. The meaning that Robert finds in the image is that if he can just get close enough, what is frightening in its obscurity will turn out to be easily explicable: "what amazed him and bewildered him so was nothing but old wrecks." Relieved, he thinks of telling Peg about it: "They needed some new thing to talk about." But this is only a dream of relief. Robert has performed a symbolic operation as a diversion, a false lead away from Peg's problematic mind and the image that he knows is in that mind. The moral of the "old wrecks" is a moral the story cannot have: that the mystery of Peg's inner world can be cleared up, that what is so frightening is really mundane. In a powerful montage, Munro chooses at this point to introduce the constable's account, disclosing that Peg actually saw much more than she said she did, ending the tale and throwing an ironic shadow over the image Robert has just decoded.

Here again, readers themselves are free to shift to the third mode of response. It is a shift that accords with Iser's general admonition about how readers transcend particular details to grasp a general idea: "we are now prepared for a change of levels, in which the scene ceases to be just an element of the plot and becomes instead the vehicle for a much broader theme" (Iser 1978: 144). So, guided by this principle, Mr. Weeble's exploded head can be read as a frightening evocation of the violence that can lie dormant in intimate relationships and that can rise up suddenly and blow them apart. There is support for this. The narrator relates an incident from Robert's past when he and his last lover before Peg were having an argument on some trivial matter: "All of a sudden, the argument split open . . . and they found themselves saying the cruelest things to each other that they could imagine" (Munro: 450). More vivid still are the fights that Peg and her former husband had, recalled by her son Clayton who has suggested that maybe the Weebles had a fight:

> "When you and Dad used to have those fights? . . . Remember, after we first moved to town? When he would be home? . . . When you used to have those fights, you know what I used to think? I used to think one of you was going to come and kill me with a knife."

> "That's not true," said Peg.
> "It is true. I did" (448)

This moment with Clayton is the one time in the story when Peg's eerie self-containment gives way: "She who always seemed pale and silky and assenting, but hard to follow as a watermark in fine paper, looked dried out, chalky, her outlines fixed in steady, helpless, unapologetic pain" (448–49).

But do we know enough now to know why Peg would not only maintain her reserve, having seen such a sight, but also lie to her husband about what she saw? Add to this the fact that there was no need to go any further once she had seen what was left of Mr. Weeble's head. And yet she felt a need (what need?) to go into the room, dragging her coat through his blood, in order to take in the whole grisly scene. In short, more is less. We know too much about what Peg does to allow us to know just who she is. We need more narrative still. What is her secret? Did she kill her husband? Probably not, but why did he drive off to Alaska and never come back? Did their fights involve physical violence? Did they fight with knives, as Clayton's fear might imply? Or does the sight of the Weebles simply match a propensity in herself? Did her husband, then, leave for Alaska in fear of her? Or, conversely, does she see what she fears might have happened to her? Is this why she has to go into the room—to see what happened to Mrs. Weeble? Or was it emotional, not physical, damage that she suffered beyond repair?

We never learn. The questions we are left with belie any theory of a smooth transition from one level of response to the next. Munro has designed her story to steadily expand our feeling of bafflement by compelling us, right up to the end, to see and feel through the mind of Peg's captive reader. Of course, and as always, readers can read any way they want. They can speculate about Peg's state of mind just as the townsfolk speculate about the Weebles, supplying whatever inference or additional narrative detail is deemed necessary to achieve some kind of goodness of fit. But it is more likely that one function of the townsfolk's effort to explain the Weebles is to serve as a caution. The same can be said of Robert's momentary misapplication of the way a pile of castaway vehicles comes into relief. Like the presentation of that image, the final startling image that follows requires its own, albeit briefer, time lapse before coming into relief (so subtly is it conveyed). This image in turn can be construed in such a way as to release the reader from the immediacy of Robert's nightmare. But if we stay within Robert's focalizing, as I believe we should, this shift in levels is not possible. The second image trumps the first. It insures his, and our, captivity in a state of knowing enough to know that he, and we, will never know enough.

IT IS POSSIBLE that I am wrong about the intentions that guided these authors. Melville's addendum might have been deliberately intended to release his readers from the pained bafflement of Bartleby's employer, lifting them onto a level of abstract contemplation. Harrison's intention might have been to foreground an allegory of male–female relations; Munro's to make a general statement about the woe that is in marriage. But what I have sought to locate in these stories is the source of their power. And in each, I have found it in a gap that refuses to close. We may think of ways to close it, but when we go back to the story, it is the sheer insistence of the gap, as a true gap, that grips. To experience this power, I believe that, like the captive readers in these stories, a reader should be unwilling to settle for a way out.

It may be that again (as in chapter 4) narrative length can be a factor in achieving this special effect. As noted above, short story theorists have keyed the unique appeal and potentiality of the short story to its shortness.[12] Its necessary compactness can give it what Austin Wright called a genre-specific "recalcitrance" that balks the reader (Wright 1989). It is a form that specializes in gaps. This in turn means that the mystery of unreadable minds comes more naturally to the short story. As Charles May wrote, "[t]he short story's focus on mysteriously motivated behavior is at least as old as Poe's exploration of the perverse" (May 2012: 174).[13] However this may be, the formal issue brings us back to the cognitive one with which we began this chapter: our condition as needful mind readers. It is time now to look more closely at why it might sometimes be a good thing to arouse and then thwart not only this need but also our more encompassing need simply to know.

---

12. This generic distinction of the short story, and the advantages it confers, are themes that surface throughout a very helpful recent issue of *Narrative* (20.2: 201 2). In it, five theorists of the short story read and discuss a single text, Alice Munro's "Passion."

13. The novel, by contrast, has more space for detail. It need not sprawl, like the "loose baggy monsters" James deplored, but as a genre it comes equipped with room to elaborate. Even in *The Seal Wife,* despite its brevity as a novel and the intensity of its focus on the unreadability of the Aleut woman, there are pockets of novelistic diversity (meteorological detail, succeeding episodes of kite design and construction, additional characters with their own stories). There are, certainly, permanently unreadable minds whose unreadability plays a significant role in baggier novels. Perhaps the most famous of these, Albertine Simonet, plays a major role in one of the baggiest of novels, Proust's *À la recherche du temps perdu.* But it does make a difference that this novel (more than most) is "fraught with background" (Auerbach, cited in May: 173), and Albertine is one among a rich dramatis personae. Moreover, Albertine is drenched in the baroque phenomenology of her self-absorbed and self-ironizing lover. He is a narrator-lover who by his own confession has "always been more open to the world of potentiality than to the world of contingent reality" (Proust 1982: 16), whose ardor depends on the possibility that his lover has deceived him (130), and who freely talks at length about the sharp pangs of jealousy she caused him. As an enigma, Albertine is inviolate, but the contrast of impact between her novelistic packaging and Munro's spare delineation of Peg could not be sharper.

CONCLUSION

Why All This Matters

ETHICS AND THE UNREADABLE MIND

In the last chapter, I quoted Andrew Delbanco's description of the narrator of "Bartleby" as "a good man trying to become a better man in the face of another's suffering." There is something very nineteenth-century in this twenty-first-century critic's assessment, with its stress on empathy, and the conscious effort to be "a better man," and the catalytic agency of suffering. But it does not catch, in fact it displaces, our narrator's puzzlement about his emotional captivity and the role that Bartleby's unreadability, not suffering, plays in this captivity. Melville seems instead to have leapt ahead by a century, anticipating two key ideas of Emmanuel Levinas, of which the first is the recognition that the other is "absolutely other." Adriaan Peperzak's wording of this idea in his commentary on Levinas eerily chimes with the experience of Bartleby as "the irreducible Other . . . a stranger who cannot be reduced to a role or function within my world; . . . someone who comes from afar and who does not belong to it" (Peperzak 1993: 137). At the same time, the tenacity of the narrator's attention to Bartleby would seem to bear out the other side of the Levinasian ethical equation: that "[t]he I is bound up with the non-I as if the entire fate of the Other was in its hands" (Levinas 1996: 18). This is not a matter of my "trying to be a better man" but of my being somehow "obliged without this obligation having begun in me, as though an order slipped into my consciousness like a thief" (119). It is like being held "hostage even before I may know it" (Peperzak 1993: 26).

This central binary made the human face a major theme in Levinas, for it is the face that beckons the captive reader even as it screens the unreadable that lies on the other side: "A face confounds the intentionality that aims at it. . . . The epiphany of the absolutely other is a face, in which the other (*Autrui*) calls on me" (Levinas 1996: 54). Faces figure in much the same way in these texts. Our narrator searches and searches Bartleby's face, bound by an absence he cannot read:

> I looked at him steadfastly. His face was leanly composed; his gray eye dimly calm. Not a wrinkle of agitation rippled him. Had there been the least uneasiness, anger, impatience, or impertinence in his manner; in other words, had there been any thing ordinarily human about him, doubtless I should have violently dismissed him from the premises. (Melville 1957: 101)

Similarly Bigelow searches the inexpressive face of the Aleut woman and Robert searches the serenely contained face of his wife, both held hostage, not by what they can't read, but by not being able to read what they can't read.

One other closely relevant theme in Levinas has to do with what I have been calling the fall-back or default ways that readers cope with the unreadability of the unreadable mind. For Levinas, the deep motive behind the need to read others is the fear of losing the integrity of the self under the spell of the other. The coping mechanism is to absorb the other by incorporating it into the terms of the self's own understanding, "to annex otherness to itself by knowledge, possession, mastery" (M. Smith 2005: 37). Levinas was writing about relations in general—how we read each other almost as a rule. And it could be argued that most narrative fiction abets this process of annexation by depending on it as a condition that gives fiction its readability and appeal. Unreadable characters intrude on this compact by removing the veil of readability and exposing the need for mastery that is generally hidden from us. The urgency of this need and the pain of its frustration is vividly expressed in Bigelow's dream when he cuts open the Aleut woman, and "a stream of writing spills from her veins, letters and runes, . . . a cipher he is to translate into meaning. Except he can't fathom the writing inside the woman" (Harrison 2002: 70).

Harrison's complex metaphor is much the same as the one J. M. Coetzee used in *Waiting for the Barbarians* (1982) when he made the magistrate an amateur archeologist, struggling to read barbarian runes even as he struggles to read the captive woman who holds him captive by her unreadability. In this novel, as in Harrison's, sexual penetration leads nowhere. Bigelow tells himself that by having sex with the Aleut woman, "[h]e's getting what he hoped . . . but it isn't at all what he expected, and a desolation seizes him" (70). The same desolation afflicts the magistrate. As many have noted, the physical contact that the magistrate "enjoys" with the barbarian woman, and that is described at length, is an index not of contact but of the absence of contact. In this light, the most intimate forms of physical contact—sex (sex as taking, using) and torture—are aligned as two desperate expressions of the same desire.

> [T]o desire her has meant to enfold her and enter her, to pierce her surface and stir the quiet of her interior into an ecstatic storm; then to retreat, to subside, to wait for desire to reconstitute itself. But with this woman it is as if there is no interior, only a surface across which I hunt back and forth seeking entry. Is this how her torturers felt hunting their secret, whatever they thought it was? For the first time I feel a dry pity for them: how natural a mistake to believe that you can burn or tear or hack your way into the secret body of the other! (Coetzee 1982: 43)

Coetzee preserves intact the secret body of this other from both the magistrate and from us right up to their last moment together: "When I tighten my grip on her hand there is no answer. I see only too clearly what I see: a stocky girl with a broad mouth and hair cut in a fringe across her forehead staring over my shoulder into the sky; a stranger; a visitor from strange parts now on her way home after a less than happy visit. 'Goodbye,' I say. 'Goodbye,' she says. There is no more life in her voice than in mine" (73).

In drawing on the apt words of Levinas, I by no means wish to implicate his metaphysics or much else of the layered complexity of his thought in the case I have been making. As noted above, the match between Levinas and my authors quickly breaks down, beginning with the fact that, though I have been focusing on their unreadable characters, there are also characters in their novels who are clearly meant to be readable. Coetzee, of all the writers I have dealt with here, has sought to develop an ethics in connection with human unreadability, yet the unreadable characters in his novels are in general socially marginalized and often solitary others. They seem (as they are often taken to be) part of a more narrowly focused commentary on the colonial mindset. The barbarian woman is coded as both racially and ethnically distinct; Michael K in *Life and Times of Michael K* would have been recognized by South African readers as "colored"; Vercueil in *Age of Iron* is homeless; Friday in *Foe* is a black man from a distant island, mute, and exotically unreadable: "In the grip of dancing he is not himself. He is beyond human reach. I call his name and am ignored, I put out a hand and am brushed aside. All the while he dances he makes a humming noise in his throat, deeper than his usual voice; sometimes he seems to be singing" (Coetzee 1987: 92).[1]

The word "barbarian" is itself a generic type. It works as a performative, swallowing up an entire people. A central focus of *Waiting for the Barbarians* is the condition that gives rise to the term and sustains the behavior it enables. In this regard, the magistrate mirrors his vicious antagonist, Colonel Joll. Moreover, we are allowed the sense that we can read both men: the magistrate from the inside, Colonel Joll from the outside. When these two have their final encounter after the defeat of Joll's forces, it begins with a tableau, the two of them separated by the window of Joll's carriage.

> His face is naked, washed clean, perhaps by the blue moonlight, perhaps by physical exhaustion. I stare at his pale high temples. Memories of his mother's soft breast, of the tug in his hand of the first kite he flew, as well as of those intimate cruelties for which I abhor him, shelter in that beehive. (Coetzee 1982: 146)

There is a complexity emerging here that suggests a multitude of possible Jolls in that "beehive." But look what happens once the magistrate literally grabs Colonel Joll by the arm and forces him to talk:

> "Let me go!" he sobs. He is no stronger than a child.
>
> "In a minute. How could it be that the barbarians did this to you?"
>
> "We froze in the mountains! We starved in the desert! Why did no one tell us it would be like that?" (147)

1. Coetzee renders the same implicit judgment on our relations with animals, who could be described as having the absolute of unreadable minds. In an essay that has become a classic, Thomas Nagel contended that we will never "know what it is like for a *bat* to be a bat" (1970; cited in Coetzee 1999a: 31). In *The Lives of Animals* (1999a), a slippery document at best, Coetzee's fictional surrogate, the famous novelist Elizabeth Costello, struggles to make a stand for animal rights against an onslaught of academic reasoners. Her position is that, whatever their unreadability, one is obliged to assume that animals have "fullness of being" and as such deserve the honor and respect and care that comes with that status. "Fullness of being" would then be the common denominator shared by humans and animals, just as fullness of *human* being is the common denominator shared by Europeans and barbarians. One could extrapolate further from this that the word "animal" has worked like the word "barbarian," in that it is a performative that, among other things, excludes. It has allowed those animals of the species *Homo sapiens* to slip from under the term while retaining its application to the rest of their fellow creatures.

The tableau gives way to the busy, discursive intermental interchange of narrative action, and at the same time Colonel Joll shrinks back into a type, the would-be bully crying with self-pity. In the context of a searching critique of empire, it works. But at the same time it reinforces the impression that in the storyworld of this novel the exclusivity of Otherness is reserved for its unreadable barbarians.[2]

To repeat, the experience of unreadable fictional minds, meant as such, is very hard to maintain. Jesse Bering writes that people "cannot turn off their mind-reading skills even if they want to. All human actions are forevermore perceived to be the products of unobservable mental states, and every behavior, therefore, is subject to intense sociocognitive scrutiny" (Bering 2002: 12). This intense scrutiny can be extended to any bizarre event, which can be read as a signifier, sent perhaps from the mind of God (Bering 2002, 2011). Correlatively, in fiction we often find signifiers of this sort and often attribute them to the mind of the author. This is the symbolic default whereby the unreadable becomes readable at another level of signification. In fact, in *Life and Times of Michael K*, it is hard *not* to read Michael K symbolically, with his seeds in his pocket. He does it himself: "It excited him, he found, to say, recklessly, *the truth, the truth about me. 'I am a gardener'*" (181; original emphasis). Similarly, we are invited to see Vercueil as the Angel of Death, wrapping Mrs. Curren in his cold embrace at the end of *Age of Iron*. Failing these, there is still the term "other," which can work as a familiar signifying tag, conveying its own minimal degree of readable displacement.

The ethical move that I am promoting here is to read the barbarian woman, the Aleut woman, Bartleby, Heathcliff, Kurtz, John and Kathy Wade,

2. It is quite possible to see the generic type of the barbarian overlain in this novel by another generic type, woman, which may well be the dominant element in the magistrate's obsessive need to breach an impenetrable otherness. This possibility snapped into sharper focus with the publication of Coetzee's *Disgrace* (1999b), a novel whose protagonist, David Lurie, is captive to the same overriding combination of need and mindset, though with less awareness and more devastating personal consequences. William Butler Yeats, a famous real-life captive, generalized its sexual dimension, claiming that the "tragedy of sexual intercourse is the perpetual virginity of the soul" (to John Sparrow, cited by Christopher Ricks 1974: 64). For Yeats, "the finest description of sexual intercourse ever written" could be found in lines by Lucretius as translated by Dryden:

> They gripe, they squeeze, their humid tongues they dart,
> As each would force their way to t'others heart:
> In vain they only cruze about the coast,
> For bodies cannot pierce, nor be in bodies lost . . .
> All ways they try, successless all they prove,
> To cure the secret sore of lingring love. (Dryden, "Lucretius, the Fourth Book,
> Concerning the Nature of Love," ll. 75–78, 91–92; cited in Ricks 1974: 64)

Peg and the Weebles in a full acceptance of their insistent unreadability. I am arguing that there is value in not allowing default responses to override the immediate experience of an unreadable fictional mind. This does not preclude the symbolic, but requires that it not displace the experience of unreadability. This does, however, preclude empathy, at least insofar as empathy involves the presumption of a readable mind. To release one's understanding even from the claims of empathy is to adopt a stance of humility and respect before the human unknowable that I believe to some extent governs each of these texts.

THE DARK SIDE OF "THEORY OF MIND"

To reword the point above that I abstracted from Levinas, the "promiscuous, voracious, and proactive" cognitive imperative that makes us want to read minds (Zunshine 2011: 66),[3] and that has played and continues to play such an important role in our survival as a species, can run in tandem with a need for mastery over others that has been the cause of great suffering over the same long course of our history. In these fictions, the two needs often appear to be fused, as in Bigelow's dream of cutting up the Aleut woman in order to find her secret self. The "dry pity" that the magistrate feels for the men who tortured his barbarian "lover" is a recognition that they were motivated by the same need as he is in his love making—a refusal to accept her impenetrable otherness. Like Coetzee, though even more explicitly, O'Brien's narrator in *In the Lake of the Woods* extends this insight to the atrocities of wartime. Struggling to enumerate the possible causes for the fury that led to My Lai, O'Brien's narrator winds up with "[t]he unknown, the unknowable. The blank faces. The overwhelming otherness" (O'Brien 1994: 199).

As Conrad understood, the heroic quest to penetrate the unknown can be hard to separate from the desire to appropriate and to tame—in effect, to spread knowability. Edward Said spent many years arguing the same point as well as its corollary: that what was being spread in that quest was not actual knowability but an illusion of knowability built on preexisting terms. It was, as it were, an accredited knowability, and its failure can augment the fusion

3. The potentially confusing phrase, "Theory of Mind," derives from Premack and Woodruff's (1978) seminal question, "Does the chimpanzee have a theory of mind?" The "theory" is formulated as a gift acquired early in our lives that allows us to understand that people other than ourselves have minds. But it is a gift that comes with a need. We not only assume that others have minds but we crave reading those minds. Much of the impact of Zunshine's *Why We Read Fiction* lay in the way she connected this evolutionary acquirement with the art of narrative and its universal appeal.

of fury and fear that grips a soldier fighting in a strange land. It is here that the reading of faces and the inability to do so, which was so important a subject for Levinas, is critical. We are face-reading mammals even before we are mindreaders. An infant begins reading her mother's face within minutes of being born, laying the foundation for the set of skills required to read the mind that lies behind the face. Well before the acquirement of language, the infant enters with her mother into an evolving communicative matrix with its own complexity and precision.[4] So when one is sent into a land where one not only does not know the language of the people but cannot read their faces, the effect goes deep. In Vietnam, of course, American soldiers, having lost so many of their friends in terrible ways, had good reason to be both frightened and furious. A death-dealing enemy could be hidden anywhere, not just in the jungle but among the villagers one has been sent to defend. But these soldiers were also in an aboriginal state of not knowing, where the "overwhelming otherness" of the entire situation is perhaps felt most acutely in their inability to read anything in the "blank faces" they encounter.[5]

---

4. For an overview of recent literature on infants' recognition and reading of the mother's face see Grossmann and Vaish 2008.

5. Just to be clear, there is no argument here that to understand is to forgive. Whatever French nuances inflect the as-yet unsourced expression "Tout comprendre, c'est tout pardoner," in context the word that is belied is generally translated as "to forgive" but also could be "to pardon" or "to let off the hook." When David Edelman suggested to O'Brien that his "empathy" for soldiers under the stress of combat indicated something like this, O'Brien's reaction was emphatic:

> I understand what they went through. . . . You can explain it. It doesn't mean you can justify it. I tried in the book to carefully show the circumstances that led up to it, the men dying, anger and everything. My own unit, we went through the same things they went through, land mines and snipers and deaths, but we didn't cross the line between rage and homicide.
>
> Murder's murder, and I've always felt the same. (Edelman 1994)

In his memoir, "The Vietnam in Me," which was published in the *New York Times Magazine* at roughly the same time as the interview with Edelman, O'Brien developed this point in greater detail and along with it the anger he felt:

> [I]t's to say that I more or less understand what happened on that day in March 1968, how it happened, the wickedness that soaks into your blood and heats up and starts to sizzle. I know the boil that precedes butchery. At the same time, however, the men in Alpha [O'Brien's] Company did not commit murder. We did not turn our machine guns on civilians; we did not cross that conspicuous line between rage and homicide. I know what occurred here, yes, but I also feel betrayed by a nation that so widely shrugs off barbarity, by a military judicial system that treats murderers and common soldiers as one and the same. Apparently we're all innocent—those who exercise moral restraint and those who do not, officers who control their troops and officers who do not. In a way, America has declared itself innocent. (O'Brien, 1994b)

I argued in chapter 5 that two of the challenges O'Brien set himself in his admiring competition with Conrad was, on the one hand, to give detailed documentary representation of the human capacity for horror carried out as warfare in a foreign land, and, on the other, to show with a gathering narrativized intensity how the same terrible aggression could replicate at the level of personal relations at home in one's own land. More than that, I argued that, though a medical diagnosis of PTSD *might* account for the way Wade's tenuous sanity *might* have cracked in the middle of the night, the reader's willing collaboration in imagining an openly hypothetical horror extends the significance of the scene beyond its medical accounting. We, I argued, who are neither crazy nor criminals, play the role of virtual accomplices in the recreation of imagined horror.

I now want to suggest that, with regard to the theme of the volatility of frustrated Theory of Mind, O'Brien lays down similar parallel tracks in *In the Lake of the Woods,* so that the dangerous frustration felt by soldiers among unreadable faces can be seen to resonate in an individual life story that begins well before the war. Here again, Wade is a special case that brings out a general human potentiality. A dominant theme of his childhood is his inability to pierce the barrier between himself and his father, an aloof alcoholic whose self-contempt translates into contempt for a slightly overweight son whose absorbing interest is not the manly sports of physical prowess but the childish games of magic. Wade's anxiety to read his father's mind is so great that he takes to spying on him:

> [It] was like an elaborate detective game, a way of crawling into his father's mind and spending some time there. He'd inspect the scenery, poke around for clues. Where did the anger come from? What *was* it exactly? And why didn't anything ever please him, or make him smile, or stop the drinking? Nothing ever got solved—no answers at all—but still the spying made things better. It brought him close to his father. It was a bond. It was something they shared, something intimate and loving. (1994a: 209–210)

What is latent in this stealthy, one-sided illusion of intimacy and love is a dangerous anger that echoes the mysterious anger of Wade's father. When his father commits suicide, leaving his fourteen-year-old son permanently excluded from any access to his father's mind, the effect is lethal. "What he felt that night, and for many nights afterward, was the desire to kill. At the funeral he wanted to kill everybody who was crying and everybody who wasn't. He wanted to take a hammer and crawl into the casket and kill his father for dying" (14).

When John Wade falls in love with the "[f]iercely private, fiercely independent" Kathy Hood, a woman who had the trick of vanishing, "cleanly and purely gone, as if plucked off the planet" (33), he takes up spying on her as well. And, as he felt toward his father, though now with an erotic sensual element, he wants to "crawl inside" her. His desire carries the same off-hand menace as Bigelow's dream of cutting up his unreadable lover. "There were times when [he] wanted to open up Kathy's belly and crawl inside and stay there forever. He wanted to swim through her blood and climb up and down her spine and drink from her ovaries and press his gums against the firm red muscle of her heart. He wanted to suture their lives together" (71). Again, however easily Wade may be slotted into clinical categories of narcissism or arrested development, for O'Brien these conditions create opportunities for a more general understanding, in the same way the analysis of human psychopathologies did for Freud. The sickness reveals the deep structure of a condition we acquire by virtue of being human.

This implicit commentary on the dark side of the gift of Theory of Mind organizes much of O'Brien's rich and complex novel. Moreover, the story it tells resides within a drama of the narrator's own long losing battle to penetrate the mind of the man he is so arduously tracking. As this exhausted would-be historian wields the power of narrative, how much is his considerable gift guided in turn by anger? To what extent is he artfully stacking the evidence against his prey? Given the way O'Brien has woven together the themes of mind-reading and aggression, I don't think this reading of the narrator stretches credibility. The act of imagining Wade's terrible retribution on the hiddenness of Kathy may itself be an act of retribution—a lurid hypothesis inflicted by an intolerably frustrated biographer who, after accumulating "oceans of hapless fact," still finds his subject "beyond knowing. He's an other" (101).

STILL, Wade is indeed an extreme case. And it is worth asking if his unusually obsessive need governs this novel to the point of skewing the presentation of its theme, infecting its narrator, and perhaps even implicating the author himself. The same could be asked of the world as imagined by the notoriously shy J. M. Coetzee, whose avatars in his later autobiographical fictions and fictional autobiographies endure painful feelings of being set apart and unable to share in the lives of others.[6] Moreover, it would be foolish to deny not only

6. After Coetzee's first two novels, a prevailing coldness of temperament seems to have set in, a trait which he has subjected to withering scrutiny. One of Coetzee's strengths (among many) may be that he keeps to the feelings which, by his own account, he knows best. Warmer

that human beings are endowed by their nature to understand the minds of other human beings, but that by and large they do so with considerable success. Both the ability and the need to exercise it have been essential for our species survival. More than this, it is a moral strength that we seek to understand others as we would wish to be understood ourselves. Adding to its luster, the impulse to read minds has also been loosely associated with empathy, a concept that has enjoyed largely positive connotations and has often been used interchangeably with "sympathy." Thus the discovery of mirror neurons by Giacomo Rizzolatti and his colleagues (1996) was met not only with wonderment but in some quarters with rejoicing. It seemed to make empathy demonstrably neurological (Gallese 2001; Preston and de Waal 2002; Decety and Jackson 2004), giving renewed support to the long thread of evolutionary theory from Peter Kropotkin to Frans de Waal that has put our sociality at the center of our evolutionary success.[7] But the main point in our context is that the gift can fail even as the need to exercise it persists and fulfillment crystalizes into an imperative. For readers and interpreters, what this means is that an alertness to intentionally unfilled gaps of action and characterization should be worked into our methods of reading complex fictions lest we fabricate a mind behind a face meant to be left unread.

One final point before going on. It is not hopelessly old-fashioned to maintain that an essential part of being human, perhaps *the* essential part, is the sense we have of being free. Whether or not this sense of freedom is wholly an illusion has yet to be determined and may never be. But for now, in the present context, it means being free of the presumption that we are wholly knowable. So you might say that a perfected operation of our Theory of Mind would have to include a counter-presumption of unknowability, granted to others in the same way one grants it to oneself. This consideration should

---

emotions of affection and even love will leak through the crevices of his novels, often sighted from afar; but Coetzee's specialties are the feelings of isolation: of shame, humiliation, embarrassment, disgrace, alienation, fear, pain, and the general weight of emotional repression, relieved by the familiar comforts of thought, irony, and an exquisitely dry humor.

7. What empathy can do for readers is actually a vexed issue. As Suzanne Keen (2007) has shown in her magisterial study of empathy and the novel, there is no unanimity in the research. For Keen, at least, the empathy that we feel for fictional characters is neither sufficiently nor inevitably productive of sympathy for real people in the real world or, by extension, of altruism. This point bears directly on the revisionary side of Keen's study, which is to unsettle firm convictions about whether or not the arousal of empathy in fiction can lead to altruistic behavior. Her working definition of empathy is "a vicarious, spontaneous sharing of affect, [which] can be provoked by witnessing another's emotional state, by hearing about another's condition, or even by reading" (Keen 2007: 4). Fritz Breithaupt provides another serviceable, if barer, definition: "the capacity of an observer to receive access to the emotional state or intellectual awareness of another being or fictional construct" (Breithaupt 2011: 273).

also, I think, inflect our methods of interpretation, insofar as they grant a degree of unknowability to the intentions behind a fictional text. To do so is to recognize a freedom to be that, in a strange unbidden way, authors in their turn often recognize in the characters they create. As I suggested in my reflections on Morrison's *Beloved* and García Márquez's tales, and as I have argued elsewhere (H. P. Abbott 2011), there is an unpredictability in the creative process that can be felt even in the texture of a finished, packaged, published work of art.

WHAT I HAVE TRIED TO DO IN THIS BOOK

In this chapter and the two before it, I have sought to sketch an analytics of egregious narrative gaps, currently a hole in an otherwise immensely profitable ongoing cognitive inquiry into what goes on in our transactions with narrative storyworlds. There is much else to be inquired into, beginning with the historical issue of why unreadable characters began proliferating in twentieth-century literature. But I have focused in this last chapter on what I believe are genuine ethical considerations that link the way we relate to the unreadable characters of fiction with the way we relate to real people, both near at hand and around the globe.

But just as this last chapter is nested in the two before it, these three chapters are in turn nested in the chapters that precede them. When I set out to put this book together, I felt that to make the points I was intending to make in my concluding chapters required a frame that was both important in itself and also important as a context for those chapters. Our abiding lack of knowledge encompasses more than what we don't and won't know about what goes on in the minds of others. The enigmas of self that I took up in Parts One and Two are enigmas that are always with us and therefore always, in that sense, available, if easily ignored or replaced with what passes for knowledge. The minds of others, including the enigmas of self that must abide in those minds, constitute a different kind of unknowability. It is the unknowability that comes with one's being, to some extent, locked out from the minds of others. It, too, can be easily ignored or superscribed with certainty.

If a constant reference of this book has been our cognitive limits as human beings living our lives in what we call the real world, the focus of the book has been the experience of fiction. Could I have as easily drawn on nonfiction? It's a good question and worth pursuing. After all, when Tim O'Brien said of *In the Lake of the Woods* that he wanted to write a real mystery, the context might suggest that nonfiction could serve the same purpose:

"I think that's the way life usually operates. I wanted to write a real mystery, as opposed to a mystery that's solved, and then it's not a mystery anymore" (Edelman 1994). O'Brien mentions the unsolved mysteries of the disappearance of Amelia Earhart and the assassination of Jack Kennedy as immediate examples of "the way life operates." But life also operates with the ever-present possibility that these mysteries will be solved, even though we will all go to our graves with a thousand other such mysteries unsolved. Nonfiction carries with it this same possibility. Unlike fiction, nonfiction is "falsifiable" and always subject to correction; its mysteries may be solved. But in fiction, the author reigns, and a mystery can, if the author chooses, remain a mystery forever.

Of course, if all that is at issue are whodunits (Who killed Kennedy?), then I would not have written this book. Nor, I think would O'Brien have written his, because in the same paragraph of the same interview he goes on to mention "the greater mysteries the book's about, the mysteries of love. How much do people love us? What do they really feel about us? You live with someone for twenty years and you never really know." Even if she did not disappear, there would still be this and more about what goes on in the heart and mind of Kathy that Wade would never really know. Nor would we—and not only about her, but about Wade as well. What Kathy's disappearance helps do is write these mysteries large. It is here that O'Brien comes closer to the kind of mystery that Conrad is dealing with through Marlow, a narrator who will never penetrate the heart and mind of Kurtz. Both authors exercise their license as fictionists to keep their narrators permanently weighed down by the burden of unknowing.

I began Part One with Beckett and then picked him up again in chapter 4 not only because he was a specialist in permanent mysteries, but also because of the thoroughgoing, multifaceted ways his "art of failure" served him—keeping his readers poised along the knife edge of knowledge and ignorance. When he told Georges Duthuit that "to be an artist is to fail, as no other dare fail" (Beckett 1983: 145), he was speaking literally, not metaphorically. Failure by itself, of course, is easy. It is an experience we have on a daily basis—and writers, painters, dramatists, and cinematographers are no exception to this rule. It is why we have critics. It is also why the other term in Beckett's oxymoron, Art, is so important. Taken together, the two terms encompass not only Beckett's refusal to give audiences what they were designed by nature and trained by culture to want, and not only his own need to feel the strangeness of the human condition, but also the daunting task of bending to his purposes what he had to hand—that is, the materials of his craft and his immense powers of invention.

The other authors I have chosen for this book have not (to my knowledge) and probably would not describe their art as an art of failure. And yet the experience of a failure to know is something that they clearly have prized as an object of their art. To borrow words from Flannery O'Connor, they have pursued a kind of fiction that "will always be pushing its own limits outward towards the limits of mystery, because for this kind of writer, the meaning of a story does not begin except at a depth where adequate motivation and adequate psychology and the various determinations have been exhausted" (1961: 41). I have lifted O'Connor's words from a context of belief that is not in my reading intended by the authors I have selected for this book. O'Connor falls more nearly among the Christian apophatic writers, for whom there is one final metaphysical certainty that contains the mysteries that are so important for her and her fiction. But despite the absence of any such containment and the assurance that goes with it, the mysteries evoked in the works I have chosen are no less wonderful for that. In this book, I have tried to show that an art dedicated to these mysteries, an art so radically and variously practiced by Beckett, was also skillfully practiced by others in their often quite different ways.

It only remains to ask: is this project at all useful? Is it useful to know what it feels like to experience the kinds of cognitive failure that I have claimed are available to the willing reader? Is it good to be immersed in the experience of our ignorance: to sustain a felt awareness of not knowing why or who we are, or to feel the breakdown of syntax in pursuit of the inexpressible, or to honor with full acceptance the deep unreadability of the minds of others? Or are these states of mind in fact debilitating, undermining a cognitive efficiency that we have relied on extensively for our current success as a species? After all, without convictions—beginning with the conviction that we can rely on our convictions—we cannot make the decisions we need to make simply to survive. Does an acceptance of failure in the areas I have dealt with in this book encroach on this necessity? Or are all these questions moot, since we are the way we are?

Well, to the extent that we are genetically hard-wired by evolution, reading these authors in the spirit I have advocated will not change us. After such knowledge, we go on much the same. But I believe our individual development is also governed by a flexible and many-stranded "genetic leash," to use E. O. Wilson's coinage (Wilson 1998: 128, 157–58). It has given us a freedom of cultural evolution that even a self-confessed "diehard hereditarian" (158) freely acknowledges. It has allowed the production of a superabundance of behavioral variety. And it is here, along the indefinable extent and complexity of this leash, that one finds the large and complex issue of how literature functions in the context of our lives. At its best, I believe literature is indeed a "machine to think with": that is, a way of growing knowledge in a vast, collective, evolving conversation. And a key terrain of that growing knowledge is the knowledge of our common humanity and the great range of behavior and cultural practice that falls within it. What I am arguing is, to begin with, that a vital part of that knowledge is the knowledge that there are important things we will never know and questions we will never answer. But what I am also arguing is that it is vital to feel this. We can talk about this knowledge, yet in doing so we occlude the experience of it. We slip in "aboutness" where we felt "isness." What the authors in this study do (if we permit them) is disengage us from the attitude of such "aboutness" by techniques of total immersion.

So, my answer to the question I asked above is that such experiential knowledge is at the present time not only useful but urgent. After all, the planet on which our reflex capabilities took shape was a big one with lots of room in which pockets of opposing cultural certainties could thrive and do the necessary work of social cohesion that culture can do so well. If those were much more violent times than our own, as Steven Pinker (2011) and Joshua Goldstein (2011) have recently shown with abundant evidence, it is still very hard to predict where we'll be, violence-wise, when the global population has gone from 7 billion to 10 or 11 billion. The planet we live on now is already a crowded one in which constant contact brings with it threats of cultural relativism, which in turn seem increasingly to provoke a backlash of cultural absolutism (Robertson 1992, Waters 2001, Campbell 2005). Such absolutism brings with it a strenuous, aggressive, and often violent certainty on issues of who we are, what we can know, and what in the course of human events we have the power to control. In such a world, the awareness these authors offer is at the least chastening. They remind us that what wisdom we have is incomplete without the awareness of our ignorance. This is a point that Socrates made long ago. But Socrates made the case logically, confounding in argument all the so-called wise men of Athens. These authors go about the task much differently. They do not make the case but let the case make itself simply by asking of their readers that they "let go" as their authors had done before them. Letting go sounds easy, but for these authors this kind of letting go required a remarkable degree of creative independence. It was an independence not simply from the pressures of the literary marketplace but from the well-grooved imperatives of their own minds.

WORKS CITED

Abbott, Barbara. *Reference.* New York: Oxford University Press, 2010.

Abbott, H. Porter. *Diary Fiction: Writing as Action.* Ithaca, NY: Cornell University Press, 1984.

———. *Beckett Writing Beckett: The Author in the Autograph.* Ithaca, NY: Cornell University Press, 1996.

———."Beckett's Lawlessness: Evolutionary Psychology and Genre." *Samuel Beckett Aujourd'hui/Today* 8 (1999): 131–42.

———. (2000a) "What Do We Mean When We Say 'Narrative Literature'? Looking for Answers across Disciplinary Borders." *Style* 34.2 (Summer 2000): 260–73.

———. (2000b) "The Evolutionary Origins of the Storied Mind: Modeling the Prehistory of Narrative Consciousness and its Discontents." *Narrative* 8.3 (October 2000): 247–56.

———. "Narrative." In *Palgrave Advances in Samuel Beckett Studies.* Ed. Lois Oppenheim. Houndmills: Palgrave Macmillan, 2004. 7–29.

———. *The Cambridge Introduction to Narrative.* 2nd ed. Cambridge: Cambridge University Press [2002] 2008.

———. "Immersions in the Cognitive Sublime: The Textual Experience of the Extratextual Unknown in García Márquez and Beckett." *Narrative* 17.2 (spring 2009): 131–42.

———. "Reading Intended Meaning Where None is Intended: A Cognitivist Reappraisal of the Implied Author." *Poetics Today* 32.3 (2011): 459–85.

Abelson, Robert. "Psychological Status of the Script Concept." *American Psychology* 36 (1981): 715–29.

Admussen, Richard L. *The Samuel Beckett Manuscripts: A Study.* Boston: G. K. Hall, 1979.

Alber, Jan. "Impossible Storyworlds—and What to Do with Them." *Storyworlds* 1 (2009): 79–96.

Alston, W. P. "Ineffability." *Philosophical Review* 65 (1956): 506–22.

Altmann, Gerry T. M., and Jelena Mirković. "Incrementality and Prediction in Human Sentence Processing." *Cognitive Science* 33.4 (2009): 583–609.
Amodio, Mark C. *Writing the Oral Tradition.* Notre Dame, IN: University of Notre Dame Press, 2004.
Amossy, Ruth, and Elisheva Rosen. *Les discours du cliché.* Paris: Société d'édition d'enseignement supérieur, 1982.
Anderson, Sam. "The Underground Man." *New York Times Magazine* (October 23, 2011): 37–41, 63.
Aristotle. "Poetica." *Introduction to Aristotle.* Ed. Richard McKeon. New York: Random House, 1947. 624–67.
Ashberry, John. "The Impossible." *Poetry* 90 (1957): 250–54.
Atran, Scott. *Cognitive Foundations of Natural History: Toward an Anthropology of Science.* Cambridge: Cambridge University Press, 1990.
Atwood, Margaret. "Haunted by Their Nightmares." *The New York Times Book Review.* September 13, 1987: 45–47.
Augustine. *De Doctrina Christiana.* Trans. D. W. Robertson, Jr. Indianapolis, IN: Bobbs-Merrill, 1958.
Bair, Deirdre. *Samuel Beckett: A Biography.* New York: Harcourt, Brace, Jovanovich, 1978.
Bal, Mieke. *Narratology: Introduction to the Theory of Narrative.* 3rd ed. Toronto: University of Toronto Press, 2009.
Baldwin, Hélène. *Samuel Beckett's Real Silence.* University Park, PA: Pennsylvania University Press, 1981.
Ballard, J. G. "The Drowned Giant." In *Chronopolis and Other Stories.* New York: Putnam's, 1971. 33–42.
Banfield, Ann. "Describing the Unobserved: Events Grouped around an Empty Centre." In *The Linguistics of Writing: Arguments between Language and Literature.* Ed. Nigel Fabb et al. New York: Methuen, 1987. 265–85.
———. "Beckett's Tattered Syntax." *Representations* 84 (November 2004): 6–29.
Barge, Laura. *God, the Quest, the Hero: Thematic Structures in Beckett's Fiction.* Chapel Hill: University of North Carolina Department of Romance Languages, 1988.
Barker, Pat. *Regeneration.* New York: Penguin, 1992.
Baron-Cohen, Simon. *Mindblindness: An Essay on Autism and "Theory of Mind."* Cambridge, MA: MIT University Press, 1995.
———. *The Essential Difference: The Truth about the Male and Female Brain.* New York: Perseus Books, 2003.
Barry, Elizabeth. *Beckett and Authority: The Uses of Cliché.* Houndmills: Palgrave Macmillan, 2006.
Barthes, Roland. *S/Z.* Trans. Richard Miller. New York: Hill and Wang, 1974.
Beckett, Samuel. "Dante . . . Bruno. Vico . . . Joyce." In *Our Exagmination Round his Factification for Incamination of Work in Progress.* London: Faber & Faber, 1929. 1–22.
———. *Proust.* New York: Grove, [1931] 1957.
———. *Three Novels: Molloy, Malone Dies, The Unnamable.* New York: Grove, 1965.
———. *More Pricks Than Kicks.* New York: Grove, [1934] 1972.
———. *Disjecta: Miscellaneous Writings and a Dramatic Fragment.* Ed. Ruby Cohn. London: Calder, 1983.
———. *The Collected Shorter Plays of Samuel Beckett.* New York: Grove, 1984.
———. *As the Story Was Told: Uncollected and Late Prose.* London: Calder, 1990.
———. *Eleuthéria.* Trans. Michael Brodsky. New York: Grove, 1995.

———. *Nohow on*. New York: Grove, 1996.

Bell, Michael. "García Márquez, Magical Realism, and World Literature." In *The Cambridge Companion to Gabriel García Márquez*. Ed. Philip Swanson. Cambridge: Cambridge University Press, 2010. 179–95.

Benford, Criscillia. "'Listen to my Tale': Multilevel Structure, Narrative Sense Making, and the Inassimilable in Mary Shelley's *Frankenstein*." *Narrative* 18.3 (2010): 324–46.

Bering, Jesse M. "The Existential Theory of Mind." *Review of General Psychology* 6 (2002): 3–24.

———. *The Belief Instinct: The Psychology of Souls, Destiny, and the Meaning of Life*. New York: Norton, 2011.

Bermudez, Jose Louis. *The Paradox of Self-Consciousness*. Cambridge, MA: MIT Press, 2000.

Blanchot, Maurice. "The Essential Solitude." In *In the Space of Literature*. Trans. Ann Smock. Lincoln: University of Nebraska Press, 1982. 1–34.

Boardman, Michael M. *Narrative Innovation and Incoherence: Ideology in Defoe, Goldsmith, Austen, Eliot, and Hemingway*. Durham: Duke University Press, 1992.

Bordwell, David. "Film Futures." *Substance* 31.1 (2002): 88–104.

Bowers, Susan. "*Beloved* and the New Apocalypse." *Journal of Ethnic Studies* 18.1 (1990): 61–75.

Boyd, Brian. *On the Origin of Stories: Evolution, Cognition, and Fiction*. Cambridge, MA: Harvard University Press, 2009.

Boyle, T. Coraghessan. *Talk Talk*. New York: Penguin, 2006.

Branigan, Edward. "Nearly True: Forking Plots, Forking Interpretations." *SubStance* 31.1 (2002): 105–14.

———. *Projecting a Camera: Language-Games in Film Theory*. New York: Routledge, 2006.

Breithaupt, Fritz. "How Is It Possible to Have Empathy? Four Models." In *Theory of Mind and Literature*. Ed. Paula Leverage et al. Lafayette, IN: Purdue University Press, 2011. 273–88.

Brontë, Emily. *Wuthering Heights*. London: Penguin, 1995.

Brooks, Peter. *Reading for the Plot: Design and Intention in Narrative*. Cambridge: Harvard University Press, 1984.

Brosch, Renate. "The Secret Self: Reading Minds in the Modernist Short Story: Virginia Woolf's 'The Lady in the Looking Glass.'" *The Literary Mind REAL—Yearbook of Research in English and American Literature*. Vol. 24 (2008). Ed. Juergen Schlaeger: 195–214.

Bruner, Jerome. *Actual Minds, Possible Worlds*. Cambridge, MA: Harvard University Press, 1986.

———. *Acts of Meaning*. Cambridge, MA: Harvard University Press, 1991.

———. *Making Stories: Law, Literature, Life*. Cambridge, MA: Harvard University Press, 2003.

Bryden, Mary. *Samuel Beckett and the Idea of God*. Houndmills: Macmillan, 1998.

Buckland, Warren, ed. *Puzzle Films: Complex Storytelling in Contemporary Cinema*. Oxford: Wiley Blackwell, 2009.

Buning, Marius. "The 'Via Negativa' and its First Stirrings in *Eleutheria*." In *Beckett and Religion: Beckett, Aesthetics, Politics/Beckett et la religion: Beckett, l'esthétique, la politique*. Ed. Marius Buning et al. Amsterdam & Atlanta: Rodopi, 2000. 43–54.

Butte, George. *I Know that You Know that I Know: Narrating Subjects from* Moll Flanders *to* Marnie. Columbus: The Ohio State University Press, 2004.

Cameron, Allan. *Modular Narratives in Contemporary Cinema*. London: Palgrave Macmillan, 2008.

Campbell, George van Pelt. *Everything You Know Seems Wrong: Globalization and the Revitalizing of Tradition*. Lanham, MD: University Press of America, 2005.

Chafe, Wallace. *Discourse, Consciousness, and Time: The Flow and Displacement of Conscious Experience in Speaking and Writing.* Chicago: Chicago University Press, 1994.
Chase, Richard. *Herman Melville: a Critical Study.* New York: Macmillan, 1949.
Chatman, Seymour. *Story and Discourse: Narrative Structure in Fiction and Film.* Ithaca, NY: Cornell University Press, 1978.
———. *Coming to Terms: The Rhetoric of Narrative in Fiction and Film.* Ithaca, NY: Cornell University Press, 1990.
Chomsky, Noam. *Syntactic Structures.* The Hague: Mouton, 1957.
Clark, Andy. *Being There: Putting Brain, Body, and World Together Again.* Cambridge, MA: MIT Press, 1997.
Clark, James Midgley. *Meister Eckhart: An Introduction to the Study of His Works with an Anthology of His Sermons.* Edinburgh: Thomas Nelson, 1957.
Coetzee, J. M. *Waiting for the Barbarians.* Harmondsworth: Penguin, 1982.
———. *Life and Times of Michael K.* New York: Viking Penguin, 1985.
———. *Foe.* London: Penguin, 1987.
———. (1999a) *The Lives of Animals.* Princeton: Princeton University Press, 1999.
———. (1999b) *Disgrace.* London: Secker & Warburg, 1999.
Cohn, Dorrit. *Transparent Minds: Narrative Modes for Presenting Consciousness in Fiction.* Princeton, NJ: Princeton University Press, 1978.
———. *The Distinction of Fiction.* Baltimore: Johns Hopkins University Press, 1998.
Coleridge, Samuel Taylor. *Biographia Literaria.* Ed. James Engell and W. Jackson Bate. London: Routledge & Kegan Paul, 1983.
Conrad, Joseph. *Heart of Darkness.* 2nd ed. Ed. D. C. R. A. Goonetilleke. Peterborough, Ont.: Broadview Press, 1999.
Crick, Francis. *The Astonishing Hypothesis: The Scientific Search for the Soul.* New York: Scribner, 1995.
Culler, Jonathan. *Structuralist Poetics: Structuralism, Linguistics, and the Study of Literature.* Ithaca, NY: Cornell University Press, 1975.
———. *The Pursuit of Signs: Semiotics, Literature, Deconstruction.* Ithaca, NY: Cornell University Press, 1981.
Damasio, Antonio. *The Feeling of What Happens: Body and Emotion in the Making of Consciousness.* New York: Harcourt, 1999.
———. *Self Comes to Mind: Constructing the Conscious Brain.* New York: Pantheon, 2010.
Dante Alighieri. *The Divine Comedy.* Trans. C. H. Sisson. Manchester: Carcanet, 1980.
Darwin, Charles. *The Origin of Species by Means of Natural Selection; The Descent of Man and Selection in Relation to Sex.* Chicago: Encyclopedia Britannica, 1952.
Davis, Mary E. "The Voyage Beyond the Map: 'El Ahogado Más Hermoso del Mundo.'" In *Critical Essays on Gabriel García Márquez.* Ed. George R. MacMurray. Boston: G. K. Hall, 1987. 159–68.
Dawkins, Richard. *The Selfish Gene.* 2nd ed. Oxford: Oxford University Press, 1989.
Decety, Jean, and P. L. Jackson. "The Functional Architecture of Human Empathy." *Behavioral and Cognitive Neuroscience Reviews* 3 (2004): 71–100.
Delbanco, Andrew. *Melville: His World and Work.* New York: Knopf, 2005.
Deleuze, Gilles. "L'épuisé." In Samuel Beckett, *Quad et autres pièces pour la television.* Paris: Minuit, 1992. 55–106.
Denard, Carolyn C., ed. *Toni Morrison: Conversations.* Jackson: University Press of Mississippi, 2008.
Dennett, Daniel C. *Consciousness Explained.* Boston: Little, Brown, 1991.

Derrida, Jacques. *Acts of Literature.* Ed. Derek Attridge. New York: Routledge, 1990.
DiMaggio, Paul. "Culture and Cognition." *Annual Review of Sociology* 23 (1997): 263–85.
Dissanayake, Ellen. *Homo Aestheticus: Where Art Comes from and Why.* New York: Free Press, 1992.
Doležel, Lubomír. *Heterocosmica: Fiction and Possible Worlds.* Baltimore: Johns Hopkins University Press, 1998.
Donald, Merlin. *The Origins of the Modern Mind.* Cambridge, MA: Harvard University Press, 1991.
Dubrow, Heather. "The Interplay of Narrative and Lyric: Competition, Cooperation, and the Case of the Anticipatory Amalgam." *Narrative* 14.3 (2006): 264–71.
Eckhart, Meister. *Meister Eckhart: the Complete Works.* Trans. M. O. C. Walsh. Longmead: Element Books, 1987.
Eco, Umberto. *The Role of the Reader: Explorations in the Semiotics of Texts.* Bloomington: Indiana University Press, 1979.
———. *The Open Work.* Trans. Anna Cancogni. Cambridge, MA: Harvard University Press, 1989.
Edelman, David Louis. "Tim O'Brien Full Interview Transcript." October 1, 1994. http://www.davidlouisedelman.com/author-interviews/tim-obrien-full/
Edelman, Gerald, and Jiulio Tononi. *A Universe of Consciousness: How Matter Becomes Imagination.* New York: Basic Books, 2001.
Elsaesser, Thomas. "The Mind-Game Film." In *Puzzle Films.* Ed. Warren Buckland, 2009. 13–41.
Emonds, Joseph E. *Lexicon and Grammar: The English Syntacticon.* Berlin: DeGruyter, 2000.
Esslin, Martin. *The Theatre of the Absurd.* New York: Doubleday, 1961.
Faris, Wendy B. *Ordinary Enchantments: Magical Realism and the Remystification of Narrative.* Nashville, TN: Vanderbilt University Press, 2004.
Filmore, Charles J. *Lectures on Deixis.* Stanford, CA: CSLI Publications, 1997.
Fish, Stanley. *Is There a Text in this Class? The Authority of Interpretive Communities.* Cambridge, MA: Harvard University Press, 1980.
Fludernik, Monica. *Towards a "Natural" Narratology.* London: Routledge, 1996.
———. *An Introduction to Narratology.* New York: Routledge, 2009.
Franke, William, ed. *On What Cannot Be Said: Apophatic Discourses in Philosophy, Religion, and the Arts.* Vol. 1, *Classic Formulations.* Notre Dame: University of Notre Dame Press, 2007.
Freeland, Cynthia A. "The Sublime in Cinema." In *Passionate Views: Film, Cognition, and Emotion.* Ed. Carl Plantiga and Greg M. Smith. Baltimore: Johns Hopkins University Press, 1999. 65–83.
Gallese, Vittorio. "The 'Shared Manifold' Hypothesis: from Mirror Neurons to Empathy." *Journal of Consciousness Studies* 8 (2001): 33–50.
García Márquez, Gabriel. "El ahogado mas hermoso del mundo." *Todos los cuentos de Gabriel García Márquez (1947–1972).* Barcelona: Plaza y Janés, [1968]1978. 239–45.
———. *Collected Stories.* Trans. Gregory Rabassa. New York: HarperCollins, 1999.
———. *Conversations with Gabriel García Márquez.* Ed. Gene H. Bell-Villada. Jackson, MS: University Press of Mississippi, 2006.
———. "Nobel Lecture: The Solitude of Latin America." *Nobelprize.org.* 8-26-2012. http://www.nobelprize.org/nobel_prizes/literature/laureates/1982/marquez-lecture.html.
Gazzaniga, Michael S. *The Mind's Past.* Berkeley: University of California Press, 1998.
———. *The Ethical Brain.* New York: Dana Press, 2005.

Gelman, Susan A., Marianne Taylor, and Simone Nguyen. *Mother-Child Conversations about Gender: Understanding the Acquisition of Essentialist Beliefs.* Oxford: Blackwell, 2004.

Genette, Girard. *Narrative Discourse: An Essay in Method.* Trans. Jane E. Lewin. Ithaca, NY: Cornell University Press, 1980.

Gerrig, Richard. *Experiencing Narrative Worlds: On the Psychological Activities of Reading.* New Haven: Yale University Press, 1993.

Gladwell, Malcolm. *Outliers: The Story of Success.* New York: Back Bay Books, 2011.

Goffman, Erving. *Frame Analysis: An Essay on the Organization of Experience.* Boston: Northeastern University Press, 1986.

Goichman, Samuel. [Review of *In the Lake of the Woods*]. *Publishers Weekly* (October 1994). http://www.publishersweekly.com/978-0-395-48889-8

Goldstein, Joshua. *Winning the War on War: The Decline of Armed Conflict Worldwide.* New York: Dutton/Plume, 2011.

Goodman, Nelson. *Ways of World-Making.* Indianapolis: Hackett, 1978.

Goody, Jack. *The Interface between the Written and the Oral.* Cambridge: Cambridge University Press, 1987.

Grewal, Gurleen. *Circles of Sorrow, Lines of Struggle: The Novels of Toni Morrison.* Baton Rouge: Louisiana State University Press, 1998.

Grice, Paul. "Logic and Conversation" [1975]. In *Studies in the Way of Words.* Cambridge, MA: Harvard University Press, 1989. 22–40.

Grossmann, Tobias, and Amrisha Vaish. "Reading Faces in Infancy: Developing a Multi-Level Analysis of a Social Stimulus." In *Social Cognition: Development, Neuroscience and Autism.* Ed. T. Striano and V. Reid. Oxford: Blackwell, 2008. 167–80.

Haddon, Mark. *The Curious Incident of the Dog in the Night-Time.* New York: Vintage, 2004.

Hamburger, Käte. *The Logic of Fiction.* Trans. Marilynn Rose. Bloomington: Indiana University Press, 1973.

Haneke, Michael. "Documentary on Director Michael Haneke." *Caché.* DVD: Sony Pictures Classic Films, 2006.

Hanson, Clare. "'Things Out of Words': Towards a Poetics of Short Fiction." In *Rereading the Short Story.* Ed. Clare Hanson. Houndmills: Macmillan, 1989. 22–33.

Harding, Sandra, and Jean F. O'Barr. *Sex and Scientific Inquiry.* Chicago: University of Chicago Press, 1987.

Harrison, Kathryn. *The Seal Wife.* New York: Random House, 2002.

Hauser, Marc D. *Moral Minds: How Nature Designed our Universal Sense of Right and Wrong.* Boston: Little, Brown, 2008.

Havelock, Eric. *Preface to Plato.* Cambridge, MA: Belknap Press of Harvard University Press, 1963.

———. *The Muse Learns to Write: Reflections on Orality and Literacy from Antiquity to the Present.* New Haven: Yale University Press, 1986.

Hawkins, Peter S., and Anne H. Schotter, eds. *Ineffability: Naming the Unnamable from Dante to Beckett.* Brooklyn: AMS Press, 1984.

Heidegger, Martin. *Grundprobleme der Phänomenologie (1919–1920).* Gesamtausgaba Band 58. Frankfort: Germany: Vittorio Klostermann, 1993.

Hemingway, Ernest. *The Sun Also Rises.* New York: Scribner's, 1926.

———. *The Short Stories.* New York: Scribner's, 1966.

———. *Death in the Afternoon.* New York: Scribner's, [1932] 1996.

Herman, David, ed. *Narratologies: New Perspectives on Narrative Analysis.* Columbus: The Ohio State University Press, 1999.

———. *Story Logic: Problems and Possibilities of Narrative.* Lincoln: University of Nebraska Press, 2002.

———. "Introduction." In *Narrative Theory and the Cognitive Sciences.* Ed. David Herman. Stanford: CSLI Publications, 2003. 1–30.

———. "Narrative Theory and the Intentional Stance." *Partial Answers* 6.2 (2008): 233–60.

Hernadi, Paul. "The Erotics of Retrospection: Historytelling, Audience Response, and the Strategies of Desire." *New Literary History* 12 (1981): 243–52.

———. "Why is Literature: A Co-Evolutionary Perspective on Imaginative World-Making." *Poetics Today* 23.1 (2002): 21–42.

Hogan, Patrick Colm. *On Interpretation: Meaning and Inference in Law, Psychoanalysis, and Literature.* Athens: University of Georgia Press, 1996.

———. *The Mind and Its Stories: Narrative Universals and Human Emotion.* Cambridge: Cambridge University Press, 2003.

———. *Affective Narratology: The Emotional Structure of Stories.* Lincoln: University of Nebraska Press, 2011.

Holy Bible Containing the Old and New Testament. Boston: Whittemore Associates, 1949.

Huettel, Scott A. et al. "Prefrontal Cortex Activation is Evoked by the Violation of Local Stimulus Expectations." <wysiwyg://39http://www.biac.duke.edu/research/talks/SFN_2001.asp>).

Hutto, Daniel. *The Presence of Mind.* Philadelphia: John Benjamins, 1999.

Ingarden, Roman. *Das literarische Kunstwerk. Eine Untersuchung aus dem Grenzgebiet der Ontologie, Logik und Literaturwissenschaft.* Halle: Niemeyer, 1931.

Innis, Harold A. *The Bias of Communication.* Toronto: University of Toronto Press, 1951.

Intrator, J., et al. "A Brain Imaging (SPECT) Study of Semantic and Affective Processing in Psychopaths." *Biological Psychiatry* 42 (1997): 96–103.

Iser, Wolfgang. *The Implied Reader: Patterns of communication in Prose Fiction from Bunyan to Beckett.* Baltimore: Johns Hopkins University Press, 1974.

———. *The Act of Reading: A Theory of Aesthetic Response.* Baltimore: Johns Hopkins University Press, 1978.

———. *The Range of Interpretation.* New York: Columbia University Press, 2000.

Jackendoff, Ray. *Semantics and Cognition.* Cambridge, MA: MIT Press, 1983.

———. *Consciousness and the Computational Mind.* Cambridge, MA: MIT Press, 1987.

Jackson, Tony. *The Technology of the Novel: Writing and Narrative in British Fiction.* Baltimore: Johns Hopkins University Press, 2009.

Jacobson, Roman. "Shifters, Verbal Categories, and the Russian Verb." In *Selected Writings.* Vol. 2. The Hague: Mouton, 1971. 103–47.

Jahn, Manfred. "Speak Friend and Enter: Garden Paths, Artificial Intelligence, and Cognitive Narratology." In *Narratologies.* Ed. David Herman, 1999. 167–94.

James, Henry. "The Art of Fiction." In *The Future of the Novel.* Ed. Leon Edel. New York: Vintage, 1956. 3–27.

James, William. *The Varieties of Religious Experience.* Ed. Martin E. Marty. Harmondsworth: Penguin, 1983.

Jameson, Fredric. *The Political Unconscious: Narrative as a Socially Symbolic Act.* Ithaca, NY: Cornell University Press, 1981.

Jesperson, Otto. *Language: Its Nature, Development and Origin.* London: Allen and Unwin, 1922.

Johansson, Birgitta. "Beckett and the Apophatic in Selected Shorter Texts." In *Beckett and Religion: Beckett, Aesthetics, Politics/Beckett et la religion: Beckett, l'esthétique, la politique.* Ed. Marius Buning, et al. Amsterdam & Atlanta: Rodopi, 2000. 55–66.

Juliet, Charles. *Rencontre avec Samuel Beckett.* Paris: Fata Morgana, 1986.
Keen, Suzanne. *Empathy and the Novel.* Oxford: Oxford University Press, 2007.
Kellogg, Ronald. *The Psychology of Writing.* Oxford: Oxford University Press, 1994.
Kenner, Hugh. *Samuel Beckett: A Critical Study.* New York: Grove, 1961.
———."Who Else but Sam?" *New York Times Book Review.* 4 December 1977.
———. "Beckett at Eighty." *Historical Fictions.* San Francisco: Northpoint Press, 1990. 289–95.
Kenyon, Frederick C. *Books and Readers in Ancient Greece and Rome.* Oxford: Clarendon Press, 1937.
Kermode, Frank. *The Genesis of Secrecy: On the Interpretation of Narrative.* Cambridge, MA: Harvard University Press, 1979.
Kierkegaard, Søren. *Philosophical Fragments, or a Fragment of Philosophy.* Trans. David F. Swenson. Princeton, NJ: Princeton University Press, 1936.
Klein, Stanley B., Leda Cosmides, and K. Costabile. "Preserved Knowledge of Self in a Case of Alzheimer's Dementia." *Social Cognition* 21 (2003): 157–65.
Klein, Stanley B., and C. E. Gangi. "The Multiplicity of Self: Neuropsychological Evidence and its Implications for the Self as a Construct in Psychological Research." *The Year in Cognitive Neuroscience 2010: Annals of the New York Academy of Sciences* 1191 (2010): 1–15.
Koch, Christoff. *The Quest for Consciousness: A Neurobiological Approach.* Greenwood Village, CO: Roberts, 2004.
Krebs, Paula M. "Next Time, Fail Better." *The Chronicle of Higher Education* (May 6, 2012) http://chronicle.com/article/Next-Time-Fail-Better/131790/
Kukla, André. *Ineffability and Philosophy.* Abingdon: Routledge, 2005.
Laass, Eva. *Broken Taboos, Subjective Truths: Forms and Functions of Unreliable Narration in Contemporary American Cinema.* Trier: Wissenschaftlicher Verlag Trier, 2008.
Lakoff, George, and Mark Johnson. *Metaphors We Live By.* Chicago: Chicago University Press, 1980.
———. *Philosophy in the Flesh: The Embodied Mind and its Challenge to Western Thought.* New York: Basic Books, 1999.
Lawson, Mark. "Guilt, Lies, and Videotape." *The Guardian,* January 20, 2006. http://arts.guardian.co.uk/features/story/0,,16904280,00.html
Lerner, Laurence. "Cliché and Commonplace." *Essays in Criticism* 6.1 (1956): 249–65.
Levinas, Emmanuel. *Emmanuel Levinas: Basic Philosophical Writings.* Ed. Adriaan T. Peperzak, Simon Critchley, and Robert Bernasconi. Bloomington: Indiana University Press, 1996.
Li, Stephanie. *Toni Morrison: A Biography.* Santa Barbara, CA: ABC/CLIO, 2010.
Lodge, David. *The Modes of Modern Writing: Metaphor, Metonymy, and the Typology of Modern Literature.* Chicago: University of Chicago Press, 1977.
Lohafer, Susan. *Reading for Storyness: Preclosure Theory, Empirical Poetics, and Culture in the Short Story.* Baltimore: Johns Hopkins University Press, 2003.
Lorant, Laurie Robertson. *Melville: A Biography.* New York: Clarkson Potter, 1996.
Ludwin, Dawn M. *Blaise Pascal's Quest for the Ineffable.* New York: Peter Lang, 2001.
Mahafey, Vicki. *Modernist Literature: Challenging Fictions.* Oxford: Blackwell, 2007.
Malina, Debra. *Breaking the Frame: Metalepsis and the Construction of the Subject.* Columbus: The Ohio State University Press, 2002.
Mandler, George. *Mind and Body: Psychology of Emotion and Stress.* New York: Norton, 1984.
Mansfield, Katherine. "At the Bay." In *Stories.* New York: Norton, 1991. 97–134.

Mar, Raymond A. "The Neuropsychology of Narrative: Story Comprehension, Story Production and their Interrelation." *Neuropsychologia* 42.10 (2004): 1414–1434.

———. "The Neural Bases of Social Cognition and Story Comprehension." *Annual Review of Psychology* 62 (2011): 103–34.

Mar, Raymond A., and Keith Oatley. "The Function of Fiction is the Abstraction and Simulation of Social Experience." *Perspectives on Psychological Science* 3 (2008): 173–92.

Margolin, Uri. "Cognitive Science, the Thinking Mind, and Literary Narrative." In *Narrative Theory and the Cognitive Sciences.* Ed. David Herman. Stanford: CSLI Publications, 2003. 271–94.

Marcus, Matthew. "Wait-and-See Strategies for Parsing Natural Language." Working—MIT Paper 75, 1974. http://dspace.mit.edu/bitstream/handle/1721.1/41110/AI_WP_075.pdf?sequence=4

———. *A Theory of Syntactic Recognition for Natural Language.* Cambridge, MA: MIT Press, 1980.

Martin, Henri-Jean. *The History and Power of Writing.* Trans. Lydia Cochrane. Chicago: Chicago University Press, 1994.

Mathis, Gilles, ed. *Le cliché.* Toulouse: Presses universitaires du Mirail, 1998.

Maturana, Humberto, and Francisco Varela. *The Tree of Knowledge: The Roots of Human Understanding.* Boston: Shambhala Press, 1998 [1987].

Mauss, Marcel. "A category of the human mind: the notion of person; the notion of Self." In *The category of the person: Anthropology, Philosophy, History.* Trans. W. D. Halls. Ed. Michael Carrithers, Steven Collins, and Steven Lukes. Cambridge: Cambridge University Press, 1985. 1–25.

Mayr, Ernst. *What Evolution Is.* New York: Basic Books, 2001.

McHale, Brian. *Postmodernist Fiction.* London: Routledge, 1987.

———. "Beginning to Think about Narrative in Poetry." *Narrative* 17.1 (2009): 11–27.

Melville, Herman. "Bartleby the Scrivener." In *Selected Tales and Poems.* Ed. Richard Chase. New York: Rinehart, 1957. 92–131.

Mendoza, Plinio Apuleyo, and Gabriel García Márquez. *El olor de la guayaba.* Barcelona: Mondadori, [1982] 1994.

Miall, David S. *Literary Reading: Empirical and Theoretical Studies.* New York: Peter Lang, 2006.

Mignon, Paul-Louis. "Le théâtre de A jusqu'à Z: Samuel Beckett." *L'avant-scène du théâtre* 313 (15 juin 1964): 8.

Milius, John, and Francis Ford Coppola. *Apocalypse Now Redux.* New York: Hyperion, 2000.

Miller, J. Hillis. *Hawthorne and History: Defacing It.* Cambridge, MA: Basil Blackwell, 1991.

Miller, Joseph D. "The 'Novel' Novel: A Sociobiological Analysis of the Novelty Drive as Expressed in Science Fiction." In *Biopoetics: Evolutionary Explorations in the Arts.* Ed. Brett Cook and Frederick Turner. Lexington, KY: ICUS Books, 1999. 315–34.

Milton, John. *The Student's Milton.* Ed. Frank Allen Patterson. New York: Appleton-Century-Crofts, 1957.

Minsky, Marvin. *The Society of Mind.* New York: Simon & Schuster, 1988.

Mithin, Steven. *The Singing Neanderthals: The Origins of Music, Language, Mind, and Body.* Cambridge, MA: Harvard University Press, 2006.

Morgan, Monique R. *Narrative Means, Lyric Ends: Temporality in the Nineteenth-Century British Long Poem.* Columbus: The Ohio State University Press, 2009.

Morrison, Toni. (1987a) *Beloved.* New York: Knopf, 1987.

———. (1987b) "The Site of Memory." In *Inventing the Truth: The Art and Craft of Memoir.* Ed. Willam Zinsser. Boston: 1987. 103–24.

———. "Unspeakable Things Unspoken: The Afro-American Presence in American Literature." *Michigan Quarterly Review* 28.1 (1988): 1–34.

Munro, Alice. "Fits." In *Selected Stories.* New York: Vintage, 1996. 429–53.

Ng, David. "Memories of Murder Hidden in Plain Sight: Austrian Director Michael Haneke Evokes the Power of Nightmares." *Village Voice* (2005): http://www.villagevoice.com/2005-12-06/film/memories-of-murder/full/

Nelles, William. *Frameworks: Narrative Levels and Embedded Narrative.* New York: Peter Lang, 1997.

Nuckolls, Charles W. "Cognitive Anthropology." In *A Companion to Cognitive Science.* Ed. William Bechtel and George Graham. Oxford: Blackwell, 1999. 140–45.

Oatley, Keith. "Theory of Mind and Theory of Minds in Literature." In *Theory of Mind and Literature.* Ed. Paula Leverage et al. West Lafayette, IN: Purdue University Press, 2011. 13–26.

O'Brien, Tim. "The Magic Show." In *Writers on Writing.* Ed. Robert Pack and Jay Parini. Middlebury, VT: Middlebury College Press, 1991. 175–83.

———. (1994a) *In the Lake of the Woods.* New York: Penguin, 1994.

———. (1994b) "The Vietnam in Me." *New York Times Magazine* (October 2, 1994). http://www.nytimes.com/books/98/09/20/specials/obrien-vietnam.html

O'Connor, Flannery. *Mystery and Manners: Occasional Prose.* Ed. Sally Fitzgerald and Robert Fitzgerald. New York: Farrar, Straus, and Giroux, 1961.

Ohmann, Richard. "Speech, Literature, and the Space Between." *New Literary History* 4 (1972): 47–63.

Olson, David. *The World on Paper: The Conceptual and Cognitive Implications of Writing and Reading.* Cambridge: Cambridge University Press, 1994.

Ong, Walter. *Orality and Literacy: The Technologizing of the Word.* London: Methuen, 1982.

———. "Writing is a Technology that Restructures Thought." In *The Written Word: Literacy in Transition.* Ed. Gerd Baumann. Oxford: Clarendon Press, 1986. 23–50.

Oyama, Susan. *Evolution's Eye: A Systems View of the Biology-Culture Divide.* Durham: Duke University Press, 2000.

Palmer, Alan. *Fictional Minds.* Lincoln: University of Nebraska Press, 2004.

———. *Social Minds in the Novel.* Columbus: The Ohio State University Press, 2010.

Pavel, Thomas. *Fictional Worlds.* Cambridge, MA: Harvard University Press, 1986.

Penrose, Roger. *The Emperor's New Mind: Concerning Computers, Minds, and the Laws of Physics.* Oxford: Oxford University Press, 1989.

Peperzak, Adriaan. *To the Other: An Introduction to the Philosophy of Emmanuel Levinas.* West Lafayette, IN: Purdue University Press, 1993.

Pérez-Peña, Richard. "Commencement Speakers: Familiar Faces Offering Advice, Idealism, and Humor." *New York Times,* June 16, 2012. http://www.nytimes.com/2012/06/17/us/graduation-speakers-offer-advice-idealism-and-humor.html?pagewanted=all&_r=0

Perloff, Marjorie. *The Poetics of Indeterminacy: Rimbaud to Cage.* Evanston, IL: Northwestern University Press, 1983.

Perry, Menakhem, and Meir Sternberg. "The King Through Ironic Eyes: Biblical Narrative and the Literary Reading Process." *Poetics Today* 7.2 [1968] (1986): 275–322.

Phelan, James. *Reading People, Reading Plots: Character, Progression, and the Interpretation of Narrative.* Chicago: University of Chicago Press: 1989.

———. *Narrative as Rhetoric: Technique, Audiences, Ethics, Ideology.* Columbus: The Ohio State University Press, 1996.

———. *Experiencing Fiction: Judgments, Progressions, and the Rhetorical Theory of Narrative.* Columbus: The Ohio State University Press, 2007.
———. "'I Affirm Nothing': *Lord Jim* and the Uses of Textual Recalcitrance." In *Joseph Conrad: Voice, Sequence, History, Genre.* Ed. Jakob Lothe, Jeremy Hawthorn, and James Phelan. Columbus: The Ohio State University Press, 2008. 41–59.
———. "Progression, Speed, and Judgment in 'Das Urteil.'" In *Franz Kafka: Narration, Rhetoric, and Reading.* Ed. Jakob Lothe, Beatrice Sandberg, and Ronald Speirs. Columbus: The Ohio State University Press: 2011. 22–29.
Pinker, Steven. *The Language Instinct: How the Mind Creates Language.* New York: William Morrow, 1994.
———. *How the Mind Works.* New York: Norton, 1997.
———. *The Blank Slate.* New York: Viking, 2002.
———. *The Better Angels of Our Nature: Why Violence Has Declined.* New York: Viking, 2011.
Plimpton, George, ed. "Ernest Hemingway" [interview]. *Writers at Work: The* Paris Review *Interviews: Second Series.* New York: Viking, 1965. 215–39.
Plotnitsky, Arkady. *The Knowable and the Unknowable: Modern Science, Nonclassical Thought, and the "Two Cultures."* Ann Arbor: University of Michigan Press, 2002.
Porton, Richard. "Collective Guilt and Individual Responsibility: An Interview with Michael Haneke." *Cinéaste* 31 (2005): 50–51.
Pound, Ezra. *ABC of Reading.* London: Faber & Faber, 1961.
Pratt, Mary Louise. *Toward a Speech-Act Theory of Literary Discourse.* Bloomington: Indiana University Press, 1977.
Premack, David G., and Guy Woodruff. "Does the Chimpanzee Have a Theory of Mind?" *Behavioral and Brain Sciences* 1 (1978): 515–26.
Preston, Stephanie, and Frans de Waal. "Empathy: Its Ultimate and Proximate Bases." *Behavioral and Brain Sciences* 25 (2002): 1–72.
Prince, Gerald. *Dictionary of Narratology.* 2nd ed. Lincoln: University of Nebraska Press, [1987] 2003.
Proust, Marcel. *Remembrance of Things Past.* Vol. 3. Trans. C. K. Scott Moncrieff and Terence Kilmartin. New York: Vintage, 1982.
Pseudo-Dionysius. *The Complete Works.* Trans. Colm Luibheid. New York: Paulist Press, 1987.
Rabinowitz, Peter J. *Before Reading: Narrative Conventions and the Politics of Interpretration.* Ithaca, NY: Cornell University Press, 1987.
———. "'A Lot has been built Up': Omission and Rhetorical Realism in Dostoevsky's *The Gambler.*" *Narrative* 9.2 (May 2001): 203–9.
Rader, Ralph. *Fact, Fiction, and Form: Selected Essays.* Ed. James Phelan and David H. Richter. Columbus: The Ohio State University Press, 2011.
Redfern, Walter. *Clichés and Coinages.* Oxford: Basil Blackwell, 1989.
Reid, Alec. *All I Can Manage, More than I Could: An Approach to the Plays of Samuel Beckett.* Dublin: Dolmen Press, 1968.
Richards, I. A. *Principles of Literary Criticism.* London: Kegan Paul, 1924.
Richardson, Alan. *The Neural Sublime: Cognitive Theories and Romantic Texts.* Baltimore: Johns Hopkins University Press, 2010.
Richardson, Brian. *Unnatural Voices: Extreme Narration in Modern and Contemporary Fiction.* Columbus: The Ohio State University Press, 2006.
Ricks, Christopher. *Keats and Embarrassment.* Oxford: Oxford University Press, 1974.
Ricoeur, Paul. *Time and Narrative, Vol. I.* Trans. Kathleen McLaughlin and David Pellauer. Chicago: University of Chicago Press, 1984.

Risser, James. *Hermeneutics and the Voice of the Other: Re-Reading Gadamer's Philosophical Hermeneutics.* Albany: SUNY Press, 1997.

Rizzolatti, Giacomo, Luciano Fadiga, Vittorio Gallese, and Leonardo Fogassi. "Premotor Cortex and the Recognition of Motor Actions." *Cognitive Brain Research* 3 (1996): 131–41.

Robbe-Grillet, Alain. "Samuel Beckett, or Presence on the Stage." In *For a New Novel: Essays on Fiction.* Trans. Richard Howard. New York: Grove, 1965. 111–25.

Robertson, Roland. *Globalization: Social Theory and Social Culture.* London: Sage, 1992.

Rumelhart, David E. "Notes on a Schema for Stories." In *Representations and Understanding.* Ed. D. G. Bobrow and A. Collins. New York: Academic Press, 1975. 211–36.

Ryan, Marie-Laure. *Possible Worlds, Artificial Intelligence, and Narrative Theory.* Bloomington: Indiana University Press, 1991.

Sacks, Oliver. *The Man Who Mistook his Wife for a Hat.* New York: Summit Books, 1985.

Savarese, Ralph James. *Reasonable People: A Memoir of Autism and Adoption.* New York: Other Press, 2007.

Savarese, Ralph James, and Lisa Zunshine. "The Critic as Neurocosmopolite; Or, What Cognitive Approaches to Literature Can Learn from Disability Studies: Lisa Zunshine in conversation with Ralph James Savarese." *Narrative* 22.1 (January 2014).

Schank, Roger C. *Tell Me a Story: Narrative and Intelligence.* Evanston: Northwestern University Press, 1990.

Schank, Roger C., and Robert Abelson. *Scripts, Plans, and Goals.* Hillsdale, NJ: Erlbaum, 1977.

Schjeldahl, Peter. "Words and Pictures." *The New Yorker* 82.32 (2005): 162–68.

Seidenberg, M. S., Tanenhaus, M. K., Leiman, J. M., and Bienkowski, M. "Automatic access of the meaning of ambiguous words in context: Some limitations of knowledge-based processing." *Cognitive Psychology* 14 (1982): 489–537.

Shepard, Roger. "Ecological Constraints on Internal Representation: Resonant Kinematics of Perceiving, Imagining, Thinking, and Dreaming." *Psychological Review* 91.4 (October 1984): 417–47.

Shklovsky, Viktor. *Theory of the Novel.* Trans. Benjamin Sher. Elmwood Park, IL: Dalkey Archive, 1990.

Smith, Barbara Herrnstein. "Narrative Versions, Narrative Theories." In *On Narrative.* Ed. W. J. T. Mitchell. Chicago: University of Chicago Press, 1981. 209–32.

Smith, Michael B. *Toward the Outside: Concepts and Themes in Emmanuel Levinas.* Pittsburgh: Duquesne University Press, 2005.

Spolsky, Ellen. *Gaps in Nature: Literary Interpretation and the Modular Mind.* Albany: SUNY Press, 1993.

Stein, Gertrude. *Look at Me Now and Here I Am: Writings and Lectures 1909–1945.* Ed. Patricia Meyerowitz. Harmondsworth: Penguin, 1971.

———. (1998a) *Tender Buttons.* In *Writings: 1903–1932.* Ed. Catharine R. Stimpson and Harriet Chessman. New York: Library of America, 1998. 313–55.

———. (1998b) "What Are Master-Pieces and Why are There so Few of Them." In *Writings: 1932–1946.* Ed. Catharine R. Stimpson and Harriet Chessman. New York: Library of America, 1998. 355–63.

Steinecke, Hartmut. "The Novel and the Individual: The Significance of Goethe's *Wilhelm Meister* in the Debate about the Bildungsroman." In *Reflection and Action: Essays on the Bildungsroman.* Ed. James Harden. Columbia: University of South Carolina Press, 1991.

Steiner, Wendy. *Exact Resemblance to Exact Resemblance: The Literary Portraiture of Gertrude Stein.* New Haven: Yale University Press, 1978.

Sternberg, Meir. *Expositional Modes and Temporal Ordering in Fiction.* Baltimore: Johns Hopkins University Press, 1978.

———. "Telling in Time (II): Chronology, Teleology, Narrativity." *Poetics Today* 13.3 (1992): 463–561.

———. "Telling in Time (III): Chronology, Estrangement, and Stories of Literary History." *Poetics Today* 27.1 (2006): 125–235.

Stewart, Garrett. *Reading Voices: Literature and the Phonotext*. Berkeley: University of California Press, 1990.

Stockwell, Peter. "Scripts and Schemas." *Cognitive Poetics: An Introduction*. London: Routledge, 2002. 75–89.

Stoker, Bram. *Dracula*. New York: Barnes & Noble, 1992.

Strawson, Galen. "Against Narrativity." *Ratio* 17.4 (2004): 428–52.

Swinney, D. A. "Lexical Access During Sentence Comprehension: (Re)consideration of Context Effects." *Journal of Verbal Learning and Verbal Behavior* 18 (1979): 645–60.

Taleb, Nassim Nicholas. *The Black Swan: The Impact of the Highly Improbable*. New York: Random House, 2007.

Taylor, Claire. "García Márquez and Film." In *The Cambridge Companion to Gabriel García Márquez*. Ed. Philip Swanson. Cambridge: Cambridge University Press, 2010. 160–78.

Thorndyke, P. W. "Cognitive Structures in Comprehension and Memory of Narrative Discourse." *Cognitive Psychology* 9 (1977): 77–110.

Trollope, Anthony. *Barchester Towers*. London: Dent, nd.

Tsur, Reuven. "Two Critical Attitudes: Quest for Certitude and Negative Capability." *College English* 36/7 (March 1975): 776–88.

Turner, Mark. *Reading Minds: The Study of English in the Age of Cognitive Science*. Princeton: Princeton University Press, 1991.

Van der Hoeden, Jean. *Samuel Beckett et la question de Dieu*. Paris: Éditions du Cerf, 1997.

Varela, Francisco, Evan Thompson, and Eleanor Rosche. *The Embodied Mind: Cognitive Science and Human Experience*. Cambridge, MA: MIT Press, 1991.

Verplaetse, Jan, et al. *The Moral Brain: Essays on the Evolutionary and Neuroscientific Aspects of Morality*. New York: Springer, 2009.

Walsh, Richard. "The Common Basis of Narrative and Music: Somatic, Social, and Affective Foundations." *Storyworlds* 3 (2011): 49–72.

Warhol, Robyn. "Neonarrative: or, How to Render the Unnarratable in Realist Fiction and Contemporary Film." In *A Companion to Narrative Theory*. Ed. James Phelan and Peter Rabinowitz. Oxford: Blackwell, 2005. 220–31.

Waters, Malcolm. *Globalization*. 2nd ed. London: Routledge, [1995] 2001.

Wegner, Daniel M. *The Illusion of Conscious Will*. Cambridge, MA: MIT Press, 2003.

Weinstein, Philip. *Unknowing: The Work of Modernist Fiction*. Ithaca, NY: Cornell University Press, 2005.

Wheatley, Catherine. "Secrets, Lies, and Videotapes." *Sight & Sound* 16.2 (2006): 32–36.

White, Allon. *The Uses of Obscurity: The Fiction of Early Modernism*. London: Routledge & Kegan Paul, 1981.

White, Emily. "Seasons of Lust: *The Seal Wife* by Kathryn Harrison." *The Village Voice* (May 7, 2002): www3.villagevoice.com/vls/177/white.shtml—8k

Williamson, S., T. Harpur, and R. Hare. "Abnormal Processing of Affective Words by Psychopaths." *Psychopathology* 28 (1991): 260–73.

Wilson, E. O. *Consilience: The Unity of Knowledge*. New York: Knopf, 1998.

Wilson, Edmund. "The Ambiguity of Henry James." *The Triple Thinkers: Twelve Essays on Literary Subjects*. London: Oxford University Press, 1948. 88–132.

Winterson, Jeanette. "The White Room," 2008. http://www.jeanettewinterson.com/pages/content/index.asp?PageID=275

Wittgenstein, Ludwig. *Philosophical Investigations.* Trans. G. E. M. Anscombe. Oxford: Blackwell, 1997.

———. *Tractatus Logico-Philosophicus.* Trans. C. K. Ogden. New York: Cosimo, 2007.

Wolf, Werner. "Framing Borders in Frame Stories." In *Framing Borders in Literature and Other Media.* Ed. Werner Wolf and Walter Bernhard. Amsterdam: Rodopi, 2006. 1–40.

Wolosky, Shira. *Language Mysticism: The Negative Way of Language in Eliot, Beckett, and Celan.* Stanford, CA: Stanford University Press, 1995.

Wordsworth, William. "Prospectus to *The Recluse*." In *The Norton Anthology of English Literature, Volume 2,* 5th ed. Ed. M. H. Abrams, et al. New York: Norton: 1986. 224–26.

Wright, Austin. "Recalcitrance in the Short Story." In *Short Story Theory at the Crossroads.* Ed. Susan Lohafer, and Joellen Clarey. Baton Rouge: Louisiana State University Press, 1989.

Wynands, Sandra. *Iconic Spaces: The Dark Theology of Samuel Beckett's Drama.* Notre Dame, IN: University of Notre Dame Press, 2007.

Young, Kay. *Imagining Minds: The Neuro-Aesthetic of Austin, Eliot, and Hardy.* Columbus: The Ohio State University Press, 2010.

Young, Kay, and Jeffrey L. Saver. "The Neurology of Narrative." (2001). In Young, *Imagining Minds,* 185–94.

Zijderveld, Anton. *On Clichés: The Supersedure of Meaning by Function in Modernity.* London: Routledge & Kegan Paul, 1979.

Zunshine, Lisa. *Why We Read Fiction: Theory of Mind and the Novel.* Columbus: The Ohio State University Press, 2006.

———. *Strange Concepts and the Stories They Make Possible.* Baltimore: Johns Hopkins University Press, 2009.

———. "Theory of Mind and Fictions of Embodied Transparency." In *Theory of Mind and Literature.* Ed. Paula Leverage et al. West Lafayette, IN: Purdue University Press, 2011. 63–91.

———. *Getting Inside Your Head: What Cognitive Science Can Tell Us about Popular Culture.* Baltimore, MD: University of Johns Hopkins Press, 2012.

INDEX

THEORY AND INTERPRETATION OF NARRATIVE

James Phelan, Peter J. Rabinowitz, and Robyn Warhol, Series Editors

Because the series editors believe that the most significant work in narrative studies today contributes both to our knowledge of specific narratives and to our understanding of narrative in general, studies in the series typically offer interpretations of individual narratives and address significant theoretical issues underlying those interpretations. The series does not privilege one critical perspective but is open to work from any strong theoretical position.

A Poetics of Unnatural Narrative
EDITED BY JAN ALBER, HENRIK SKOV NIELSEN, AND BRIAN RICHARDSON

Narrative Discourse: Authors and Narrators in Literature, Film, and Art
PATRICK COLM HOGAN

An Aesthetics of Narrative Performance: Transnational Theater, Literature, and Film in Contemporary Germany
CLAUDIA BREGER

Literary Identification from Charlotte Brontë to Tsitsi Dangarembga
LAURA GREEN

Narrative Theory: Core Concepts and Critical Debates
DAVID HERMAN, JAMES PHELAN AND PETER J. RABINOWITZ, BRIAN RICHARDSON, AND ROBYN WARHOL

After Testimony: The Ethics and Aesthetics of Holocaust Narrative for the Future
EDITED BY JAKOB LOTHE, SUSAN RUBIN SULEIMAN, AND JAMES PHELAN

The Vitality of Allegory: Figural Narrative in Modern and Contemporary Fiction
GARY JOHNSON

Narrative Middles: Navigating the Nineteenth-Century British Novel
EDITED BY CAROLINE LEVINE AND MARIO ORTIZ-ROBLES

Fact, Fiction, and Form: Selected Essays
RALPH W. RADER. EDITED BY JAMES PHELAN AND DAVID H. RICHTER

The Real, the True, and the Told: Postmodern Historical Narrative and the Ethics of Representation
ERIC L. BERLATSKY

Franz Kafka: Narration, Rhetoric, and Reading
EDITED BY JAKOB LOTHE, BEATRICE SANDBERG, AND RONALD SPEIRS

Social Minds in the Novel
ALAN PALMER

Narrative Structures and the Language of the Self
MATTHEW CLARK

Imagining Minds: The Neuro-Aesthetics of Austen, Eliot, and Hardy
KAY YOUNG

Postclassical Narratology: Approaches and Analyses
EDITED BY JAN ALBER AND MONIKA FLUDERNIK

Techniques for Living: Fiction and Theory in the Work of Christine Brooke-Rose
KAREN R. LAWRENCE

Towards the Ethics of Form in Fiction: Narratives of Cultural Remission
LEONA TOKER

Tabloid, Inc.: Crimes, Newspapers, Narratives
V. PENELOPE PELIZZON AND NANCY M. WEST

Narrative Means, Lyric Ends: Temporality in the Nineteenth-Century British Long Poem
MONIQUE R. MORGAN

Joseph Conrad: Voice, Sequence, History, Genre
EDITED BY JAKOB LOTHE, JEREMY HAWTHORN, AND JAMES PHELAN

Understanding Nationalism: On Narrative, Cognitive Science, and Identity
PATRICK COLM HOGAN

The Rhetoric of Fictionality: Narrative Theory and the Idea of Fiction
RICHARD WALSH

Experiencing Fiction: Judgments, Progressions, and the Rhetorical Theory of Narrative
JAMES PHELAN

Unnatural Voices: Extreme Narration in Modern and Contemporary Fiction
BRIAN RICHARDSON

Narrative Causalities
EMMA KAFALENOS

Why We Read Fiction: Theory of Mind and the Novel
LISA ZUNSHINE

I Know That You Know That I Know: Narrating Subjects from Moll Flanders *to* Marnie
GEORGE BUTTE

Bloodscripts: Writing the Violent Subject
ELANA GOMEL

Surprised by Shame: Dostoevsky's Liars and Narrative Exposure
DEBORAH A. MARTINSEN

Having a Good Cry: Effeminate Feelings and Pop-Culture Forms
ROBYN R. WARHOL

Politics, Persuasion, and Pragmatism: A Rhetoric of Feminist Utopian Fiction
ELLEN PEEL

Telling Tales: Gender and Narrative Form in Victorian Literature and Culture
ELIZABETH LANGLAND

Narrative Dynamics: Essays on Time, Plot, Closure, and Frames
EDITED BY BRIAN RICHARDSON

Breaking the Frame: Metalepsis and the Construction of the Subject
DEBRA MALINA

Invisible Author: Last Essays
CHRISTINE BROOKE-ROSE

Ordinary Pleasures: Couples, Conversation, and Comedy
KAY YOUNG

Narratologies: New Perspectives on Narrative Analysis
EDITED BY DAVID HERMAN

Before Reading: Narrative Conventions and the Politics of Interpretation
PETER J. RABINOWITZ

Matters of Fact: Reading Nonfiction over the Edge
DANIEL W. LEHMAN

The Progress of Romance: Literary Historiography and the Gothic Novel
DAVID H. RICHTER

A Glance Beyond Doubt: Narration, Representation, Subjectivity
SHLOMITH RIMMON-KENAN

Narrative as Rhetoric: Technique, Audiences, Ethics, Ideology
JAMES PHELAN

Misreading Jane Eyre: *A Postformalist Paradigm*
JEROME BEATY

Psychological Politics of the American Dream: The Commodification of Subjectivity in Twentieth-Century American Literature
LOIS TYSON

Understanding Narrative
EDITED BY JAMES PHELAN AND PETER J. RABINOWITZ

Framing Anna Karenina: *Tolstoy, the Woman Question, and the Victorian Novel*
AMY MANDELKER

Gendered Interventions: Narrative Discourse in the Victorian Novel
ROBYN R. WARHOL

Reading People, Reading Plots: Character, Progression, and the Interpretation of Narrative
JAMES PHELAN

CPSIA information can be obtained
at www.ICGtesting.com
Printed in the USA
FFHW021818031218
49731117-54181FF

9 780814 252741